NON SANZ DROICT.

ALL'S
Well, that Ends Well.

Decorative headband and title of the first printed version, in the First Folio (1623)

William Shakespeare

All's Well
That Ends Well

With New and Updated Critical
Essays and a Revised Bibliography

THE SIGNET CLASSICS SHAKESPEARE
General Editor: Sylvan Barnet

SIGNET CLASSICS

SIGNET CLASSICS
Published by New American Library, a division of
Penguin Group (USA) Inc., 375 Hudson Street,
New York, New York 10014, USA
Penguin Group (Canada), 90 Eglinton Avenue East, Suite 700, Toronto,
Ontario M4P 2Y3, Canada (a division of Pearson Penguin Canada Inc.)
Penguin Books Ltd., 80 Strand, London WC2R 0RL, England
Penguin Ireland, 25 St. Stephen's Green, Dublin 2,
Ireland (a division of Penguin Books Ltd.)
Penguin Group (Australia), 250 Camberwell Road, Camberwell, Victoria 3124,
Australia (a division of Pearson Australia Group Pty. Ltd.)
Penguin Books India Pvt. Ltd., 11 Community Centre, Panchsheel Park,
New Delhi - 110 017, India
Penguin Books (NZ), Cnr Airborne and Rosedale Roads, Albany,
Auckland 1310, New Zealand (a division of Pearson New Zealand Ltd.)
Penguin Books (South Africa) (Pty.) Ltd., 24 Sturdee Avenue,
Rosebank, Johannesburg 2196, South Africa

Penguin Books Ltd., Registered Offices:
80 Strand, London WC2R 0RL, England

Published by Signet Classics, an imprint of New American Library,
a division of Penguin Group (USA) Inc.

First Signet Classics Printing (Second Revised Edition), October 2005
10 9 8 7 6 5 4 3 2 1

Contents

Shakespeare: An Overview

Biographical Sketch

Between the record of his baptism in Stratford on 26 April 1564 and the record of his burial in Stratford on 25 April 1616, some forty official documents name Shakespeare, and many others name his parents, his children, and his grandchildren. Further, there are at least fifty literary references to him in the works of his contemporaries. More facts are known about William Shakespeare than about any other playwright of the period except Ben Jonson. The facts should, however, be distinguished from the legends. The latter, inevitably more engaging and better known, tell us that the Stratford boy killed a calf in high style, poached deer and rabbits, and was forced to flee to London, where he held horses outside a playhouse. These traditions are only traditions; they may be true, but no evidence supports them, and it is well to stick to the facts.

Mary Arden, the dramatist's mother, was the daughter of a substantial landowner; about 1557 she married John Shakespeare, a tanner, glove maker, and trader in wool, grain, and other farm commodities. In 1557 John Shakespeare was a member of the council (the governing body of Stratford), in 1558 a constable of the borough, in 1561 one of the two town chamberlains, in 1565 an alderman (entitling him to the appellation of "Mr."), in 1568 high bailiff— the town's highest political office, equivalent to mayor. After 1577, for an unknown reason he drops out of local politics. What *is* known is that he had to mortgage his wife's property, and that he was involved in serious litigation.

The birthday of William Shakespeare, the third child and the eldest son of this locally prominent man, is unrecorded, but the Stratford parish register records that the infant was baptized on 26 April 1564. (It is quite possible that he was born on 23 April, but this date has probably been assigned by tradition because it is the date on which, fifty-two years later, he died, and perhaps because it is the feast day of St. George, patron saint of England.) The attendance records of the Stratford grammar school of the period are not extant, but it is reasonable to assume that the son of a prominent local official attended the free school—it had been established for the purpose of educating males precisely of his class—and received substantial training in Latin. The masters of the school from Shakespeare's seventh to fifteenth years held Oxford degrees; the Elizabethan curriculum excluded mathematics and the natural sciences but taught a good deal of Latin rhetoric, logic, and literature, including plays by Plautus, Terence, and Seneca.

On 27 November 1582 a marriage license was issued for the marriage of Shakespeare and Anne Hathaway, eight years his senior. The couple had a daughter, Susanna, in May 1583. Perhaps the marriage was necessary, but perhaps the couple had earlier engaged, in the presence of witnesses, in a formal "troth plight," which would render their children legitimate even if no further ceremony were performed. In February 1585, Anne Hathaway bore Shakespeare twins, Hamnet and Judith.

That Shakespeare was born is excellent; that he married and had children is pleasant; but that we know nothing about his departure from Stratford to London or about the beginning of his theatrical career is lamentable and must be admitted. We would gladly sacrifice details about his children's baptism for details about his earliest days in the theater. Perhaps the poaching episode is true (but it is first reported almost a century after Shakespeare's death), or perhaps he left Stratford to be a schoolmaster, as another tradition holds; perhaps he was moved (like Petruchio in *The Taming of the Shrew*) by

> Such wind as scatters young men through the world,
> To seek their fortunes farther than at home
> Where small experience grows.   (1.2.49–51)

In 1592, thanks to the cantankerousness of Robert Greene, we have our first reference, a snarling one, to Shakespeare as an actor and playwright. Greene, a graduate of St. John's College, Cambridge, had become a playwright and a pamphleteer in London, and in one of his pamphlets he warns three university-educated playwrights against an actor who has presumed to turn playwright:

> There is an upstart crow, beautified with our feathers, that with his *tiger's heart wrapped in a player's hide* supposes he is as well able to bombast out a blank verse as the best of you, and being an absolute Johannes-factotum [i.e., jack-of-all-trades] is in his own conceit the only Shake-scene in a country.

The reference to the player, as well as the allusion to Aesop's crow (who strutted in borrowed plumage, as an actor struts in fine words not his own), makes it clear that by this date Shakespeare had both acted and written. That Shakespeare is meant is indicated not only by *Shake-scene* but also by the parody of a line from one of Shakespeare's plays, *3 Henry VI*: "O, tiger's heart wrapped in a woman's hide" (1.4.137). If in 1592 Shakespeare was prominent enough to be attacked by an envious dramatist, he probably had served an apprenticeship in the theater for at least a few years.

In any case, although there are no extant references to Shakespeare between the record of the baptism of his twins in 1585 and Greene's hostile comment about "Shake-scene" in 1592, it is evident that during some of these "dark years" or "lost years" Shakespeare had acted and written. There are a number of subsequent references to him as an actor. Documents indicate that in 1598 he is a "principal comedian," in 1603 a "principal tragedian," in 1608 he is one of the "men players." (We do not have, however, any solid information about which roles he may have played; later traditions say he played Adam in *As You Like It* and the ghost in *Hamlet*, but nothing supports the assertions. Probably his role as dramatist came to supersede his role as actor.) The profession of actor was not for a gentleman, and it occasionally drew the scorn of university men like Greene, who resented writing speeches for persons less educated than themselves, but it was respectable enough; players, if prosperous, were in effect members of the bourgeoisie, and there is nothing to suggest that Stratford considered William Shakespeare less than a solid citizen. When, in 1596, the Shakespeares were granted a coat of arms—i.e., the right to be considered gentlemen—the grant was made to Shakespeare's father, but probably William Shakespeare had arranged the matter on his own behalf. In subsequent transactions he is occasionally styled a gentleman.

Although in 1593 and 1594 Shakespeare published two narrative poems dedicated to the Earl of Southampton, *Venus and Adonis* and *The Rape of Lucrece*, and may well have written most or all of his sonnets in the middle nineties, Shakespeare's literary activity seems to have been almost entirely devoted to the theater. (It may be significant that the two narrative poems were written in years when the plague closed the theaters for several months.) In 1594 he was a charter member of a theatrical company called the Chamberlain's Men, which in 1603 became the royal company, the King's Men, making Shakespeare the king's playwright. Until he retired to Stratford (about 1611, apparently), he was with this remarkably stable company. From 1599 the company acted primarily at the Globe theater, in which Shakespeare held a one-tenth interest. Other Elizabethan dramatists are known to have acted, but no other is known also to have been entitled to a share of the profits.

Shakespeare's first eight published plays did not have his name on them, but this is not remarkable; the most popular play of the period, Thomas Kyd's *The Spanish Tragedy*, went through many editions without naming Kyd, and Kyd's authorship is known only because a book on the profession of acting happens to quote (and attribute to Kyd) some lines on the interest of Roman emperors in the drama. What is remarkable is that after 1598 Shakespeare's name commonly appears on printed plays—some of which are not his. Presumably his name was a drawing card, and publishers used it to attract potential buyers. Another indication of his popularity comes from Francis Meres, author of *Palladis Tamia: Wit's Treasury* (1598). In this anthology of snippets accompanied by an essay on literature, many playwrights are mentioned, but Shakespeare's name occurs more often than any other, and Shakespeare is the only play-wright whose plays are listed.

From his acting, his playwriting, and his share in a playhouse, Shakespeare seems to have made considerable money. He put it to work, making substantial investments in Stratford real estate. As early as 1597 he bought New Place, the second-largest house in Stratford. His family moved in soon afterward, and the house remained in the family until a granddaughter died in 1670. When Shakespeare made his will in 1616, less than a month before he died, he sought to leave his property intact to his descendants. Of small bequests to relatives and to friends (including three actors, Richard Burbage, John Heminges, and Henry Condell), that to his wife of the second-best bed has provoked the most comment. It has sometimes been taken as a sign of an unhappy marriage (other supposed signs are the apparently hasty marriage, his wife's seniority of eight years, and his residence in London without his family). Perhaps the second-best bed was the bed the couple had slept in, the best bed being reserved for visitors. In any case, had Shakespeare not excepted it, the bed would have gone (with the rest of his household possessions) to his daughter and her husband.

On 25 April 1616 Shakespeare was buried within the chancel of the church at Stratford. An unattractive monument to his memory, placed on a wall near the grave, says that he died on 23 April. Over the grave itself are the lines, perhaps by Shakespeare, that (more than his literary fame) have kept his bones undisturbed in the crowded burial ground, where old bones were often dislodged to make way for new:

> Good friend, for Jesus' sake forbear
> To dig the dust enclosed here.
> Blessed be the man that spares these stones
> And cursed be he that moves my bones.

A Note on the Anti-Stratfordians, Especially Baconians and Oxfordians

Not until 1769—more than a hundred and fifty years after Shakespeare's death—is there any record of anyone expressing doubt about Shakespeare's authorship of the plays and poems. In 1769, however, Herbert Lawrence nominated Francis Bacon (1561–1626) in *The Life and Adventures of Common Sense*. Since then, at least two dozen other nominees have been offered, including Christopher Marlowe, Sir Walter Raleigh, Queen Elizabeth I, and Edward de Vere, 17th earl of Oxford. The impulse behind all anti-Stratfordian movements is the scarcely concealed snobbish opinion that "the man from Stratford" simply could not have written the plays because he was a country fellow without a university education and without access to high society. Anyone, the argument goes, who used so many legal terms, medical terms, nautical terms, and so forth, and who showed some familiarity with classical writing, must have attended a university, and anyone who knew so much about courtly elegance and courtly deceit must himself have moved among courtiers. The plays do indeed reveal an author whose interests were exceptionally broad, but specialists in any given field—law, medicine, arms and armor, and so on—soon find that the plays do not reveal deep knowledge in specialized matters; indeed, the playwright often gets technical details wrong.

The claim on behalf of Bacon, forgotten almost as soon as it was put forth in 1769, was independently reasserted by Joseph C. Hart in 1848. In 1856 it was reaffirmed by W. H. Smith in a book, and also by Delia Bacon in an article; in 1857 Delia Bacon published a book, arguing that Francis Bacon had directed a group of intellectuals who wrote the plays.

Francis Bacon's claim has largely faded, perhaps because it was advanced with such evident craziness by Ignatius Donnelly, who in *The Great Cryptogram* (1888) claimed to break a code in the plays that proved Bacon had written not only the plays attributed to Shakespeare but also other Renaissance works, for instance the plays of Christopher Marlowe and the essays of Montaigne.

Consider the last two lines of the Epilogue in *The Tempest*:

As you from crimes would pardoned be,
Let your indulgence set me free.

What was Shakespeare—sorry, Francis Bacon, Baron Verulam—*really* saying in these two lines? According to Baconians, the lines are an anagram reading, "Tempest of Francis Bacon, Lord Verulam; do ye ne'er divulge me, ye words." Ingenious, and it is a pity that in the quotation the letter *a* appears only twice in the cryptogram, whereas in the deciphered message it appears three times. Oh, no problem; just alter "Verulam" to "Verul'm" and it works out very nicely.

Most people understand that with sufficient ingenuity one can torture any text and find in it what one wishes. For instance: Did Shakespeare have a hand in the King James Version of the Bible? It was nearing completion in 1610, when Shakespeare was forty-six years old. If you look at the 46th Psalm and count forward for forty-six words, you will find the word *shake*. Now if you go to the end of the psalm and count backward forty-six words, you will find the word *spear*. Clear evidence, according to some, that Shakespeare slyly left his mark in the book.

Bacon's candidacy has largely been replaced in the twentieth century by the candidacy of Edward de Vere (1550–1604), 17th earl of Oxford. The basic ideas behind the Oxford theory, advanced at greatest length by Dorothy and Charlton Ogburn in *This Star of England* (1952, rev. 1955), a book of 1297 pages, and by Charlton Ogburn in *The Mysterious William Shakespeare* (1984), a book of 892 pages, are these: (1) The man from Stratford could not possibly have had the mental equipment and the experience to have written the plays—only a courtier could have written them; (2) Oxford had the requisite background (social position, education, years at Queen Elizabeth's court); (3) Oxford did not wish his authorship to be known for two basic reasons: writing for the public theater was a vulgar pursuit, and the plays show so much courtly and royal disreputable behavior that they would have compromised Oxford's position at court. Oxfordians offer countless details to support the claim. For example, Hamlet's phrase "that ever I was born to set it right" (1.5.89) barely conceals "E. Ver, I was born to set it right," an unambiguous announcement of de Vere's authorship, according to *This Star of England* (p. 654). A second example: Consider Ben

Jonson's poem entitled "To the Memory of My Beloved
Master William Shakespeare," prefixed to the first collected
edition of Shakespeare's plays in 1623. According to Oxfordians, when Jonson in this poem speaks of the author of
the plays as the "swan of Avon," he is alluding not to William Shakespeare, who was born and died in Stratford-on-
Avon and who throughout his adult life owned property
there; rather, he is alluding to Oxford, who, the Ogburns say,
used "William Shakespeare" as his pen name, and whose
manor at Bilton was on the Avon River. Oxfordians do not
offer any evidence that Oxford took a pen name, and they
do not care that Oxford had sold the manor in 1581, forty-
two years before Jonson wrote his poem. Surely a reference
to the Shakespeare who was born in Stratford, who had
returned to Stratford, and who had died there only seven
years before Jonson wrote the poem is more plausible. And
exactly why Jonson, who elsewhere also spoke of Shakespeare as a playwright, and why Heminges and Condell,
who had acted with Shakespeare for about twenty years,
should speak of Shakespeare as the author in their dedication
in the 1623 volume of collected plays is never adequately
explained by Oxfordians. Either Jonson, Heminges and
Condell, and numerous others were in on the conspiracy, or
they were all duped—equally unlikely alternatives. Another
difficulty in the Oxford theory is that Oxford died in 1604,
and some of the plays are clearly indebted to works and
events later than 1604. Among the Oxfordian responses are:
At his death Oxford left some plays, and in later years these
were touched up by hacks, who added the material that
points to later dates. *The Tempest*, almost universally
regarded as one of Shakespeare's greatest plays and pretty
clearly dated to 1611, does indeed date from a period after
the death of Oxford, but it is a crude piece of work that
should not be included in the canon of works by Oxford.

The anti-Stratfordians, in addition to assuming that the
author must have been a man of rank and a university man,
usually assume two conspiracies: (1) a conspiracy in Elizabethan and Jacobean times, in which a surprisingly large
number of persons connected with the theater knew that the
actor Shakespeare did not write the plays attributed to him
but for some reason or other pretended that he did; (2) a con-

spiracy of today's Stratfordians, the professors who teach Shakespeare in the colleges and universities, who are said to have a vested interest in preserving Shakespeare as the author of the plays they teach. In fact, (1) it is inconceivable that the secret of Shakespeare's nonauthorship could have been preserved by all of the people who supposedly were in on the conspiracy, and (2) academic fame awaits any scholar today who can disprove Shakespeare's authorship.

The Stratfordian case is convincing not only because hundreds or even thousands of anti-Stratford arguments—of the sort that say "ever I was born" has the secret double meaning "E. Ver, I was born"—add up to nothing at all but also because irrefutable evidence connects the man from Stratford with the London theater and with the authorship of particular plays. The anti-Stratfordians do not seem to understand that it is not enough to dismiss the Stratford case by saying that a fellow from the provinces simply couldn't have written the plays. Nor do they understand that it is not enough to dismiss all of the evidence connecting Shakespeare with the plays by asserting that it is perjured.

The Shakespeare Canon

We return to William Shakespeare. Thirty-seven plays as well as some nondramatic poems are generally held to constitute the Shakespeare canon, the body of authentic works. The exact dates of composition of most of the works are highly uncertain, but evidence of a starting point and/or of a final limiting point often provides a framework for informed guessing. For example, *Richard II* cannot be earlier than 1595, the publication date of some material to which it is indebted; *The Merchant of Venice* cannot be later than 1598, the year Francis Meres mentioned it. Sometimes arguments for a date hang on an alleged topical allusion, such as the lines about the unseasonable weather in *A Midsummer Night's Dream*, 2.1.81–117, but such an allusion, if indeed it is an allusion to an event in the real world, can be variously interpreted, and in any case there is always the possibility that a topical allusion was inserted years later, to bring the play up-to-date. (The issue of alterations in a text between the time that Shakespeare drafted it and the time that it was printed—alterations due to censorship or playhouse practice or Shakespeare's own second thoughts—will be discussed in "The Play Text as a Collaboration" later in this overview.) Dates are often attributed on the basis of style, and although conjectures about style usually rest on other conjectures (such as Shakespeare's development as a playwright, or the appropriateness of lines to character), sooner or later one must rely on one's literary sense. There is no documentary proof, for example, that *Othello* is not as early as *Romeo and Juliet*, but one feels that *Othello* is a later, more mature work, and because the first record of its performance is 1604, one is glad enough to set its composition at that date and not push it back into Shakespeare's early years. (*Romeo and Juliet* was first published in 1597, but evidence suggests that it was written a little earlier.) The following chronology, then, is indebted not only to facts but also to informed guesswork and sensitivity. The dates, necessarily imprecise for some works, indicate something like a scholarly consensus concerning the time of original composition. Some plays show evidence of later revision.

Plays. The first collected edition of Shakespeare, published in 1623, included thirty-six plays. These are all accepted as Shakespeare's, though for one of them, *Henry VIII*, he is thought to have had a collaborator. A thirty-seventh play, *Pericles*, published in 1609 and attributed to Shakespeare on the title page, is also widely accepted as being partly by Shakespeare even though it is not included in the 1623 volume. Still another play not in the 1623 volume, *The Two Noble Kinsmen*, was first published in 1634, with a title page attributing it to John Fletcher and Shakespeare. Probably most students of the subject now believe that Shakespeare did indeed have a hand in it. Of the remaining plays attributed at one time or another to Shakespeare, only one, *Edward III*, anonymously published in 1596, is now regarded by some scholars as a serious candidate. The prevailing opinion, however, is that this rather simple-minded play is not Shakespeare's; at most he may have revised some passages, chiefly scenes with the Countess of

Salisbury. We include *The Two Noble Kinsmen* but do not include *Edward III* in the following list.

1588–94	*The Comedy of Errors*
1588–94	*Love's Labor's Lost*
1589–91	*2 Henry VI*
1590–91	*3 Henry VI*
1589–92	*1 Henry VI*
1592–93	*Richard III*
1589–94	*Titus Andronicus*
1593–94	*The Taming of the Shrew*
1592–94	*The Two Gentlemen of Verona*
1594–96	*Romeo and Juliet*
1594–96	*The Merchant of Venice*
1595	*Richard II*
1595–96	*A Midsummer Night's Dream*
1596–97	*King John*
1596–97	*1 Henry IV*
1597	*The Merry Wives of Windsor*
1597–98	*2 Henry IV*
1598–99	*Much Ado About Nothing*
1598–99	*Henry V*
1599	*Julius Caesar*
1599–1600	*As You Like It*
1599–1600	*Twelfth Night*
1600–1601	*Hamlet*
1601–1602	*Troilus and Cressida*
1602–1604	*All's Well That Ends Well*
1603–1604	*Othello*
1604	*Measure for Measure*
1605–1606	*King Lear*
1605–1606	*Macbeth*
1606–1607	*Antony and Cleopatra*
1605–1608	*Timon of Athens*
1607–1608	*Coriolanus*
1607–1608	*Pericles*
1609–10	*Cymbeline*
1610–11	*The Winter's Tale*
1611	*The Tempest*

| 1612–13 | *Henry VIII* |
| 1613 | *The Two Noble Kinsmen* |

Poems. In 1989 Donald W. Foster published a book in which he argued that "A Funeral Elegy for Master William Peter," published in 1612, ascribed only to the initials W.S., *may* be by Shakespeare. Foster later published an article in a scholarly journal, *PMLA* 111 (1996), in which he asserted the claim more positively. The evidence begins with the initials, and includes the fact that the publisher and the printer of the elegy had published Shakespeare's *Sonnets* in 1609. But such facts add up to rather little, especially because no one has found any connection between Shakespeare and William Peter (an Oxford graduate about whom little is known, who was murdered at the age of twenty-nine). The argument is based chiefly on statistical examinations of word patterns, which are said to correlate with Shakespeare's known work. Despite such correlations, however, many readers feel that the poem does not sound like Shakespeare. True, Shakespeare has a great range of styles, but his work is consistently imaginative and interesting. Many readers find neither of these qualities in "A Funeral Elegy." The poem is now attributed to John Ford.

1592–93	*Venus and Adonis*
1593–94	*The Rape of Lucrece*
1593–1600	*Sonnets*
1600–1601	*The Phoenix and the Turtle*

Shakespeare's English

1. Spelling and Pronunciation. From the philologist's point of view, Shakespeare's English is modern English. It requires footnotes, but the inexperienced reader can comprehend substantial passages with very little help, whereas for the same reader Chaucer's Middle English is a foreign language. By the beginning of the fifteenth century the chief grammatical changes in English had taken place, and the final unaccented -*e* of Middle English had been lost (though it survives even today in spelling, as in *name*); during the fifteenth century the dialect of London, the commercial and political center, gradually displaced the provincial dialects, at least in writing; by the end of the century, printing had helped to regularize and stabilize the language, especially spelling. Elizabethan spelling may seem erratic to us (there were dozens of spellings of *Shakespeare*, and a simple word like *been* was also spelled *beene* and *bin*), but it had much in common with our spelling. Elizabethan spelling was conservative in that for the most part it reflected an older pronunciation (Middle English) rather than the sound of the language as it was then spoken, just as our spelling continues to reflect medieval pronunciation—most obviously in the now silent but formerly pronounced letters in a word such as *knight*. Elizabethan pronunciation, though not identical with ours, was much closer to ours than to that of the Middle Ages. Incidentally, though no one can be certain about what Elizabethan English sounded like, specialists tend to believe it was rather like the speech of a modern stage Irishman (*time* apparently was pronounced *toime*, *old* pronounced *awld*, *day* pronounced *die*, and *join* pronounced *jine*) and not at all like the Oxford speech that most of us think it was.

An awareness of the difference between our pronunciation and Shakespeare's is crucial in three areas—in accent, or number of syllables (many metrically regular lines may look irregular to us); in rhymes (which may not look like rhymes); and in puns (which may not look like puns). Examples will be useful. Some words that were at least on occasion stressed differently from today are *aspèct*, *còmplete*, *fòrlorn*, *revènue*, and *sepùlcher*. Words that sometimes had an additional syllable are *emp[e]ress*, *Hen[e]ry*, *mòn[e]th*, and *villain* (three syllables, *vil-lay-in*). An additional syllable is often found in possessives, like *moon's* (pronounced *moones*), and in words ending in *-tion* or *-sion*. Words that had one less syllable than they now have are *needle* (pronounced *neel*) and *violet* (pronounced *vilet*). Among rhymes now lost are *one* with *loan*, *love* with *prove*, *beast* with *jest*, *eat* with *great*. (In reading, trust your sense of metrics and your ear, more than your eye.) An example of a pun that has become obliterated by a change in pronunciation is Falstaff's reply to Prince Hal's "Come, tell us your reason" in *1 Henry IV*: "Give you a reason on compulsion? If reasons were as plentiful as blackberries, I would give no man a reason upon compulsion, I" (2.4.237–40). The *ea* in *reason* was pronounced rather like a long *a,* like the *ai* in *raisin*, hence the comparison with blackberries.

Puns are not merely attempts to be funny; like metaphors they often involve bringing into a meaningful relationship areas of experience normally seen as remote. In *2 Henry IV,* when Feeble is conscripted, he stoically says, "I care not. A man can die but once. We owe God a death" (3.2.242–43), punning on *debt,* which was the way *death* was pronounced. Here an enormously significant fact of life is put into simple commercial imagery, suggesting its commonplace quality. Shakespeare used the same pun earlier in *1 Henry IV,* when Prince Hal says to Falstaff, "Why, thou owest God a death," and Falstaff replies, " 'Tis not due yet: I would be loath to pay him before his day. What need I be so forward with him that calls not on me?" (5.1.126–29).

Sometimes the puns reveal a delightful playfulness; sometimes they reveal aggressiveness, as when, replying to Claudius's "But now, my cousin Hamlet, and my son," Hamlet says, "A little more than kin, and less than kind!" (1.2.64–65). These are Hamlet's first words in the play, and we already hear him warring verbally against Claudius. Hamlet's "less than kind" probably means (1) Hamlet is not of Claudius's family or nature, *kind* having the sense it still has in our word *mankind*; (2) Hamlet is not kindly (affectionately) disposed toward Claudius; (3) Claudius is not naturally (but rather unnaturally, in a legal sense incestuously) Hamlet's father. The puns evidently were not put in as sops to the groundlings; they are an important way of communicating a complex meaning.

2. Vocabulary. A conspicuous difficulty in reading Shakespeare is rooted in the fact that some of his words are no longer in common use—for example, words concerned with armor, astrology, clothing, coinage, hawking, horsemanship, law, medicine, sailing, and war. Shakespeare had a large vocabulary—something near thirty thousand words— but it was not so much a vocabulary of big words as a vocabulary drawn from a wide range of life, and it is partly his ability to call upon a great body of concrete language that gives his plays the sense of being in close contact with life. When the right word did not already exist, he made it up. Among words thought to be his coinages are *accommodation, all-knowing, amazement, bare-faced, countless, dexterously, dislocate, dwindle, fancy-free, frugal, indistinguishable, lackluster, laughable, overawe, premeditated, sea change, star-crossed*. Among those that have not survived are the verb *convive*, meaning to feast together, and *smilet*, a little smile.

Less overtly troublesome than the technical words but more treacherous are the words that seem readily intelligible to us but whose Elizabethan meanings differ from their modern ones. When Horatio describes the Ghost as an "erring spirit," he is saying not that the ghost has sinned or made an error but that it is wandering. Here is a short list of some of the most common words in Shakespeare's plays that often (but not always) have a meaning other than their most usual modern meaning:

'a	he
abuse	deceive
accident	occurrence
advertise	inform
an, and	if
annoy	harm
appeal	accuse
artificial	skillful
brave	fine, splendid
censure	opinion
cheer	(1) face (2) frame of mind
chorus	a single person who comments on the events
closet	small private room
competitor	partner
conceit	idea, imagination
cousin	kinsman
cunning	skillful
disaster	evil astrological influence
doom	judgment
entertain	receive into service

envy	malice
event	outcome
excrement	outgrowth (of hair)
fact	evil deed
fancy	(1) love (2) imagination
fell	cruel
fellow	(1) companion (2) low person (often an insulting term if addressed to someone of approximately equal rank)
fond	foolish
free	(1) innocent (2) generous
glass	mirror
hap, haply	chance, by chance
head	army
humor	(1) mood (2) bodily fluid thought to control one's psychology
imp	child
intelligence	news
kind	natural, acting according to nature
let	hinder
lewd	base
mere(ly)	utter(ly)
modern	commonplace
natural	a fool, an idiot
naughty	(1) wicked (2) worthless
next	nearest
nice	(1) trivial (2) fussy
noise	music
policy	(1) prudence (2) stratagem
presently	immediately
prevent	anticipate
proper	handsome
prove	test
quick	alive
sad	serious
saw	proverb
secure	without care, incautious
silly	innocent

sensible	capable of being perceived by the senses
shrewd	sharp
so	provided that
starve	die
still	always
success	that which follows
tall	brave
tell	count
tonight	last night
wanton	playful, careless
watch	keep awake
will	lust
wink	close both eyes
wit	mind, intelligence

All glosses, of course, are mere approximations; sometimes one of Shakespeare's words may hover between an older meaning and a modern one, and as we have seen, his words often have multiple meanings.

3. Grammar. A few matters of grammar may be surveyed, though it should be noted at the outset that Shakespeare sometimes made up his own grammar. As E. A. Abbott says in *A Shakespearian Grammar,* "Almost any part of speech can be used as any other part of speech": a noun as a verb ("he childed as I fathered"); a verb as a noun ("She hath made compare"); or an adverb as an adjective ("a seldom pleasure"). There are hundreds, perhaps thousands, of such instances in the plays, many of which at first glance would not seem at all irregular and would trouble only a pedant. Here are a few broad matters.

Nouns: The Elizabethans thought the *-s* genitive ending for nouns (as in *man's*) derived from *his*; thus the line " 'gainst the count his galleys I did some service," for "the count's galleys."

Adjectives: By Shakespeare's time adjectives had lost the endings that once indicated gender, number, and case. About the only difference between Shakespeare's adjectives and ours is the use of the now redundant *more* or *most* with the comparative ("some more fitter place") or superlative

("This was the most unkindest cut of all"). Like double comparatives and double superlatives, double negatives were acceptable; Mercutio "will not budge for no man's pleasure."

Pronouns: The greatest change was in pronouns. In Middle English *thou, thy,* and *thee* were used among familiars and in speaking to children and inferiors; *ye, your,* and *you* were used in speaking to superiors (servants to masters, nobles to the king) or to equals with whom the speaker was not familiar. Increasingly the "polite" forms were used in all direct address, regardless of rank, and the accusative *you* displaced the nominative *ye.* Shakespeare sometimes uses *ye* instead of *you,* but even in Shakespeare's day *ye* was archaic, and it occurs mostly in rhetorical appeals.

Thou, thy, and *thee* were not completely displaced, however, and Shakespeare occasionally makes significant use of them, sometimes to connote familiarity or intimacy and sometimes to connote contempt. In *Twelfth Night* Sir Toby advises Sir Andrew to insult Cesario by addressing him as *thou:* "If thou thou'st him some thrice, it shall not be amiss" (3.2.46–47). In *Othello* when Brabantio is addressing an unidentified voice in the dark he says, "What are you?" (1.1.91), but when the voice identifies itself as the foolish suitor Roderigo, Brabantio uses the contemptuous form, saying, "I have charged thee not to haunt about my doors" (93). He uses this form for a while, but later in the scene, when he comes to regard Roderigo as an ally, he shifts back to the polite *you,* beginning in line 163, "What said she to you?" and on to the end of the scene. For reasons not yet satisfactorily explained, Elizabethans used *thou* in addresses to God—"O God, thy arm was here," the king says in *Henry V* (4.8.108)—and to supernatural characters such as ghosts and witches. A subtle variation occurs in *Hamlet.* When Hamlet first talks with the Ghost in 1.5, he uses *thou,* but when he sees the Ghost in his mother's room, in 3.4, he uses *you,* presumably because he is now convinced that the Ghost is not a counterfeit but is his father.

Perhaps the most unusual use of pronouns, from our point of view, is the neuter singular. In place of our *its, his* was often used, as in "How far that little candle throws *his* beams." But the use of a masculine pronoun for a neuter noun came to seem unnatural, and so *it* was used for the possessive as well as the nominative: "The hedge-sparrow fed the cuckoo so long / That it had it head bit off by it young." In the late sixteenth century the possessive form *its* developed, apparently by analogy with the *-s* ending used to indicate a genitive noun, as in *book*'s, but *its* was not yet common usage in Shakespeare's day. He seems to have used *its* only ten times, mostly in his later plays. Other usages, such as "you have seen Cassio and she together" or the substitution of *who* for *whom*, cause little problem even when noticed.

Verbs, Adverbs, and Prepositions: Verbs cause almost no difficulty: The third person singular present form commonly ends in *-s*, as in modern English (e.g., "He blesses"), but sometimes in *-eth* (Portia explains to Shylock that mercy "blesseth him that gives and him that takes"). Broadly speaking, the *-eth* ending was old-fashioned or dignified or "literary" rather than colloquial, except for the words *doth*, *hath*, and *saith*. The *-eth* ending (regularly used in the King James Bible, 1611) is very rare in Shakespeare's dramatic prose, though not surprisingly it occurs twice in the rather formal prose summary of the narrative poem *Lucrece*. Sometimes a plural subject, especially if it has collective force, takes a verb ending in *-s*, as in "My old bones aches." Some of our strong or irregular preterites (such as *broke*) have a different form in Shakespeare (*brake*); some verbs that now have a weak or regular preterite (such as *helped*) in Shakespeare have a strong or irregular preterite (*holp*). Some adverbs that today end in *-ly* were not inflected: "grievous sick," "wondrous strange." Finally, prepositions often are not the ones we expect: "We are such stuff as dreams are made on," "I have a king here to my flatterer."

Again, none of the differences (except meanings that have substantially changed or been lost) will cause much difficulty. But it must be confessed that for some elliptical passages there is no widespread agreement on meaning. Wise editors resist saying more than they know, and when they are uncertain they add a question mark to their gloss.

Shakespeare's Theater

In Shakespeare's infancy, Elizabethan actors performed wherever they could — in great halls, at court, in the court-yards of inns. These venues implied not only different audiences but also different playing conditions. The innyards must have made rather unsatisfactory theaters: on some days they were unavailable because carters bringing goods to London used them as depots; when available, they had to be rented from the innkeeper. In 1567, presumably to avoid such difficulties, and also to avoid regulation by the Common Council of London, which was not well disposed toward theatricals, one John Brayne, brother-in-law of the carpenter turned actor James Burbage, built the Red Lion in an eastern suburb of London. We know nothing about its shape or its capacity; we can say only that it may have been the first building in Europe constructed for the purpose of giving plays since the end of antiquity, a thousand years earlier. Even after the building of the Red Lion theatrical activity continued in London in makeshift circumstances, in marketplaces and inns, and always uneasily. In 1574 the Common Council required that plays and playing places in London be licensed because

> sundry great disorders and inconveniences have been found to ensue to this city by the inordinate haunting of great multitudes of people, specially youth, to plays, interludes, and shows, namely occasion of frays and quarrels, evil practices of incontinency in great inns having chambers and secret places adjoining to their open stages and galleries.

The Common Council ordered that innkeepers who wished licenses to hold performance put up a bond and make contributions to the poor.

The requirement that plays and innyard theaters be licensed, along with the other drawbacks of playing at inns and presumably along with the success of the Red Lion, led James Burbage to rent a plot of land northeast of the city walls, on property outside the jurisdiction of the city. Here he built England's second playhouse, called simply the Theatre. About all that is known of its construction is that it was wood. It soon had imitators, the most famous being the Globe (1599), essentially an amphitheater built across the Thames (again outside the city's jurisdiction), constructed with timbers of the Theatre, which had been dismantled when Burbage's lease ran out.

Admission to the theater was one penny, which allowed spectators to stand at the sides and front of the stage that jutted into the yard. An additional penny bought a seat in a covered part of the theater, and a third penny bought a more comfortable seat and a better location. It is notoriously difficult to translate prices into today's money, since some things that are inexpensive today would have been expensive in the past and vice versa—a pipeful of tobacco (imported, of course) cost a lot of money, about three pennies, and an orange (also imported) cost two or three times what a chicken cost—but perhaps we can get some idea of the low cost of the penny admission when we realize that a penny could also buy a pot of ale. An unskilled laborer made about five or sixpence a day, an artisan about twelve pence a day, and the hired actors (as opposed to the sharers in the company, such as Shakespeare) made about ten pence a performance. A printed play cost five or sixpence. Of course a visit to the theater (like a visit to a baseball game today) usually cost more than the admission since the spectator probably would also buy food and drink. Still, the low entrance fee meant that the theater was available to all except the very poorest people, rather as movies and most athletic events are today. Evidence indicates that the audience ranged from apprentices who somehow managed to scrape together the minimum entrance fee and to escape from their masters for a few hours, to prosperous members of the middle class and aristocrats who paid the additional fee for admission to the galleries. The exact proportion of men to women cannot be determined, but women of all classes certainly were present. Theaters were open every afternoon but Sundays for much of the year, except in times of plague, when they were closed because of fear of infection. By the way, no evidence suggests the presence of toilet facilities. Presumably the patrons relieved themselves by making a quick trip to the fields surrounding the playhouses.

There are four important sources of information about the

structure of Elizabethan public playhouses—drawings, a contract, recent excavations, and stage directions in the plays. Of drawings, only the so-called de Witt drawing (c. 1596) of the Swan—really his friend Aernout van Buchell's copy of Johannes de Witt's drawing—is of much significance. The drawing, the only extant representation of the interior of an Elizabethan theater, shows an amphitheater of three tiers, with a stage jutting from a wall into the yard or

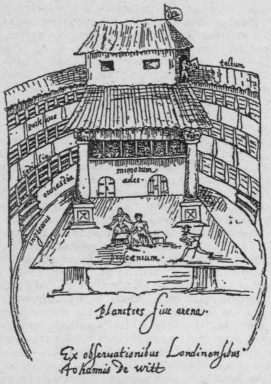

Johannes de Witt, a Continental visitor to London, made a drawing of the Swan theater in about the year 1596. The original drawing is lost; this is Aernout van Buchell's copy of it.

center of the building. The tiers are roofed, and part of the stage is covered by a roof that projects from the rear and is supported at its front on two posts, but the groundlings, who paid a penny to stand in front of the stage or at its sides, were exposed to the sky. (Performances in such a playhouse were held only in the daytime; artificial illumination was not used.) At the rear of the stage are two massive doors; above the stage is a gallery.

The second major source of information, the contract for the Fortune (built in 1600), specifies that although the Globe (built in 1599) is to be the model, the Fortune is to be square, eighty feet outside and fifty-five inside. The stage is to be forty-three feet broad, and is to extend into the middle of the yard, i.e., it is twenty-seven and a half feet deep.

The third source of information, the 1989 excavations of the Rose (built in 1587), indicate that the Rose was fourteen-sided, about seventy-two feet in diameter with an inner yard almost fifty feet in diameter. The stage at the Rose was about sixteen feet deep, thirty-seven feet wide at the rear, and twenty-seven feet wide downstage. The relatively small dimensions and the tapering stage, in contrast to the rectangular stage in the Swan drawing, surprised theater historians and have made them more cautious in generalizing about the Elizabethan theater. Excavations at the Globe have not yielded much information, though some historians believe that the fragmentary evidence suggests a larger theater, perhaps one hundred feet in diameter.

From the fourth chief source, stage directions in the plays, one learns that entrance to the stage was by the doors at the rear (*"Enter one citizen at one door, and another at the other"*). A curtain hanging across the doorway — or a curtain hanging between the two doorways — could provide a place where a character could conceal himself, as Polonius does, when he wishes to overhear the conversation between Hamlet and Gertrude. Similarly, withdrawing a curtain from the doorway could "discover" (reveal) a character or two. Such discovery scenes are very rare in Elizabethan drama, but a good example occurs in *The Tempest* (5.1.171), where a stage direction tells us, *"Here Prospero discovers Ferdinand and Miranda playing at chess."* There was also some sort of playing space "aloft" or "above" to represent, for instance, the top of a city's walls or a room above the street. Doubtless each theater had its own peculiarities, but perhaps we can talk about a "typical" Elizabethan theater if we realize that no theater need exactly fit the description, just as no mother is the average mother with 2.7 children.

This hypothetical theater is wooden, round, or polygonal (in *Henry V* Shakespeare calls it a "wooden *O*"), capable of holding some eight hundred spectators who stood in the yard around the projecting elevated stage—these spectators were the "groundlings"—and some fifteen hundred additional spectators who sat in the three roofed galleries. The stage, protected by a "shadow" or "heavens" or roof, is entered from two doors; behind the doors is the "tiring house" (attiring house, i.e., dressing room), and above the stage is some sort of gallery that may sometimes hold spectators but can be used (for example) as the bedroom from which Romeo—according to a stage direction in one text—"goeth down." Some evidence suggests that a throne can be lowered onto the platform stage, perhaps from the "shadow"; certainly characters can descend from the stage through a trap or traps into the cellar or "hell." Sometimes this space beneath the stage accommodates a sound-effects man or musician (in *Antony and Cleopatra "music of the hautboys* [oboes] *is under the stage"*) or an actor (in *Hamlet* the *"Ghost cries under the stage"*). Most characters simply walk on and off through the doors, but because there is no curtain in front of the platform, corpses will have to be carried off (Hamlet obligingly clears the stage of Polonius's corpse, when he says, "I'll lug the guts into the neighbor room"). Other characters may have fallen at the rear, where a curtain on a doorway could be drawn to conceal them.

Such may have been the "public theater," so called because its inexpensive admission made it available to a wide range of the populace. Another kind of theater has been called the "private theater" because its much greater admission charge (sixpence versus the penny for general admission at the public theater) limited its audience to the wealthy or the prodigal. The private theater was basically a large room, entirely roofed and therefore artificially illuminated, with a stage at one end. The theaters thus were distinct in two ways: One was essentially an amphitheater that catered to the general public; the other was a hall that catered to the wealthy. In 1576 a hall theater was established in Blackfriars, a Dominican priory in London that had been suppressed in 1538 and confiscated by the Crown and thus was not under the city's jurisdiction. All the actors in this Blackfriars theater were boys about eight to thirteen years old (in the public theaters similar boys played female parts; a boy Lady Macbeth played to a man Macbeth). Near the end of this section on Shakespeare's theater we will talk at some length about possible implications in this convention of using boys to play female roles, but for the moment we should say that it doubtless accounts for the relative lack of female roles in Elizabethan drama. Thus, in *A Midsummer Night's Dream*, out of twenty-one named roles, only four are female; in *Hamlet*, out of twenty-four, only two (Gertrude and Ophelia) are female. Many of Shakespeare's characters have fathers but no mothers—for instance, King Lear's daughters. We need not bring in Freud to explain the disparity; a dramatic company had only a few boys in it.

To return to the private theaters, in some of which all of the performers were children—the "eyrie of . . . little eyases" (nest of unfledged hawks—2.2.347–48) which Rosencrantz mentions when he and Guildenstern talk with Hamlet. The theater in Blackfriars had a precarious existence, and ceased operations in 1584. In 1596 James Burbage, who had already made theatrical history by building the Theatre, began to construct a second Blackfriars theater. He died in 1597, and for several years this second Blackfriars theater was used by a troupe of boys, but in 1608 two of Burbage's sons and five other actors (including Shakespeare) became joint operators of the theater, using it in the winter when the open-air Globe was unsuitable. Perhaps such a smaller theater, roofed, artificially illuminated, and with a tradition of a wealthy audience, exerted an influence in Shakespeare's late plays.

Performances in the private theaters may well have had intermissions during which music was played, but in the public theaters the action was probably uninterrupted, flowing from scene to scene almost without a break. Actors would enter, speak, exit, and others would immediately enter and establish (if necessary) the new locale by a few properties and by words and gestures. To indicate that the scene took place at night, a player or two would carry a torch. Here are some samples of Shakespeare establishing the scene:

> This is Illyria, lady.   (*Twelfth Night*, 1.2.2)

> Well, this is the Forest of Arden.   (*As You Like It*, 2.4.14)

> This castle has a pleasant seat; the air
> Nimbly and sweetly recommends itself
> Unto our gentle senses.   (*Macbeth*, 1.6.1–3)

> The west yet glimmers with some streaks of day.
>   (*Macbeth*, 3.3.5)

Sometimes a speech will go far beyond evoking the minimal setting of place and time, and will, so to speak, evoke the social world in which the characters move. For instance, early in the first scene of *The Merchant of Venice* Salerio suggests an explanation for Antonio's melancholy. (In the following passage, *pageants* are decorated wagons, floats, and *cursy* is the verb "to curtsy," or "to bow.")

> Your mind is tossing on the ocean,
> There where your argosies with portly sail—
> Like signiors and rich burghers on the flood,
> Or as it were the pageants of the sea—
> Do overpeer the petty traffickers
> That cursy to them, do them reverence,
> As they fly by them with their woven wings.   (1.1.8–14)

Late in the nineteenth century, when Henry Irving produced the play with elaborate illusionistic sets, the first scene showed a ship moored in the harbor, with fruit vendors and dock laborers, in an effort to evoke the bustling and exotic life of Venice. But Shakespeare's words give us this exotic, rich world of commerce in his highly descriptive language when Salerio speaks of "argosies with portly sail" that fly with "woven wings"; equally important, through Salerio Shakespeare conveys a sense of the orderly, hierarchical society in which the lesser ships, "the petty traffickers," curtsy and thereby "do . . . reverence" to their superiors, the merchant prince's ships, which are "Like signiors and rich burghers."

On the other hand, it is a mistake to think that except for verbal pictures the Elizabethan stage was bare. Although Shakespeare's Chorus in *Henry V* calls the stage an "unworthy scaffold" (Prologue 1.10) and urges the spectators to "eke out our performance with your mind" (Prologue 3.35), there was considerable spectacle. The last act of *Macbeth*, for instance, has five stage directions calling for *"drum and colors,"* and another sort of appeal to the eye is indicated by the stage direction *"Enter Macduff, with Macbeth's head."* Some scenery and properties may have been substantial; doubtless a throne was used, but the pillars supporting the roof would have served for the trees on which Orlando pins his poems in *As You Like It*.

Having talked about the public theater—"this wooden *O*"—at some length, we should mention again that Shakespeare's plays were performed also in other locales. Alvin Kernan, in *Shakespeare, the King's Playwright: Theater in the Stuart Court 1603–1613* (1995), points out that "several of [Shakespeare's] plays contain brief theatrical performances, set always in a court or some noble house. When Shakespeare portrayed a theater, he did not, except for the choruses in *Henry V*, imagine a public theater" (p. 195). (Examples include episodes in *The Taming of the Shrew*, *A Midsummer Night's Dream*, *Hamlet*, and *The Tempest*.)

A Note on the Use of Boy Actors in Female Roles

Until fairly recently, scholars were content to mention that the convention existed; they sometimes also mentioned that it continued the medieval practice of using males in female roles, and that other theaters, notably in ancient Greece and in China and Japan, also used males in female roles. (In classical Noh drama in Japan, males still play the female roles.) Prudery may have been at the root of the academic failure to talk much about the use of boy actors, or maybe there really is not much more to say than that it was a convention of a male-centered culture (Stephen Greenblatt's view, in *Shakespearean Negotiations* [1988]). Further, the very nature of a convention is that it is not thought about: Hamlet is a Dane and Julius Caesar is a Roman, but in Shakespeare's plays they speak English, and we in the audience never give this odd fact a thought. Similarly, a character may speak in the presence of others and we understand, again without thinking about it, that he or she is not heard by the figures on the stage (the aside); a character alone on the stage may speak (the soliloquy), and we do not take the character to be unhinged; in a realistic (box) set, the fourth wall, which allows us to see what is going on, is miraculously missing. The no-nonsense view, then, is that the boy actor was an accepted convention, accepted unthinkingly—just as today we know that Kenneth Branagh is not Hamlet, Al Pacino is not Richard III, and Denzel Washington is not the Prince of Aragon. In this view, the audience takes the performer for the role, and that is that; such is the argument we now make for race-free casting, in which African-Americans and Asians can play roles of persons who lived in medieval Denmark and ancient Rome. But gender perhaps is different, at least today. It is a matter of abundant academic study: The Elizabethan theater is now sometimes called a transvestite theater, and we hear much about cross-dressing.

Shakespeare himself in a very few passages calls attention to the use of boys in female roles. At the end of *As You Like It* the boy who played Rosalind addresses the audience, and says, "O men, . . . if I were a woman, I would kiss as many of you as had beards that pleased me." But this is in the Epilogue; the plot is over, and the actor is stepping out of the play and into the audience's everyday world. A second reference to the practice of boys playing female roles occurs in *Antony and Cleopatra*, when Cleopatra imagines that she and Antony will be the subject of crude plays, her role being performed by a boy:

> The quick comedians
> Extemporally will stage us, and present
> Our Alexandrian revels: Antony
> Shall be brought drunken forth, and I shall see
> Some squeaking Cleopatra boy my greatness.   (5.2.216–20)

In a few other passages, Shakespeare is more indirect. For instance, in *Twelfth Night* Viola, played of course by a boy, disguises herself as a young man and seeks service in the house of a lord. She enlists the help of a Captain, and (by way of explaining away her voice and her beardlessness) says,

> I'll serve this duke
> Thou shalt present me as an eunuch to him.   (1.2.55–56)

In *Hamlet*, when the players arrive in 2.2, Hamlet jokes with the boy who plays a female role. The boy has grown since Hamlet last saw him: "By'r Lady, your ladyship is nearer to heaven than when I saw you last by the altitude of a chopine" (a lady's thick-soled shoe). He goes on: "Pray God your voice . . . be not cracked" (434–38).

Exactly how sexual, how erotic, this material was and is, is now much disputed. Again, the use of boys may have been unnoticed, or rather not thought about—an unexamined convention—by most or all spectators most of the time, perhaps *all* of the time, except when Shakespeare calls the convention to the attention of the audience, as in the passages just quoted. Still, an occasional bit seems to invite erotic thoughts. The clearest example is the name that Rosalind takes in *As You Like It*, Ganymede—the beautiful youth whom Zeus abducted. Did boys dressed to play female roles carry homoerotic appeal for straight men (Lisa Jardine's view, in *Still Harping on Daughters* [1983]), or for gay men, or for some or all women in the audience? Further, when the boy actor played a woman who (for the purposes of the plot) disguised herself as a male, as Rosalind, Viola, and Portia do—so we get a boy playing a woman playing a man—what sort of appeal was generated, and for what sort of spectator?

Some scholars have argued that the convention empowered women by letting female characters display a freedom unavailable in Renaissance patriarchal society; the convention, it is said, undermined rigid gender distinctions. In this view, the convention (along with plots in which female characters for a while disguised themselves as young men) allowed Shakespeare to say what some modern gender

critics say: Gender is a constructed role rather than a bio-
logical given, something we make, rather than a fixed binary
opposition of male and female (see Juliet Dusinberre, in
Shakespeare and the Nature of Women [1975]). On the other
hand, some scholars have maintained that the male disguise
assumed by some female characters serves only to reaffirm
traditional social distinctions since female characters who
don male garb (notably Portia in *The Merchant of Venice*
and Rosalind in *As You Like It*) return to their female garb
and at least implicitly (these critics say) reaffirm the status
quo. (For this last view, see Clara Claiborne Park, in an
essay in *The Woman's Part*, ed. Carolyn Ruth Swift Lenz et
al. [1980].) Perhaps no one answer is right for all plays; in
As You Like It cross-dressing empowers Rosalind, but in
Twelfth Night cross-dressing comically traps Viola.

Shakespeare's Dramatic Language: Costumes, Gestures and Silences; Prose and Poetry

Because Shakespeare was a dramatist, not merely a poet,
he worked not only with language but also with costume,
sound effects, gestures, and even silences. We have already
discussed some kinds of spectacle in the preceding section,
and now we will begin with other aspects of visual language;
a theater, after all, is literally a "place for seeing." Consider
the opening stage direction in *The Tempest*, the first play in
the first published collection of Shakespeare's plays: *"A
tempestuous noise of thunder and Lightning heard: Enter a
Ship-master, and a Boteswain."*

Costumes: What did that shipmaster and that boatswain
wear? Doubtless they wore something that identified them
as men of the sea. Not much is known about the costumes
that Elizabethan actors wore, but at least three points are
clear: (1) many of the costumes were splendid versions of
contemporary Elizabethan dress; (2) some attempts were
made to approximate the dress of certain occupations and of
antique or exotic characters such as Romans, Turks, and
Jews; (3) some costumes indicated that the wearer was

supernatural. Evidence for elaborate Elizabethan clothing can be found in the plays themselves and in contemporary comments about the "sumptuous" players who wore the discarded clothing of noblemen, as well as in account books that itemize such things as "a scarlet cloak with two broad gold laces, with gold buttons down the sides."

The attempts at approximation of the dress of certain occupations and nationalities also can be documented from the plays themselves, and it derives additional confirmation from a drawing of the first scene of Shakespeare's *Titus Andronicus*—the only extant Elizabethan picture of an identifiable episode in a play. (See pp. xxxviii–xxxix.) The drawing, probably done in 1594 or 1595, shows Queen Tamora pleading for mercy. She wears a somewhat medieval-looking robe and a crown; Titus wears a toga and a wreath, but two soldiers behind him wear costumes fairly close to Elizabethan dress. We do not know, however, if the drawing represents an actual stage production in the public theater, or perhaps a private production, or maybe only a reader's visualization of an episode. Further, there is some conflicting evidence: In *Julius Caesar* a reference is made to Caesar's doublet (a close-fitting jacket), which, if taken literally, suggests that even the protagonist did not wear Roman clothing; and certainly the lesser characters, who are said to wear hats, did not wear Roman garb.

It should be mentioned, too, that even ordinary clothing can be symbolic: Hamlet's "inky cloak," for example, sets him apart from the brightly dressed members of Claudius's court and symbolizes his mourning; the fresh clothes that are put on King Lear partly symbolize his return to sanity. Consider, too, the removal of disguises near the end of some plays. For instance, Rosalind in *As You Like It* and Portia and Nerissa in *The Merchant of Venice* remove their male attire, thus again becoming fully themselves.

Gestures and Silences: Gestures are an important part of a dramatist's language. King Lear kneels before his daughter Cordelia for a benediction (4.7.57–59), an act of humility that contrasts with his earlier speeches banishing her and that contrasts also with a comparable gesture, his ironic

kneeling before Regan (2.4.153–55). Northumberland's failure to kneel before King Richard II (3.3.71–72) speaks volumes. As for silences, consider a moment in *Coriolanus*: Before the protagonist yields to his mother's entreaties (5.3.182), there is this stage direction: *"Holds her by the hand, silent."* Another example of "speech in dumbness" occurs in *Macbeth*, when Macduff learns that his wife and children have been murdered. He is silent at first, as Malcolm's speech indicates: "What, man! Ne'er pull your hat upon your brows. Give sorrow words" (4.3.208–9). (For a discussion of such moments, see Philip C. McGuire's *Speechless Dialect: Shakespeare's Open Silences* [1985].)

Of course when we think of Shakespeare's work, we think primarily of his language, both the poetry and the prose.

Prose: Although two of his plays (*Richard II* and *King John*) have no prose at all, about half the others have at least one quarter of the dialogue in prose, and some have notably more: *1 Henry IV* and *2 Henry IV*, about half; *As You Like It*

and *Twelfth Night*, a little more than half; *Much Ado About Nothing*, more than three quarters; and *The Merry Wives of Windsor*, a little more than five-sixths. We should remember that despite Molière's joke about M. Jourdain, who was amazed to learn that he spoke prose, most of us do not speak prose. Rather, we normally utter repetitive, shapeless, and often ungrammatical torrents; prose is something very different—a sort of literary imitation of speech at its most coherent.

Today we may think of prose as "natural" for drama; or even if we think that poetry is appropriate for high tragedy we may still think that prose is the right medium for comedy. Greek, Roman, and early English comedies, however, were written in verse. In fact, prose was not generally considered a literary medium in England until the late fifteenth century; Chaucer tells even his bawdy stories in verse. By the end of the 1580s, however, prose had established itself on the English comic stage. In tragedy, Marlowe made some use of prose, not simply in the speeches of clownish servants but even in the speech of a tragic hero, Doctor Faustus. Still, before Shakespeare, prose normally was used in the theater only for special circumstances: (1) letters and proclamations, to set them off from the poetic dialogue; (2) mad characters, to indicate that normal thinking has become disordered; and (3) low comedy, or speeches uttered by clowns even when they are not being comic. Shakespeare made use of these conventions, but he also went far beyond them. Sometimes he begins a scene in prose and then shifts into verse as the emotion is heightened; or conversely, he may shift from verse to prose when a speaker is lowering the emotional level, as when Brutus speaks in the Forum.

Shakespeare's prose usually is not prosaic. Hamlet's prose includes not only small talk with Rosencrantz and Guildenstern but also princely reflections on "What a piece of work is a man" (2.2.312). In conversation with Ophelia, he shifts from light talk in verse to a passionate prose denunciation of women (3.1.103), though the shift to prose here is perhaps also intended to suggest the possibility of madness. (Consult Brian Vickers, *The Artistry of Shakespeare's Prose* [1968].)

Poetry: Drama in rhyme in England goes back to the Middle Ages, but by Shakespeare's day rhyme no longer dominated poetic drama; a finer medium, blank verse (strictly speaking, unrhymed lines of ten syllables, with the stress on every second syllable) had been adopted. But before looking at unrhymed poetry, a few things should be said about the chief uses of rhyme in Shakespeare's plays. (1) A couplet (a pair of rhyming lines) is sometimes used to convey emotional heightening at the end of a blank verse speech; (2) characters sometimes speak a couplet as they leave the stage, suggesting closure; (3) except in the latest plays, scenes fairly often conclude with a couplet, and sometimes, as in *Richard II*, 2.1.145–46, the entrance of a new character within a scene is preceded by a couplet, which wraps up the earlier portion of that scene; (4) speeches of two characters occasionally are linked by rhyme, most notably in *Romeo and Juliet*, 1.5.95–108, where the lovers speak a sonnet between them; elsewhere a taunting reply occasionally rhymes with the previous speaker's last line; (5) speeches with sententious or gnomic remarks are sometimes in rhyme, as in the duke's speech in *Othello* (1.3.199–206); (6) speeches of sardonic mockery are sometimes in rhyme—for example, Iago's speech on women in *Othello* (2.1.146–58)—and they sometimes conclude with an emphatic couplet, as in Bolingbroke's speech on comforting words in *Richard II* (1.3.301–2); (7) some characters are associated with rhyme, such as the fairies in *A Midsummer Night's Dream*; (8) in the early plays, especially *The Comedy of Errors* and *The Taming of the Shrew*, comic scenes that in later plays would be in prose are in jingling rhymes; (9) prologues, choruses, plays-within-the-play, inscriptions, vows, epilogues, and so on are often in rhyme, and the songs in the plays are rhymed.

Neither prose nor rhyme immediately comes to mind when we first think of Shakespeare's medium: It is blank verse, unrhymed iambic pentameter. (In a mechanically exact line there are five iambic feet. An iambic foot consists of two syllables, the second accented, as in *away*; five feet make a pentameter line. Thus, a strict line of iambic pentameter contains ten syllables, the even syllables being stressed more heavily than the odd syllables. Fortunately, Shakespeare usually varies the line somewhat.) The first speech in *A Midsummer Night's Dream*, spoken by Duke Theseus to his betrothed, is an example of blank verse:

> Now, fair Hippolyta, our nuptial hour
> Draws on apace. Four happy days bring in
> Another moon; but, O, methinks, how slow
> This old moon wanes! She lingers my desires,
> Like to a stepdame, or a dowager,
> Long withering out a young man's revenue.   (1.1.1–6)

As this passage shows, Shakespeare's blank verse is not mechanically unvarying. Though the predominant foot is the iamb (as in *apace* or *desires*), there are numerous variations. In the first line the stress can be placed on "fair," as the regular metrical pattern suggests, but it is likely that "Now" gets almost as much emphasis; probably in the second line "Draws" is more heavily emphasized than "on," giving us a trochee (a stressed syllable followed by an unstressed one); and in the fourth line each word in the phrase "This old moon wanes" is probably stressed fairly heavily, conveying by two spondees (two feet, each of two stresses) the oppressive tedium that Theseus feels.

In Shakespeare's early plays much of the blank verse is end-stopped (that is, it has a heavy pause at the end of each line), but he later developed the ability to write iambic pentameter verse paragraphs (rather than lines) that give the illusion of speech. His chief techniques are (1) enjambing, i.e., running the thought beyond the single line, as in the first three lines of the speech just quoted; (2) occasionally replacing an iamb with another foot; (3) varying the position of the chief pause (the caesura) within a line; (4) adding an occasional unstressed syllable at the end of a line, traditionally called a feminine ending; and (5) beginning or ending a speech with a half line.

Shakespeare's mature blank verse has much of the rhythmic flexibility of his prose; both the language, though richly figurative and sometimes dense, and the syntax seem natural. It is also often highly appropriate to a particular character. Consider, for instance, this speech from *Hamlet*, in which Claudius, King of Denmark ("the Dane"), speaks to Laertes:

> And now, Laertes, what's the news with you?
> You told us of some suit. What is't, Laertes?
> You cannot speak of reason to the Dane
> And lose your voice. What wouldst thou beg, Laertes,
> That shall not be my offer, not thy asking?   (1.2.42–46)

Notice the short sentences and the repetition of the name "Laertes," to whom the speech is addressed. Notice, too, the shift from the royal "us" in the second line to the more intimate "my" in the last line, and from "you" in the first three lines to the more intimate "thou" and "thy" in the last two lines. Claudius knows how to ingratiate himself with Laertes.

For a second example of the flexibility of Shakespeare's blank verse, consider a passage from *Macbeth*. Distressed by the doctor's inability to cure Lady Macbeth and by the imminent battle, Macbeth addresses some of his remarks to the doctor and others to the servant who is arming him. The entire speech, with its pauses, interruptions, and irresolution (in "Pull't off, I say," Macbeth orders the servant to remove the armor that the servant has been putting on him), catches Macbeth's disintegration. (In the first line, *physic* means "medicine," and in the fourth and fifth lines, *cast the water* means "analyze the urine.")

> Throw physic to the dogs, I'll none of it.
> Come, put mine armor on. Give me my staff.
> Seyton, send out.—Doctor, the thanes fly from me.—
> Come, sir, dispatch. If thou couldst, doctor, cast
> The water of my land, find her disease
> And purge it to a sound and pristine health,
> I would applaud thee to the very echo,
> That should applaud again.—Pull't off, I say.—
> What rhubarb, senna, or what purgative drug,
> Would scour these English hence? Hear'st thou of them?
>
> (5.3.47–56)

Blank verse, then, can be much more than unrhymed iambic pentameter, and even within a single play Shakespeare's blank verse often consists of several styles, depending on the speaker and on the speaker's emotion at the moment.

The Play Text as a Collaboration

Shakespeare's fellow dramatist Ben Jonson reported that the actors said of Shakespeare, "In his writing, whatsoever he penned, he never blotted out line," i.e., never crossed out material and revised his work while composing. None of Shakespeare's plays survives in manuscript (with the possible exception of a scene in *Sir Thomas More*), so we cannot fully evaluate the comment, but in a few instances the published work clearly shows that he revised his manuscript. Consider the following passage (shown here in facsimile) from the best early text of *Romeo and Juliet*, the Second Quarto (1599):

Ro. Would I were ſleepe and peace ſo ſweet to reſt
The grey eyde morne ſmiles on the frowning night,
Checking the Eaſterne Clouds with ſtreaks of light,
And darkneſſe fleckted like a drunkard reeles,
From forth daies pathway,made by *Tytans* wheeles.
Hence will I to my ghoſtly Friers cloſe cell,
His helpe to craue,and my deare hap to tell.

                                         Exit.

       Enter Frier alone with a basket.   (night,
  Fri. The grey-eyed morne ſmiles on the frowning
Checking the Eaſterne clowdes with ſtreaks of light:
And fleckeld darkneſſe like a drunkard reeles,
From forth daies path,and *Titans* burning wheeles:
Now erethe ſun aduance his burning eie,

Romeo rather elaborately tells us that the sun at dawn is dispelling the night (morning is smiling, the eastern clouds are checked with light, and the sun's chariot—Titan's wheels—advances), and he will seek out his spiritual father, the Friar. He exits and, oddly, the Friar enters and says pretty much the same thing about the sun. Both speakers say that "the gray-eyed morn smiles on the frowning night," but there are small differences, perhaps having more to do with the business of printing the book than with the author's composition: For Romeo's "checkring," "fleckted," and "pathway," we get the Friar's "checking," "fleckeld," and "path." (Notice, by the way, the inconsistency in Elizabethan spelling: Romeo's "clouds" become the Friar's "clowdes.")

Both versions must have been in the printer's copy, and it seems safe to assume that both were in Shakespeare's manuscript. He must have written one version—let's say he first wrote Romeo's closing lines for this scene—and then he decided, no, it's better to give this lyrical passage to the Friar, as the opening of a new scene, but he neglected to delete the first version. Editors must make a choice, and they may feel that the reasonable thing to do is to print the text as Shakespeare intended it. But how can we know what he intended? Almost all modern editors delete the lines from

Romeo's speech, and retain the Friar's lines. They don't do this because they know Shakespeare's intention, however. They give the lines to the Friar because the first published version (1597) of *Romeo and Juliet* gives only the Friar's version, and this text (though in many ways inferior to the 1599 text) is thought to derive from the memory of some actors, that is, it is thought to represent a performance, not just a script. Maybe during the course of rehearsals Shakespeare—an actor as well as an author—unilaterally decided that the Friar should speak the lines; if so (remember that we don't know this to be a fact) his final intention was to give the speech to the Friar. Maybe, however, the actors talked it over and settled on the Friar, with or without Shakespeare's approval. On the other hand, despite the 1597 version, one might argue (if only weakly) on behalf of giving the lines to Romeo rather than to the Friar, thus: (1) Romeo's comment on the coming of the daylight emphasizes his separation from Juliet, and (2) the figurative language seems more appropriate to Romeo than to the Friar. Having said this, in the Signet edition we have decided in this instance to draw on the evidence provided by earlier text and to give the lines to the Friar, on the grounds that since Q1 reflects a production, in the theater (at least on one occasion) the lines were spoken by the Friar.

A playwright sold a script to a theatrical company. The script thus belonged to the company, not the author, and author and company alike must have regarded this script not as a literary work but as the basis for a play that the actors would create on the stage. We speak of Shakespeare as the author of the plays, but readers should bear in mind that the texts they read, even when derived from a single text, such as the First Folio (1623), are inevitably the collaborative work not simply of Shakespeare with his company—doubtless during rehearsals the actors would suggest alterations—but also with other forces of the age. One force was governmental censorship. In 1606 parliament passed "an Act to restrain abuses of players," prohibiting the utterance of oaths and the name of God. So where the earliest text of *Othello* gives us "By heaven" (3.3.106), the first Folio gives "Alas," presumably reflecting the compliance of stage practice with the law. Similarly, the 1623 version of *King Lear* omits the oath "Fut" (probably from "By God's foot") at 1.2.142, again presumably reflecting the line as it was spoken on the stage. Editors who seek to give the reader the play that Shakespeare initially conceived—the "authentic" play conceived by the solitary Shakespeare—probably will restore the missing oaths and references to God. Other editors, who see the play as a collaborative work, a construction made not only by Shakespeare but also by actors and compositors and even government censors, may claim that what counts is the play as it was actually performed. Such editors regard the censored text as legitimate, since it is the play that was (presumably) finally put on. A performed text, they argue, has more historical reality than a text produced by an editor who has sought to get at what Shakespeare initially wrote. In this view, the text of a play is rather like the script of a film; the script is not the film, and the play text is not the performed play. Even if we want to talk about the play that Shakespeare "intended," we will find ourselves talking about a script that he handed over to a company with the intention that it be implemented by actors. The "intended" play is the one that the actors—we might almost say "society"—would help to construct.

Further, it is now widely held that a play is also the work of readers and spectators, who do not simply receive meaning, but who create it when they respond to the play. This idea is fully in accord with contemporary poststructuralist critical thinking, notably Roland Barthes's "The Death of the Author," in *Image-Music-Text* (1977), and Michel Foucault's "What Is an Author?", in *The Foucault Reader* (1984). The gist of the idea is that an author is not an isolated genius; rather, authors are subject to the politics and other social structures of their age. A dramatist especially is a worker in a collaborative project, working most obviously with actors—parts may be written for particular actors—but working also with the audience. Consider the words of Samuel Johnson, written to be spoken by the actor David Garrick at the opening of a theater in 1747:

> The stage but echoes back the public voice;
> The drama's laws, the drama's patrons give,
> For we that live to please, must please to live.

The audience—the public taste as understood by the playwright—helps to determine what the play is. Moreover, even members of the public who are not part of the playwright's immediate audience may exert an influence through censorship. We have already glanced at governmental censorship, but there are also other kinds. Take one of Shakespeare's most beloved characters, Falstaff, who appears in three of Shakespeare's plays, the two parts of *Henry IV* and *The Merry Wives of Windsor*. He appears with this name in the earliest printed version of the first of these plays, *1 Henry IV*, but we know that Shakespeare originally called him (after an historical figure) Sir John Oldcastle. Oldcastle appears in Shakespeare's source (partly reprinted in the Signet edition of *1 Henry IV*), and a trace of the name survives in Shakespeare's play, 1.2.43–44, where Prince Hal punningly addresses Falstaff as "my old lad of the castle." But for some reason—perhaps because the family of the historical Oldcastle complained—Shakespeare had to change the name. In short, the play as we have it was (at least in this detail) subject to some sort of censorship. If we think that a text should present what we take to be the author's intention, we probably will want to replace *Falstaff* with *Oldcastle*. But if we recognize that a play is a collaboration, we may welcome the change, even if it was forced on Shakespeare. Somehow *Falstaff*, with its hint of *false-staff*, i.e., inadequate prop, seems just right for this fat knight who, to our delight, entertains the young prince with untruths. We can go as far as saying that, at least so far as a play is concerned, an insistence on the author's original intention (even if we could know it) can sometimes impoverish the text.

The tiny example of Falstaff's name illustrates the point that the text we read is inevitably only a version—something in effect produced by the collaboration of the playwright with his actors, audiences, compositors, and editors—of a fluid text that Shakespeare once wrote, just as the *Hamlet* that we see on the screen starring Kenneth Branagh is not the *Hamlet* that Shakespeare saw in an open-air playhouse starring Richard Burbage. *Hamlet* itself, as we shall note in a moment, also exists in several versions. It is not surprising that there is now much talk about the *instability* of Shakespeare's texts.

Because he was not only a playwright but was also an actor and a shareholder in a theatrical company, Shakespeare probably was much involved with the translation of the play from a manuscript to a stage production. He may or may not have done some rewriting during rehearsals, and he may or may not have been happy with cuts that were made. Some plays, notably *Hamlet* and *King Lear*, are so long that it is most unlikely that the texts we read were acted in their entirety. Further, for both of these plays we have more than one early text that demands consideration. In *Hamlet*, the Second Quarto (1604) includes some two hundred lines not found in the Folio (1623). Among the passages missing from the Folio are two of Hamlet's reflective speeches, the "dram of evil" speech (1.4.13–38) and "How all occasions do inform against me" (4.4.32–66). Since the Folio has more numerous and often fuller stage directions, it certainly looks as though in the Folio we get a theatrical version of the play, a text whose cuts were probably made—this is only a hunch, of course—not because Shakespeare was changing his conception of Hamlet but because the playhouse demanded a modified play. (The problem is complicated, since the Folio not only cuts some of the Quarto but adds some material. Various explanations have been offered.)

Or take an example from *King Lear*. In the First and Second Quarto (1608, 1619), the final speech of the play is given to Albany, Lear's surviving son-in-law, but in the First Folio version (1623), the speech is given to Edgar. The Quarto version is in accord with tradition—usually the highest-ranking character in a tragedy speaks the final words. Why does the Folio give the speech to Edgar? One possible answer is this: The Folio version omits some of Albany's speeches in earlier scenes, so perhaps it was decided (by Shakespeare? by the players?) not to give the final lines to so pale a character. In fact, the discrepancies are so many between the two texts, that some scholars argue we do not simply have texts showing different theatrical productions. Rather, these scholars say, Shakespeare substantially revised the play, and we really have two versions of *King Lear* (and of *Othello* also, say some)—two different plays—not simply two texts, each of which is in some ways imperfect.

In this view, the 1608 version of *Lear* may derive from Shakespeare's manuscript, and the 1623 version may derive from his later revision. The Quartos have almost three hundred lines not in the Folio, and the Folio has about a hundred lines not in the Quartos. It used to be held that all the texts were imperfect in various ways and from various causes — some passages in the Quartos were thought to have been set from a manuscript that was not entirely legible, other passages were thought to have been set by a compositor who was new to setting plays, and still other passages were thought to have been provided by an actor who misremembered some of the lines. This traditional view held that an editor must draw on the Quartos and the Folio in order to get Shakespeare's "real" play. The new argument holds (although not without considerable strain) that we have two authentic plays, Shakespeare's early version (in the Quarto) and Shakespeare's — or his theatrical company's — revised version (in the Folio). Not only theatrical demands but also Shakespeare's own artistic sense, it is argued, called for extensive revisions. Even the titles vary: Q1 is called *True Chronicle Historie of the life and death of King Lear and his three Daughters*, whereas the Folio text is called *The Tragedie of King Lear*. To combine the two texts in order to produce what the editor thinks is the play that Shakespeare intended to write is, according to this view, to produce a text that is false to the history of the play. If the new view is correct, and we do have texts of two distinct versions of *Lear* rather than two imperfect versions of one play, it supports in a textual way the poststructuralist view that we cannot possibly have an unmediated vision of (in this case) a play by Shakespeare; we can only recognize a plurality of visions.

Editing Texts

Though eighteen of his plays were published during his lifetime, Shakespeare seems never to have supervised their publication. There is nothing unusual here; when a playwright sold a play to a theatrical company he surrendered his ownership to it. Normally a company would not publish the play, because to publish it meant to allow competitors to acquire the piece. Some plays did get published: Apparently hard-up actors sometimes pieced together a play for a publisher; sometimes a company in need of money sold a play; and sometimes a company allowed publication of a play that no longer drew audiences. That Shakespeare did not concern himself with publication is not remarkable; of his contemporaries, only Ben Jonson carefully supervised the publication of his own plays.

In 1623, seven years after Shakespeare's death, John Heminges and Henry Condell (two senior members of Shakespeare's company, who had worked with him for about twenty years) collected his plays—published and unpublished—into a large volume, of a kind called a folio. (A folio is a volume consisting of large sheets that have been folded once, each sheet thus making two leaves, or four pages. The size of the page of course depends on the size of the sheet—a folio can range in height from twelve to sixteen inches, and in width from eight to eleven; the pages in the 1623 cdition of Shakespeare, commonly called the First Folio, are approximately thirteen inches tall and eight inches wide.) The eighteen plays published during Shakespeare's lifetime had been issued one play per volume in small formats called quartos. (Each sheet in a quarto has been folded twice, making four leaves, or eight pages, each page being about nine inches tall and seven inches wide, roughly the size of a large paperback.)

Heminges and Condell suggest in an address "To the great variety of readers" that the republished plays are presented in better form than in the quartos:

> Before you were abused with diverse stolen and surreptitious copies, maimed and deformed by the frauds and stealths of injurious impostors that exposed them; even those, are now offered to your view cured and perfect of their limbs, and all the rest absolute in their numbers, as he [i.e., Shakespeare] conceived them.

There is a good deal of truth to this statement, but some of the quarto versions are better than others; some are in fact preferable to the Folio text.

Whoever was assigned to prepare the texts for publication in the first Folio seems to have taken the job seriously and yet not to have performed it with uniform care. The sources of the texts seem to have been, in general, good unpublished copies or the best published copies. The first play in the collection, *The Tempest*, is divided into acts and scenes, has unusually full stage directions and descriptions of spectacle, and concludes with a list of the characters, but the editor was not able (or willing) to present all of the succeeding texts so fully dressed. Later texts occasionally show signs of carelessness: in one scene of *Much Ado About Nothing* the names of actors, instead of characters, appear as speech prefixes, as they had in the Quarto, which the Folio reprints; proofreading throughout the Folio is spotty and apparently was done without reference to the printer's copy; the pagination of *Hamlet* jumps from 156 to 257. Further, the proofreading was done while the presses continued to print, so that each play in each volume contains a mix of corrected and uncorrected pages.

Modern editors of Shakespeare must first select their copy; no problem if the play exists only in the Folio, but a considerable problem if the relationship between a Quarto and the Folio—or an early Quarto and a later one—is unclear. In the case of *Romeo and Juliet*, the First Quarto (Q1), published in 1597, is vastly inferior to the Second (Q2), published in 1599. The basis of Q1 apparently is a version put together from memory by some actors. Not surprisingly, it garbles many passages and is much shorter than Q2. On the other hand, occasionally Q1 makes better sense than Q2. For instance, near the end of the play, when the parents have assembled and learned of the deaths of Romeo and Juliet, in Q2 the Prince says (5.3.208–9),

Come, *Montague;* for thou art early vp
To see thy sonne and heire, now earling downe.

The last three words of this speech surely do not make sense, and many editors turn to Q1, which instead of "now earling downe" has "more early downe." Some modern editors take only "early" from Q1, and print "now early down"; others take "more early," and print "more early down." Further, Q1 (though, again, quite clearly a garbled and abbreviated text) includes some stage directions that are not found in Q2, and today many editors who base their text on Q2 are glad to add these stage directions, because the directions help to give us a sense of what the play looked like on Shakespeare's stage. Thus, in 4.3.58, after Juliet drinks the potion, Q1 gives us this stage direction, not in Q2: *"She falls upon her bed within the curtains."*

In short, an editor's decisions do not end with the choice of a single copy text. First of all, editors must reckon with Elizabethan spelling. If they are not producing a facsimile, they probably modernize the spelling, but ought they to preserve the old forms of words that apparently were pronounced quite unlike their modern forms—*lanthorn, alablaster*? If they preserve these forms are they really preserving Shakespeare's forms or perhaps those of a compositor in the printing house? What is one to do when one finds *lanthorn* and *lantern* in adjacent lines? (The editors of this series in general, but not invariably, assume that words should be spelled in their modern form, unless, for instance, a rhyme is involved.) Elizabethan punctuation, too, presents problems. For example, in the First Folio, the only text for the play, Macbeth rejects his wife's idea that he can wash the blood from his hand (2.2.60–62):

> No: this my Hand will rather
> The multitudinous Seas incarnardine,
> Making the Greene one, Red.

Obviously an editor will remove the superfluous capitals, and will probably alter the spelling to "incarnadine," but what about the comma before "Red"? If we retain the comma, Macbeth is calling the sea "the green one." If we drop the comma, Macbeth is saying that his bloody hand will make the sea ("the Green") *uniformly* red.

An editor will sometimes have to change more than spelling and punctuation. Macbeth says to his wife (1.7.46–47):

> I dare do all that may become a man,
> Who dares no more, is none.

For two centuries editors have agreed that the second line is unsatisfactory, and have emended "no" to "do": "Who dares do more is none." But when in the same play (4.2.21–22) Ross says that fearful persons

> Floate vpon a wilde and violent Sea
> Each way, and moue,

need we emend the passage? On the assumption that the compositor misread the manuscript, some editors emend "each way, and move" to "and move each way"; others emend "move" to "none" (i.e., "Each way and none"). Other editors, however, let the passage stand as in the original. The editors of the Signet Classics Shakespeare have restrained themselves from making abundant emendations. In their minds they hear Samuel Johnson on the dangers of emendation: "I have adopted the Roman sentiment, that it is more honorable to save a citizen than to kill an enemy." Some departures (in addition to spelling, punctuation, and lineation) from the copy text have of course been made, but the original readings are listed in a note following the play, so that readers can evaluate the changes for themselves.

Following tradition, the editors of the Signet Classics Shakespeare have prefaced each play with a list of characters, and throughout the play have regularized the names of the speakers. Thus, in our text of *Romeo and Juliet*, all speeches by Juliet's mother are prefixed "Lady Capulet," although the 1599 Quarto of the play, which provides our copy text, uses at various points seven speech tags for this one character: *Capu. Wi.* (i.e., Capulet's wife), *Ca. Wi.*, *Wi.*, *Wife*, *Old La.* (i.e., Old Lady), *La.*, and *Mo.* (i.e., Mother). Similarly, in *All's Well That Ends Well*, the character whom we regularly call "Countess" is in the Folio (the copy text) variously identified as *Mother*, *Countess*, *Old Countess*, *Lady*, and *Old Lady*. Admittedly there is some loss in regularizing, since the various prefixes may give us a hint of the way Shakespeare (or a scribe who copied Shakespeare's manuscript) was thinking of the character in a particular scene—for instance, as a mother, or as an old lady. But too much can be made of these differing prefixes, since the social relationships implied are *not* always relevant to the given scene.

We have also added line numbers and in many cases act and scene divisions as well as indications of locale at the beginning of scenes. The Folio divided most of the plays into acts and some into scenes. Early eighteenth-century editors increased the divisions. These divisions, which provide a convenient way of referring to passages in the plays, have been retained, but when not in the text chosen as the basis for the Signet Classics text they are enclosed within square brackets, [ ], to indicate that they are editorial additions. Similarly, though no play of Shakespeare's was equipped with indications of the locale at the heads of scene divisions, locales have here been added in square brackets for the convenience of readers, who lack the information that costumes, properties, gestures, and scenery afford to spectators. Spectators can tell at a glance they are in the throne room, but without an editorial indication the reader may be puzzled for a while. It should be mentioned, incidentally, that there are a few authentic stage directions—perhaps Shakespeare's, perhaps a prompter's—that suggest locales, such as *"Enter Brutus in his orchard,"* and *"They go up into the Senate house."* It is hoped that the bracketed additions in the Signet text will provide readers with the sort of help provided by these two authentic directions, but it is equally hoped that the reader will remember that the stage was not loaded with scenery.

Shakespeare on the Stage

Each volume in the Signet Classics Shakespeare includes a brief stage (and sometimes film) history of the play. When we read about earlier productions, we are likely to find them eccentric, obviously wrongheaded—for instance, Nahum Tate's version of *King Lear*, with a happy ending, which held the stage for about a century and a half, from the late seventeenth century until the end of the first quarter of the nineteenth. We see engravings of David Garrick, the greatest actor of the eighteenth century, in eighteenth-century garb as King Lear, and we smile, thinking how absurd the production must have been. If we are more thoughtful, we say, with the English novelist L. P. Hartley, "The past is a foreign country: they do things differently there." But if the eighteenth-century staging is a foreign country, what of the plays of the late sixteenth and seventeenth centuries? A foreign language, a foreign theater, a foreign audience.

Probably all viewers of Shakespeare's plays, beginning with Shakespeare himself, at times have been unhappy with the plays on the stage. Consider three comments about production that we find in the plays themselves, which suggest Shakespeare's concerns. The Chorus in *Henry V* complains that the heroic story cannot possibly be adequately staged:

> But pardon, gentles all,
> The flat unraisèd spirits that hath dared
> On this unworthy scaffold to bring forth
> So great an object. Can this cockpit hold
> The vasty fields of France? Or may we cram
> Within this wooden *O* the very casques
> That did affright the air at Agincourt?
>
> . . . .
>
> Piece out our imperfections with your thoughts.
>
> (Prologue 1.8–14, 23)

Second, here are a few sentences (which may or may not represent Shakespeare's own views) from Hamlet's longish lecture to the players:

> Speak the speech, I pray you, as I pronounced it to you, trippingly on the tongue. But if you mouth it, as many of our players do, I had as lief the town crier spoke my lines. . . . O, it offends me to the soul to hear a robustious periwig-pated fellow tear a passion to tatters, to very rags, to split the ears of the groundlings. . . . And let those that play your clowns speak no more than is set down for them, for there be of them that will themselves laugh, to set on some quantity of barren spectators to laugh too, though in the meantime some necessary question of the play be then to be considered. That's villainous and shows a most pitiful ambition in the fool that uses it. (3.2.1–47)

Finally, we can quote again from the passage cited earlier in this introduction, concerning the boy actors who played the female roles. Cleopatra imagines with horror a theatrical version of her activities with Antony:

> The quick comedians
> Extemporally will stage us, and present
> Our Alexandrian revels: Antony
> Shall be brought drunken forth, and I shall see

Some squeaking Cleopatra boy my greatness
I' th' posture of a whore.   (5.2.216–21)

It is impossible to know how much weight to put on such
passages—perhaps Shakespeare was just being modest
about his theater's abilities—but it is easy enough to think
that he was unhappy with some aspects of Elizabethan production. Probably no production can fully satisfy a playwright, and for that matter, few productions can fully satisfy
us; we regret this or that cut, this or that way of costuming
the play, this or that bit of business.

One's first thought may be this: Why don't they just do
"authentic" Shakespeare, "straight" Shakespeare, the play
as Shakespeare wrote it? But as we read the plays—words
written to be performed—it sometimes becomes clear that
we do not know *how* to perform them. For instance, in
Antony and Cleopatra Antony, the Roman general who has
succumbed to Cleopatra and to Egyptian ways, says, "The
nobleness of life / Is to do thus" (1.1.36–37). But what is
"thus"? Does Antony at this point embrace Cleopatra? Does
he embrace and kiss her? (There are, by the way, very few
scenes of kissing on Shakespeare's stage, possibly because
boys played the female roles.) Or does he make a sweeping
gesture, indicating the Egyptian way of life?

This is not an isolated example; the plays are filled with
lines that call for gestures, but we are not sure what the gestures should be. *Interpretation* is inevitable. Consider a passage in *Hamlet.* In 3.1, Polonius persuades his daughter,
Ophelia, to talk to Hamlet while Polonius and Claudius
eavesdrop. The two men conceal themselves, and Hamlet
encounters Ophelia. At 3.1.131 Hamlet suddenly says to her,
"Where's your father?" Why does Hamlet, apparently out of
nowhere—they have not been talking about Polonius—ask
this question? Is this an example of the "antic disposition"
(fantastic behavior) that Hamlet earlier (1.5.172) had told
Horatio and others—including us—he would display? That
is, is the question about the whereabouts of her father a
seemingly irrational one, like his earlier question (3.1.103)
to Ophelia, "Ha, ha! Are you honest?" Or, on the other hand,
has Hamlet (as in many productions) suddenly glimpsed
Polonius's foot protruding from beneath a drapery at the

rear? That is, does Hamlet ask the question because he has suddenly seen something suspicious and now is testing Ophelia? (By the way, in productions that do give Hamlet a physical cue, it is almost always Polonius rather than Claudius who provides the clue. This itself is an act of interpretation on the part of the director.) Or (a third possibility) does Hamlet get a clue from Ophelia, who inadvertently betrays the spies by nervously glancing at their place of hiding? This is the interpretation used in the BBC television version, where Ophelia glances in fear toward the hiding place just after Hamlet says "Why wouldst thou be a breeder of sinners?" (121–22). Hamlet, realizing that he is being observed, glances here and there *before* he asks "Where's your father?" The question thus is a climax to what he has been doing while speaking the preceding lines. Or (a fourth interpretation) does Hamlet suddenly, without the aid of any clue whatsoever, intuitively (insightfully, mysteriously, wonderfully) sense that someone is spying? Directors must decide, of course—and so must readers.

Recall, too, the preceding discussion of the texts of the plays, which argued that the texts—though they seem to be before us in permanent black on white—are unstable. The Signet text of *Hamlet*, which draws on the Second Quarto (1604) and the First Folio (1623) is considerably longer than any version staged in Shakespeare's time. Our version, even if spoken very briskly and played without any intermission, would take close to four hours, far beyond "the two hours' traffic of our stage" mentioned in the Prologue to *Romeo and Juliet*. (There are a few contemporary references to the duration of a play, but none mentions more than three hours.) Of Shakespeare's plays, only *The Comedy of Errors*, *Macbeth*, and *The Tempest* can be done in less than three hours without cutting. And even if we take a play that exists only in a short text, *Macbeth*, we cannot claim that we are experiencing the very play that Shakespeare conceived, partly because some of the Witches' songs almost surely are non-Shakespearean additions, and partly because we are not willing to watch the play performed without an intermission and with boys in the female roles.

Further, as the earlier discussion of costumes mentioned, the plays apparently were given chiefly in contemporary, that is, in Elizabethan dress. If today we give them in the costumes that Shakespeare probably saw, the plays seem not contemporary but curiously dated. Yet if we use our own dress, we find lines of dialogue that are at odds with what we see; we may feel that the language, so clearly not our own, is inappropriate coming out of people in today's dress. A common solution, incidentally, has been to set the plays in the nineteenth century, on the grounds that this attractively distances the plays (gives them a degree of foreignness, allowing for interesting costumes) and yet doesn't put them into a museum world of Elizabethan England.

Inevitably our productions are adaptations, *our* adaptations, and inevitably they will look dated, not in a century but in twenty years, or perhaps even in a decade. Still, we cannot escape from our own conceptions. As the director Peter Brook has said, in *The Empty Space* (1968):

> It is not only the hair-styles, costumes and make-ups that look dated. All the different elements of staging—the shorthands of behavior that stand for emotions; gestures, gesticulations and tones of voice—are all fluctuating on an invisible stock exchange all the time. . . . A living theatre that thinks it can stand aloof from anything as trivial as fashion will wilt. (p. 16)

As Brook indicates, it is through today's hairstyles, costumes, makeup, gestures, gesticulations, tones of voice—this includes our *conception* of earlier hairstyles, costumes, and so forth if we stage the play in a period other than our own—that we inevitably stage the plays.

It is a truism that every age invents its own Shakespeare, just as, for instance, every age has invented its own classical world. Our view of ancient Greece, a slave-holding society in which even free Athenian women were severely circumscribed, does not much resemble the Victorians' view of ancient Greece as a glorious democracy, just as, perhaps, our view of Victorianism itself does not much resemble theirs. We cannot claim that the Shakespeare on our stage is the true Shakespeare, but in our stage productions we find a Shakespeare that speaks to us, a Shakespeare that our ancestors doubtless did not know but one that seems to us to be the true Shakespeare—at least for a while.

Our age is remarkable for the wide variety of kinds of staging that it uses for Shakespeare, but one development deserves special mention. This is the now common practice of race-blind or color-blind or nontraditional casting, which allows persons who are not white to play in Shakespeare. Previously blacks performing in Shakespeare were limited to a mere three roles, Othello, Aaron (in *Titus Andronicus*), and the Prince of Morocco (in *The Merchant of Venice*), and there were no roles at all for Asians. Indeed, African-Americans rarely could play even one of these three roles, since they were not welcome in white companies. Ira Aldridge (c.1806–1867), a black actor of undoubted talent, was forced to make his living by performing Shakespeare in England and in Europe, where he could play not only Othello but also—in whiteface—other tragic roles such as King Lear. Paul Robeson (1898–1976) made theatrical history when he played Othello in London in 1930, and there was some talk about bringing the production to the United States, but there was more talk about whether American audiences would tolerate the sight of a black man—a real black man, not a white man in blackface—kissing and then killing a white woman. The idea was tried out in summer stock in 1942, the reviews were enthusiastic, and in the following year Robeson opened on Broadway in a production that ran an astounding 296 performances. An occasional all-black company sometimes performed Shakespeare's plays, but otherwise blacks (and other minority members) were in effect shut out from performing Shakespeare. Only since about 1970 has it been common for nonwhites to play major roles along with whites. Thus, in a 1996–97 production of *Antony and Cleopatra*, a white Cleopatra, Vanessa Redgrave, played opposite a black Antony, David Harewood. Multiracial casting is now especially common at the New York Shakespeare Festival, founded in 1954 by Joseph Papp, and in England, where even siblings such as Claudio and Isabella in *Measure for Measure* or Lear's three daughters may be of different races. Probably most viewers today soon stop worrying about the lack of realism, and move beyond the color of the performers' skin to the quality of the performance.

Nontraditional casting is not only a matter of color or race; it includes sex. In the past, occasionally a distinguished woman of the theater has taken on a male role—Sarah Bernhardt (1844–1923) as Hamlet is perhaps the most famous example—but such performances were widely regarded as eccentric. Although today there have been some performances involving cross-dressing (a drag *As You Like It* staged by the National Theatre in England in 1966 and in the United States in 1974 has achieved considerable fame in the annals of stage history), what is more interesting is the casting of women in roles that traditionally are male but that need not be. Thus, a 1993–94 English production of *Henry V* used a woman—*not* cross-dressed—in the role of the governor of Harfleur. According to Peter Holland, who reviewed the production in *Shakespeare Survey* 48 (1995), "having a female Governor of Harfleur feminized the city and provided a direct response to the horrendous threat of rape and murder that Henry had offered, his language and her body in direct connection and opposition" (p. 210). Ten years from now the device may not play so effectively, but today it speaks to us. Shakespeare, born in the Elizabethan Age, has been dead nearly four hundred years, yet he is, as Ben Jonson said, "not of an age but for all time." We must understand, however, that he is "for all time" precisely because each age finds in his abundance something for itself and something of itself.

And here we come back to two issues discussed earlier in this introduction—the instability of the text and, curiously, the Bacon/Oxford heresy concerning the authorship of the plays. *Of course* Shakespeare wrote the plays, and we should daily fall on our knees to thank him for them—and yet there is something to the idea that he is not their only author. Every editor, every director and actor, and every reader to some degree shapes them, too, for when we edit, direct, act, or read, we inevitably become Shakespeare's collaborator and re-create the plays. The plays, one might say, are so cunningly contrived that they guide our responses, tell us how we ought to feel, and make a mark on us, but (for better or for worse) we also make a mark on them.

—SYLVAN BARNET
Tufts University

Introduction

It has been customary since the late nineteenth century to call *All's Well That Ends Well* a "problem play," or a "dark comedy." The first term relates it to the sort of drama we associate chiefly with Ibsen, a play about a social system in need of repair, a system with, say, faulty attitudes toward female emancipation or toward venereal disease. Because *All's Well* (like much other Elizabethan comedy) includes speeches on the nature of virtue and presents us with a picture of a virtuous but lowborn woman rejected by her snobbish husband, there was enough point in the comparison to give it some life for a century. But what is the problem? Because Shakespeare's Helena seemed to resemble Ibsen's Nora, *All's Well* gained Shaw's approval (as much of Shakespeare did not), but it is not really very like a nineteenth-century *pièce à thèse*. It does not move toward a debate in which some commonly held code is called into doubt; it does not preach the abandonment of humbug; it does not suggest that the world will go well if only people will give up romantic ideas. It does not really anatomize the problem of nobility—Does nobility reside in lineage or in deeds?—because the lowborn heroine is so clearly right and the snobbish aristocrat so clearly wrong that there is no debate.

Abandoning the hunt for this sort of "problem," then, we can turn to a different sort of problem that has vexed students of the play: Where does it fit in Shakespeare's career? Here we confront the term "dark comedy," which associates this play with an alleged period in Shakespeare's life, about 1601–06, when he supposedly lost faith in the golden world he had seen about him (and had dramatized in *A Midsummer Night's Dream, As You Like It,* and *Twelfth Night*) and fell into the bitter cynicism that—users of the term commonly say—marks this play as well as *Measure for Measure, Troilus and Cressida, Hamlet, King Lear,* and *Timon of Athens.* The late E. K. Chambers—a great scholar, with whom one may differ only humbly and reluctantly—in *Shakespeare: A Survey* puts it this way: *All's Well*

> groups itself undeniably with *Troilus and Cressida* and *Measure for Measure,* as one of the bitter comedies; for it is a comedy from which all laughter has evaporated, save the grim laughter which follows the dubious sallies of Monsieur Lavache and the contemptuous laughter which presides over the plucking bare of the ineffable Parolles. The spiritual affinities of Helena's story are indeed far less with the radiant humor of *Twelfth Night* and *As You Like It* than with the analytic psychology of the great advance-guard of tragedy, *Julius Caesar* and *Hamlet,* which was almost contemporary with these.

The theory runs that for some reason Shakespeare became unhappy and turned to tragedy and to bitter comedy. Why he did so is variously explained. For some proponents, the sonnets tell a story of the poet's discovery of betrayal; the friend's infidelity, or the Dark Lady's lust, drove Shakespeare to despair, and the despair is manifested in the plays. Or the fall of Essex shattered Shakespeare's world. (Chambers very tentatively inclines to the suggestion that "Shakespeare's world-sickness" may be most plausibly related to the failure of Essex's conspiracy.) Or the death of Shakespeare's father in 1601 was a crushing blow. Or the advent of the unimpressive James I, following the death of Queen Elizabeth in 1603, was enough to cause the poet great unhappiness. But all these speculations are based on the shaky premise that a professional dramatist's works mirror his state of mind, as a romantic lyric poet's are supposed to. He writes tragedies when tragedy has struck home, and he writes comedies when all is going well. Probably an Elizabethan dramatist would have been surprised to learn that he had been writing autobiography when all along he had thought he was writing tragedy, comedy, history, or whatever else his company wanted or was currently in vogue.

The play was first published in the Folio of 1623, seven years after Shakespeare's death. There is no external evidence of the date of *All's Well*—no reference to it by any witness, no quotation from it in a datable work, no detected allusion in it to any current event. Conjectures about its date must be based on theories about Shakespeare's progressive use of certain motifs and the development of Shakespeare's style.

To take the question of motif first: most readers find the bed trick, or the "substitute bride motif" (to use the delicate term that folklorists apply to stories in which a wife substitutes herself for another woman to deceive her would-be adulterous husband), so arresting that the play is felt to closely resemble *Measure for Measure*, in which Angelo beds with Mariana, to whom he was betrothed, rather than with Isabella, whom he thinks he has seduced. In *All's Well*, the caddish Bertram vows he will not live with his wife Helena until she can get a ring from his finger and show him a child she has had by him; Helena, taking advantage of Bertram's illicit interest in the chaste Diana, is at length able to fulfill these seemingly impossible conditions. Shakespeare, however, was a great user and re-user of folk motifs, and there is really not much strength in the argument that because the "substitute bride" is used in *All's Well* the play must be close in date to *Measure for Measure*, given at court in December 1604. After all, there is a tale of shipwreck at the start of *The Comedy of Errors* and there is an apparent shipwreck at the start of *The Tempest,* but some twenty years separate the two. Similarly, there are outlaws in *The Two Gentlemen of Verona* and in *As You Like It,* but no one would seriously argue that the plays were written in close proximity. On the other hand, *The Comedy of Errors* and *Love's Labor's Lost*—universally agreed to be among Shakespeare's earliest work—share no common motifs; *Love's Labor's Lost* does not even conclude with the unions or reunions that are almost the *sine qua non* of Shakespeare's comedies.

The bed trick in *Measure for Measure* is managed not by the bride but by a duke who advises her how to outwit a would-be seducer. The bed trick in *All's Well* is the bride's idea, and in its clever heroine *All's Well* differs from *Measure for Measure* and resembles the earlier comedies: *The Merchant of Venice* (in which Portia is more resourceful than all the Venetian men), *As You Like It* (in which Rosalind, banished to the woods, manipulates two weddings), and *Twelfth Night* (in which Viola at length weds the man whom she has loved for four and a half acts). Like these comedies, moreover, *All's Well* is a play about love and marriage: the "dark" *Troilus and Cressida,* less about love than about dishonor and disillusion, concludes with the lovers separated; *Measure for Measure* concludes with a strong hint of a marriage but the play is less about love than it is about lust and justice and mercy.

The subject matter offers no compelling argument to date the play later than the "happy" comedies and along with *Measure for Measure,* but there are abundant passages in a style more mature than the style (or, rather, styles) typical of the earliest plays. Much of the verse in *All's Well* has a complexity, weightiness, and forcefulness that resemble the verse in *Hamlet* and *Measure for Measure.* Here are two examples:

Why not a mother? When I said "a mother"
Methought you saw a serpent. What's in "mother"
That you start at it? I say I am your mother,
And put you in the catalogue of those
That were enwombèd mine. 'Tis often seen
Adoption strives with nature, and choice breeds
A native slip to us from foreign seeds.
You ne'er oppressed me with a mother's groan,
Yet I express to you a mother's care.   (1.3.142–50)

That thou didst love her, strikes some scores away
From the great compt; but love that comes too late,
Like a remorseful pardon slowly carried,
To the great sender turns a sour offense,
Crying "That's good that's gone." Our rash faults
Make trivial price of serious things we have,
Not knowing them, until we know their grave.
                                              (5.3.56–62)

But this business of choosing passages is tricky; no play is
all of a piece, and in selecting these a fair number in a different style were skipped. There are more than a few passages that are so simple, so jingling, so unsophisticated that
they seem like apprentice work:

If she, my liege, can make me know this clearly,
I'll love her dearly, ever, ever dearly.   (315–16)

Here is my hand; the premises observed,
Thy will by my performance shall be served;
So make the choice of thy own time, for I,
Thy resolved patient, on thee still rely.
More should I question thee, and more I must,
Though more to know could not be more to trust.
                                              (2.1.203–8)

Various explanations can be offered for the rhymes—that here they add to a sense of ritual, that there they are used for a letter (which must be set off), that they deal with the past, that they make a contrast with a previous speech, that they are vestiges of an old play Shakespeare is revising, etc.—but the fact remains that the style is not sufficiently uniform to allow the easy generalization that it resembles the style of *Measure for Measure.* The most noticeable sign of maturity is the high percentage of run-on lines (giving a flexibility and power lacking in much of the early highly regular verse)—but this percentage is not significantly different from that in *The Merchant of Venice,* published in 1598 and quite possibly written a year or two earlier. It should be mentioned, too, that some of the least slick, the most "weighty" passages in *All's Well* may owe part of their weight to the fact that the printer did not correctly decipher the manuscript; the text is not a particularly good one, and some of the obscurity (often associated with maturity) perhaps has its origin in printing house uncertainties.

"Obscurity" gets us back to the idea of a "dark" play. The bed trick has seemed unpleasant to most readers (though it should be noted that by this trick Helena saves Bertram from committing adultery, and ultimately restores to him the wife who, we have seen, is a loving as well as an enterprising woman), but no one in the play minds it. The virtuous widow, who would avoid "any staining act," pronounces the plan "lawful," and the King is sufficiently delighted by the outcome to reward the widow's daughter. The other allegedly "dark" aspect of the play that has attracted a good deal of comment is the beginning, which is weighty with talk of death and disease:

> *Countess.* In delivering my son from me I bury a second
> husband. (1.1.1–2)

> *Bertram.* And I in going, madam, weep o'er my father's death
> anew; but I must attend his Majesty's command. . . .
> (3–5)

Countess. What hope is there of his Majesty's amendment?

(13–14)

Lafew. He hath abandoned his physicians. . . .   (15)

The play goes on, with talk of "haggish age" that has brought about the King's illness, the death of Bertram's father, and presumably the death of Helena's father. Yet how do Elizabethan comedies usually open if not with some sorrowful problem at hand, whose dissolution will be the matter of the play? The first speech in *The Comedy of Errors* is a couplet spoken by a man who knows he will be sentenced to death (it contains the words "fall," "doom of death," and "woes"); when he is assured that he is indeed sentenced to death, he tells a woeful tale of shipwreck and separation from wife and children. *The Two Gentlemen of Verona* begins with friends separating; *Love's Labor's Lost* begins with a vigorous speech announcing a method of securing eternal fame, but this very speech is full of awareness of "brazen tombs," "disgrace of death," and "cormorant devouring Time." The fact is that the first scene of *All's Well* mingles with its references to sorrow references to renewal, rebirth—the happy ending that characterizes comedy. The Countess is losing her son, but she is assured she will find in the King "a husband"; Helena's father has died, but his prescription lives in papers that Helena possesses, and the King will soon be restored to health. Helena seems to be grieving for her dead father, but in fact her mind is on the young man whom she loves, and though her love seems hopeless she wins him as her husband. If *As You Like It* included the bed trick, which is to say if Orlando were a cad, quite possibly the embarrassed and unhappy critics would have found that play, commonly called happy and golden, as dark as *All's Well*. After all, *As You Like It* begins with the bitter complaints of a younger brother, quickly moves to a fight between the brothers and to some churlish words ("old dog") spoken to an aged faithful retainer, and then to news that the rightful duke has been banished by his brother: family treachery, the tragic stuff that makes *King Lear.* Of course Bertram, the young lover in *All's Well,* is far less engaging than Orlando, but several of Shakespeare's lovers are unamiable people (Proteus in *The Two Gentlemen,* Claudio in *Much Ado*), yet the comedies are not therefore dark. (It can even be argued that Lysander's delightful transient infidelity in *A Midsummer Night's Dream* has its affinity with Bertram's perverse desire to seduce Diana when he is furnished with Helena, but it must be admitted that the spirit of holiday foolery, dominant in *A Midsummer Night's Dream,* is sparse in *All's Well.*)

An old theory, now rarely held because of the tendency to call it a problem play and to date it about 1602, suggests that *All's Well That Ends Well* is the play Francis Meres called *Love Labor's Won* when he listed a dozen of Shakespeare's plays in 1598. Meres says that Shakespeare excels both in comedy and tragedy:

> For comedy, witness his *Gentlemen of Verona,* his *Errors,* his *Love Labor's Lost,* his *Love Labor's Won,* his *Midsummer's Night Dream,* and his *Merchant of Venice;* for tragedy his *Richard the Second, Richard the Third, Henry the Fourth, King John, Titus Andronicus,* and his *Romeo and Juliet.*

Of these, only *Love Labor's Won* has not come down to us, or has not come down to us under that title. If Meres was not mistaken (he seems to know what he is talking about), and Shakespeare had indeed written the play, it is reasonable to assume that it is included in the Folio, but under a different title. (The Folio was prepared by long-standing friends of Shakespeare, who sought to collect his plays as his memorial.) *The Taming of the Shrew* has been the favorite candidate because it is unquestionably early enough for Meres to have known of it in 1598, but the recent discovery of a page from an account book for 1603 lists—among other plays—both *The Taming of the*

Shrew and *Love's Labor Won* (sic), and so the two cannot be identical. The plot of *All's Well* makes it an eminently suitable candidate; Helena certainly labors to win her beloved. If the identity of *All's Well* and *Love's Labor's Won* (to combine Meres' spelling and that of the account book) were established, it would prove that *All's Well* had been written by 1598 and published by 1603—but no proof is available. Put it this way: if Meres was correct that Shakespeare wrote *Love's Labor's Won*, quite possibly it survives (presumably with substantial revision) as *All's Well*, and we should alter our conception of Shakespeare's development; but if Meres was mistaken, and the play was by another hand (hence omitted from the Folio), we have been wasting our time.

Although the play dramatizes the triumph of love's labor, Helena engages in activities that have distressed some readers. Her dialogue with Parolles (1.1) in which she bandies jokes about virginity may seem neither witty nor decorous to us, but we ought to recall that Bassanio's Portia, a paragon, makes off-color jokes, as do several of Shakespeare's other chaste comic heroines. This dialogue, moreover, is not mere irrelevant foolery; Helena insists that she will maintain her chastity awhile, as a virtuous heroine should, and the dialogue concludes with Parolles' advice, "Get thee a good husband, and use him as he uses thee" (221–22). The play deals with Helena's getting a husband; in one sense she does not use him as he uses her (she returns his scorn with love); in another sense she does, for she deceives him— to a good end—as he deceives her. He accepts her as his wife but fabricates a means of leaving her without consummating the marriage, and she fabricates a means of saving him from adultery and of guiding him into what we must assume will be (as in the world of all comedy) a marriage in which they live happily ever after. That Helena engages in deception is not in itself bad. Deception in Elizabethan drama is commonly used to assist a love affair. No one is upset by the "honest slanders" devised to bring Beatrice and Benedick together in *Much Ado,* and the list of heroines who in one way or another deceive their beloved for a good purpose is a long one. Helena takes advantage of Bertram's pursuit of Diana to substitute herself for Diana.

Bertram is an "unseasoned courtier," a foolish young prig whom Helena must bring to a healthy condition (he has "sick desires" for Diana) rather as she must heal the King's disease. Like Shakespeare's better-known heroines, Rosalind, Portia, Beatrice, and Viola, Helena is energetic yet thoroughly womanly. If one thinks she is too inclined to wear the pants, what of Julia, Rosalind, and Viola, all of whom—unlike Helena—literally wear pants in their efforts to bring matters to a happy ending? Helena has something of the earnestness of Brutus' Portia combined with the resourcefulness of Bassanio's Portia; she fears that her "ambitious love" has "offended," and that Bertram is "too good and fair" for her, but no character except Bertram ever speaks ill of her, and it is evident to all readers that Bertram is (until at the end when he accepts Helena) far from "good and fair."

Perhaps our chief dissatisfaction with Helena arises from the fact that we cannot laugh at her—unless we feel that Parolles has the better of the argument on virginity. Rosalind (to give only one example) is engaging partly because we enjoy her discomfort when she learns that her beloved Orlando is in the Forest of Arden:

> Alas the day! What shall I do with my doublet and hose? What did he when thou saw'st him? What said he? How looked he? Wherein went he? What makes he here? Did he ask for me? Where remains he? How parted he with thee? And when shalt thou see him again? Answer me in one word. (3.2.217–22)

We get no comedy of this sort, and we miss it. But if we never experience the delightful intimacy of laughing at one with whom we sympathize, it does not follow that we must find Helena an unpleasant man-hunter. She feigns death—

but in *Much Ado* and in *The Winter's Tale* similar false reports of death are issued for the good purpose of restoring a man to his loving wife. The women in those two plays do not themselves contrive the report, but no discredit accrues to the contrivers and none ought to accrue to Helena. It is better to say that Helena resourcefully persists in love than that (E. K. Chambers' words) she "passes from dishonor to dishonor."

The offensive person in the play is not Helena, who loves Bertram and brings him to love her, but Bertram, whose folly is abundantly remarked upon. His mother, Lafew, and the King all rebuke him, and though one can sympathize with his plea that in the choice of a wife he might reasonably be allowed the help of his own eyes, it is clear that he is blind—not only to Helena's goodness but to Parolles' folly. Bertram believes that the cowardly braggart Parolles is a soldier simply because he talks and dresses the part. Bertram squares his guesses by shows (to take a line that appears in another context), values the worthless Parolles and (a sort of corollary) scorns the virtuous Helena. Fortunately, he lives in the world of comedy; "comedy is full of purposes mistook, not 'falling on the inventor's head' but luckily misfiring altogether. In comedy, as often happens in life, people are mercifully saved from being as wicked as they meant to be."*

It is commonly said that the world of *All's Well*, like that of *Measure for Measure*, is a depraved place, a cynic's vision—again the "dark" realm of an embittered writer. Readers of the Signet edition of the latter play may also have read an appended essay by R. W. Chambers (not to be confused with E. K. Chambers); if so, they will not be likely to see *Measure for Measure* as "dark." Nor is the world of *All's Well* wretched. Bertram is a fool, Parolles is close to a scoundrel, but the rest of the characters—including the

---

*Helen Gardner, "As You Like It," in *More Talking of Shakespeare*, ed. John Garret. This essay is reprinted in the Signet edition of *As You Like It*.

Clown, whose bawdry is playful enough—are tolerable and tolerant, endowed with no more than the usual faults of men, and (if we keep in mind Helena, Lafew, the King, and the Countess) with more than the usual virtues. Bertram's failure to value Helena and his failure to see through Parolles are abundantly remarked upon, but when Parolles has been exposed and Helena is reputed dead, and nothing can come of further dwelling on Bertram's past folly, Lafew, the Countess, and the King forgive him. Lafew asserts that Bertram was "misled with [i.e., by] a snipped taffeta fellow" (4.5.1–2), the Countess (who had spoken sharply to Bertram when sharp-speaking might have been of some use) now urges the King "to make it/Natural rebellion done i' th' blade of youth,/ When oil and fire, too strong for reason's force,/O'erbears it and burns on" (5.3.5–8), and the King replies that he has "for-given and forgotten all" (9). Indeed, despite his immaturity Bertram has won repute in battle and now, apparently aware of his opprobrious behavior, he begs pardon for his "high-repented blames" (36). It is recognized that Bertram has done abundant wrong to the King, to his mother, to Helena, and

> to himself
> The greatest wrong of all. He lost a wife
> Whose beauty did astonish the survey
> Of richest eyes; whose words all ears took captive;
> Whose dear perfection hearts that scorned to serve
> Humbly called mistress.   (14–19)

But this greatest wrong has not in fact been done; love and Providence have contrived that all shall end well. "What things are we!" exclaims the First Lord, and the Second Lord replies:

> Merely our own traitors. And as in the common course of
> all treasons we still see them reveal themselves till they
> attain to their abhorred ends, so he that in this action con-

trives against his own nobility, in his proper stream o'erflows himself.   (4.3.22–27)

In another context this is the stuff of tragedy. Macbeth, for
example, urged by his wife, contrives against his own
nobility and destroys himself. The violence he does to his
king recoils upon him and he finds he has achieved not
"honor, love, obedience, troops of friends," but only curses,
false friends, and sleepless nights. In *All's Well* men are not
angels, but neither are they devils; love and forgiveness are
no less evident than folly and youthful lust. The vision is no
darker than that radiant moment in *The Merchant of Venice*
when Portia, appealing to Shylock to show mercy toward the
man who has indeed forfeited his bond, says:

> Though justice be thy plea, consider this:
> That, in the course of justice, none of us
> Should see salvation. We do pray for mercy,
> And that same prayer doth teach us all to render
> The deeds of mercy.   (4.1.197–201)

The world of *The Merchant of Venice* is more lyrical, filled
with moonlight and music—when Shylock is not onstage—
but the vision of humanity is no higher; lower, indeed, for
Shylock is malevolent where Bertram and Parolles are
foolish. In Shakespeare's comedies, folly is not something
scourged but something enjoyed. For example, in *Love's
Labor's Lost*, a delightful spoof on the folly of trying to live
as though men were disembodied minds, the King of
Navarre, leader of the scheme to form a society of scholars
who shall give no audience to women, proudly tells his fol-
lowers that they "war against affections [i.e., passions],/And
the huge army of the world's desire" (1.1.9–10). How noble,
and yet how foolish. Nor is it cynical to say that this is folly;
Berowne aptly points out that "every man with his affects is
born,/Not by might mastered, but by special grace" (148–49),

and as though to prove his point a constable brings in a clown who has already broken the vow to forswear women. The affects have their place, no less than reason. Even our faults can serve us. "The web of our life," says a French lord in *All's Well,* "is of a mingled yarn, good and ill together; our virtues would be proud if our faults whipped them not, and our crimes would despair if they were not cherished by our virtues" (4.3.74–78). If mortals are fools, Shakespeare seems to cherish them as much for their folly as Puck does, and (notably in *Much Ado,* where the clowns bring about the denouement) he turns their folly to use. The delightful thing about folly is that it insulates a man from despair and fills him with a zest for living. Othello's occupation is gone when Desdemona is (he thinks) unfaithful, but Parolles can easily enough find another livelihood when his military claims are exposed.

> If my heart were great
> 'Twould burst at this. Captain I'll be no more,
> But I will eat and drink and sleep as soft
> As captain shall. Simply the thing I am
> Shall make me live. Who knows himself a braggart,
> Let him fear this; for it will come to pass
> That every braggart shall be found an ass.
> Rust, sword; cool, blushes; and Parolles live
> Safest in shame! Being fooled, by fool'ry thrive!
> There's place and means for every man alive.
> I'll after them.   *Exit*.
>   (344–54)

Othello kills himself, "for he was great of heart," but Parolles is protected from Othello's greatness ("*If* my heart were great") and therefore from murdering a Desdemona and from committing suicide. Lafew, who had been the first to detect Parolles, treats him generously enough at last: "Though you are a fool and a knave you shall eat." Parolles, indeed, in the final act becomes an engaging fool; another comic dramatist would have whipped him from the stage, but Shakespeare exposes Parolles not merely for moral reasons but "for the love of laughter" (twice repeated), and finds a place for the braggart-turned-fool in the abundant comic world.

All ends well, partly because most of the people in the play are decent, but chiefly because of a beneficent Providence. By the time the play reaches its end, not only has the King been restored to health, Parolles cured of his pretensions, Diana equipped with a dowry, Bertram brought to his senses, but Helena is wed in deed as well as name to a loving husband. Now, it is the nature of a play, or any work of art, in contrast to real life, that the doings of the characters are remarkably coherent. In the theater we look attentively for a few hours at a few people and we see the course of a lifetime, or all that presumably is significant in a lifetime, whereas in life things go on for years, mingled with a good deal of irrelevance.

Life may or may not be a chaos; art is a pattern. Something like Fate presides in all plays, however vivid and energetic the characters may be. "Hanging and wiving goes by destiny," Nerissa lightly says, providing us with a tag that summarizes tragedy and comedy. "Who can control his fate?" Othello asks. Surely not the tragic heroes — unless we see them as men who get exactly what they deserve. No less than five of Euripides' plays include (with one variation) these lines:

> Many indeed the shapes and changes are
> Of heavenly beings. Many things the gods
> Achieve beyond our judgment. What we thought
> Is not confirmed, and what we thought not God
> Contrives. And so it happens in this story.*

*Translation by Rex Warner, in *Three Great Plays of Euripides*. New York: The New American Library of World Literature, Inc. (Mentor Books), 1958.

The comic version of Fate is Fortune or Time or beneficent Providence:

> All other doubts, by Time let them be cleared.
> Fortune brings in some boats that are not steered.
>
> > (*Cymbeline*, 4.3.45–46)

> O Time, thou must untangle this, not I;
> It is too hard a knot for me t' untie.   (*Twelfth Night*, 2.2.40–41)

In *All's Well*, numerous references to Providence make explicit the pattern that underlies all comedy. "The very hand of heaven" cures the King. Later, Helena is providentially brought to the very place and persons that can restore her to Bertram:

> > > Doubt not but heaven
> > Hath brought me up to be your daughter's dower,
> > As it hath fated her to be my motive [i.e., means]
> > And helper to a husband.   (4.4.18–21)

In Shakespeare's source—it is reprinted in this volume—the heroine "purposed to find means to attain the two things, that thereby she might recover her husband," and she set out for Florence. But in *All's Well*, when Helena sets out on her pilgrimage to St. Jaques we are not given any reason to believe that she is pursuing Bertram. Learning of the seemingly impossible conditions Bertram has imposed, she says almost nothing, allowing the Countess and others to censure him. When the Countess and Lords leave the stage, in a soliloquy she blames herself for driving Bertram to the wars where he may "be the mark/Of smoky muskets" (3.2.112–13).

> Shall I stay here to do't? No, no, although
> The air of paradise did fan the house

And angels officed all. I will be gone,
That pitiful rumor may report my flight
To consolate thine ear. Come night, end day;
For with the dark, poor thief, I'll steal away.

Exit.

(129–34)

We learn (from a letter) that she has set out on a pilgrimage, and that Bertram may thus return to Rousillon. We next meet Helena in Florence, where by chance she engages in conversation a widow who, as it turns out, is the mother of a young girl whom Bertram is courting. We have no right to assume that Helena lied in her soliloquy (to whom could she be lying?) and that she set out to catch Bertram; we can only assume that the hand of heaven has brought about the encounter in Florence with the widow, her daughter, and Bertram.

It is worth mentioning, too, that in the source the heroine meets a Florentine woman who leads her to the widow, but Shakespeare's Helena happens on the widow unaided. The effect is to increase the sense of Providence precisely because it is so improbable that Helena would encounter the widow herself. To say that in *All's Well* there is often a sense of Providence is not, of course, to say that the characters are mindless puppets who undertake nothing for themselves. Helena herself argues (1.1.223–36) to the contrary. Readiness, however, is all:

But with the word the time will bring on summer,
When briars shall have leaves as well as thorns,
And be as sweet as sharp. We must away;
Our wagon is prepared, and time revives us.
All's well that ends well; still the fine's the crown.
Whate'er the course, the end is the renown.

(4.4.31–36)

("The fine's the crown" is an idea Shakespeare stated more than once: in the second part of *Henry VI* we get "La fin couronne les oeuvres;" in *Troilus* "The end crowns all;" elsewhere there are variations.) The cooperation with time that Helena here urges she urges again at Marseilles, when the widow despairs that they have come too late.

> *Widow.* Lord, how we lose our pains!
>
> *Helena.* All's well that ends well yet,
>   Though time seems so adverse and means unfit.
>   I do beseech you, whither is he gone?
>   * * * * * * * * * * * * *
>   We must to horse again.
>   (5.1.24–37)

In 5.3 the King forgives Bertram and observes that "The time is fair again":

>   All is whole.
>   Not one word more of the consumèd time.
>   Let's take the instant by the forward top;
>   For we are old, and on our quick'st decrees
>   Th' inaudible and noiseless foot of Time
>   Steals ere we can effect them.   (5.3.37–42)

But the time (here, with a suggestion of the age, the present state) is not yet "whole," for Helena is still thought dead, hence the appropriateness of the melancholy note introduced by the King's reflections on his old age. The melancholy deepens as thoughts return to the "dead" Helena, whom Bertram now laments. The king repeats his forgiveness:

>   Well excused.
>   That thou didst love her, strikes some scores away
>   From the great compt; but love that comes too late,
>   Like a remorseful pardon slowly carried,

> To the great sender turns a sour offense,
> Crying "That's good that's gone."   (55–60)

Reluctantly skipping this near-chance to compare the motif of "That's good that's gone" with its occurrence in the tragedies, notably in *Antony and Cleopatra,* we move on and note that the last lines in the play (excluding the Epilogue) are:

> All yet seems well, and if it end so meet,
> The bitter past, more welcome is the sweet.
>
> (333–34)

The tragic lesson that the Greek dramatists often preached was "Count no man happy until he is dead"; Oedipus *seemed* happy, but because he had killed his father and married his mother he was a contaminated wretch whose *life* was tragic though he did not know it until near the end of the play. His actions (to borrow from Aristotle's ethical theories) were not in accordance with virtue and therefore he was not genuinely happy. Conversely, in *All's Well,* though Helena is dogged by misfortune, and Bertram is for a while a fool, Helena's persistent virtue, in combination with God's grace, saves Bertram from himself and brings happiness to herself and to a variety of lesser characters. "Choose thou thy husband," the delighted King says to Diana, "and I'll pay thy dower" (328).

All has ended well, which means that a happy *beginning* is in store for Helena and Bertram, and for Diana and whomever she elects. Correspondingly, the end of the play glances back to the beginning. The King's invitation to Diana to choose a husband echoes his earlier agreement to let Helena choose a husband. Still another link between end and beginning is found in the Epilogue; the King says,

> The King's a beggar now the play is done,   (1)

appealing to the audience for applause, but in his sudden loss of power our minds may travel back to the weak king in the first act; and in the full realization that he is a king only in so far as our imagination takes his clothing to be an external symbol of an internal reality, we may recall that Parolles' military garb covered nothing substantial. The story is over, the characters live happily ever after, disembodied from the actors who have presented them and who in the workaday world daily—"with strife"—seek to please the audience. For a moment the audience becomes a benevolent Providence, governing the figures on the stage by bestowing the applause which allows them to depart.

For further comment about the ending of the play, see the discussion of the stage history of *All's Well*, where something is said about the ways in which recent productions have ended.

—SYLVAN BARNET

All's Well That Ends Well

King of France
Duke of Florence
Bertram, Count of Rousillon
Lafew, an old lord
Parolles, a follower of Bertram
Steward, named Rinaldo ⎫
Clown, named Lavatch ⎭ servants to the Countess
A Page
Two French lords, the brothers Dumaine, serving in the
  Florentine army
A Gentleman, a stranger
Countess of Rousillon, mother to Bertram
Helena, an orphan protected by the Countess
A Widow of Florence
Diana, daughter to the widow
Mariana, neighbor to the widow
Lords, Officers, Soldiers, Attendants

  Scene: Rousillon; Paris; Florence; Marseilles]

All's Well That Ends Well

ACT 1

Scene 1. [*Rousillon.*°¹ *The Count's palace.*]

Enter young Bertram, Count of Rousillon, his mother [the Countess], and Helena, Lord Lafew, all in black.

Countess. In delivering° my son from me I bury a second husband.

Bertram. And I in going, madam, weep o'er my father's death anew; but I must attend his Majesty's command, to whom I am now in ward,° evermore   5
in subjection.

Lafew. You shall find of° the King a husband, madam; you, sir, a father. He that so generally° is at all times good must of necessity hold° his virtue to you, whose worthiness would stir it up   10

---

¹ The degree sign (°) indicates a footnote, which is keyed to the text by line number. Text references are printed in **boldface**; the annotation follows in roman type. 1.1.s.d. **Rousillon** formerly a province in southern France (usually spelled "Rossillion" in the Folio; the accent is on the second syllable, and -llion was probably pronounced -yun)   1 **delivering** sending away (with pun on giving birth)   5 **to whom I am now in ward** whose ward I now am   7 **of** in   8 **generally** impartially   9 **hold** continue

3

where it wanted,° rather than lack it where there is such abundance.

Countess. What hope is there of his Majesty's amendment?

15 *Lafew.* He hath abandoned his physicians, madam, under whose practices he hath persecuted time with hope, and finds no other advantage in the process but only the losing of hope by time.

Countess. This young gentlewoman had a father—O,
20 that "had," how sad a passage° 'tis—whose skill was almost as great as his honesty; had it stretched so far, would have made nature immortal, and death should have play for lack of work. Would for the King's sake he were living! I think it would
25 be the death of the King's disease.

Lafew. How called you the man you speak of, madam?

Countess. He was famous, sir, in his profession, and it was his great right to be so: Gerard de Narbon.

30 *Lafew.* He was excellent indeed, madam. The King very lately spoke of him admiringly and mourningly; he was skillful enough to have lived still, if knowledge could be set up against mortality.

Bertram. What is it, my good lord, the King lan-
35 guishes of?

Lafew. A fistula,° my lord.

Bertram. I heard not of it before.

Lafew. I would it were not notorious. Was this gentlewoman the daughter of Gerard de Narbon?

40 *Countess.* His sole child, my lord, and bequeathed to my overlooking.° I have those hopes of her good

---

11 **where it wanted** i.e., even if it (virtue) were lacking   20 **passage** (1) incident (2) passing away   36 **fistula** abscess   41 **overlooking** guardianship

that her education promises; her dispositions she
inherits, which makes fair gifts fairer; for where an
unclean mind carries virtuous qualities,° there commendations go with pity; they are virtues and   45
traitors too. In her they are the better for their
simpleness;° she derives° her honesty and achieves
her goodness.

Lafew. Your commendations, madam, get from her
tears.   50

Countess. 'Tis the best brine a maiden can season°
her praise in. The remembrance of her father never
approaches her heart but the tyranny of her sorrows takes all livelihood° from her cheek. No more
of this, Helena; go to,° no more, lest it be rather   55
thought you affect° a sorrow than to have—

Helena. I do affect a sorrow indeed, but I have it
too.

Lafew. Moderate lamentation is the right of the dead,
excessive grief the enemy to the living.   60

Countess. If the living be enemy to the grief, the ex-
cess makes it soon mortal.

Bertram. Madam, I desire your holy wishes.

Lafew. How understand we that?°

Countess. Be thou blessed, Bertram, and succeed
thy father   65
In manners° as in shape! Thy° blood and virtue
Contend for empire in thee, and thy goodness

---

44 **virtuous qualities** skills (not moral qualities)   46–47 **their simpleness** being single, unmixed   47 **derives** inherits   51 **season** preserve
54 **livelihood** (1) vitality (2) nourishment   55 **go to** (a remonstrance,
"Stop")   56 **affect** feign (Helena enigmatically replies that she both
feigns a sorrow—for her father, we later learn—and has one; her use
of the word also includes another meaning, "love")   64 **Lafew . . .
that** (perhaps this line is misplaced, and should begin Lafew's previous speech)   66 **manners** morals   66 **Thy** may thy

Share with thy birthright! Love all, trust a few,
Do wrong to none; be able for thine enemy
70 Rather in power than use,° and keep thy friend
Under thy own life's key. Be checked for silence,
But never taxed° for speech. What heaven more
        will,
That thee may furnish and my prayers pluck down,
Fall on thy head! Farewell. My lord,
75 'Tis an unseasoned courtier; good my lord,
Advise him.

Lafew.   He cannot want° the best
That shall attend his love.

Countess. Heaven bless him! Farewell, Bertram.

                                                        [*Exit.*]

Bertram. The best wishes that can be forged in your
80   thoughts be servants to you! [*To Helena*] Be com-
     fortable° to my mother, your mistress, and make
     much of her.

Lafew. Farewell, pretty lady; you must hold the credit
of your father.   [*Exit with Bertram.*]

85 *Helena.* O, were that all! I think not on my father,
And these great tears grace his remembrance more
Than those I shed for him. What was he like?
I have forgot him; my imagination
Carries no favor° in't but Bertram's.
90 I am undone; there is no living, none,
If Bertram be away; 'twere all one
That I should love a bright particular star,
And think to wed it, he is so above me.
In his bright radiance and collateral light
95 Must I be comforted, not in his sphere.°

69–70 **be able . . . use** let your strength equal your foe's in poten-
tiality, but do not use it 72 **taxed** censured 76 **want** lack
81 **comfortable** comforting 89 **favor** (1) face (2) love token 94–95
In his bright . . . sphere i.e., I must content myself with his light,
parallel to ("collateral") but above me; I cannot be in his orbit

Th' ambition in my love thus plagues itself:
The hind that would be mated by the lion
Must die for love. 'Twas pretty, though a plague,
To see him every hour, to sit and draw
His archèd brows, his hawking° eye, his curls,   100
In our heart's table;° heart too capable°
Of every line and trick of his sweet favor.
But now he's gone, and my idolatrous fancy°
Must sanctify his relics. Who comes here?

Enter Parolles.°

One that goes with him. I love him for his sake,   105
And yet I know him a notorious liar,
Think him a great way fool, solely a coward;
Yet these fixed evils sit so fit in him,
That they take place° when virtue's steely bones
Looks bleak i' th' cold wind; withal,° full oft we
    see   110
Cold wisdom waiting on superfluous folly.°

Parolles. Save° you, fair queen!

Helena. And you, monarch!

Parolles. No.

Helena. And no.   115

Parolles. Are you meditating on virginity?

Helena. Ay. You have some stain° of soldier in you;
let me ask you a question. Man is enemy to virginity; how may we barricado it against him?

Parolles. Keep him out.   120

Helena. But he assails; and our virginity, though valiant, in the defense yet is weak. Unfold to us some
warlike resistance.

100 **hawking** hawklike, keen   101 **table** flat surface on which a
picture is drawn   101–2 **capable/Of** receptive to   103 **fancy** lover's
fantasy   104s.d. **Parolles** (cf. French *paroles,* "words," i.e., Talker,
Braggart)   109 **take place** find acceptance (?)   110 **withal** besides
111 **Cold . . . folly** i.e., a threadbare wise servant attending on a rich
fool   112 **Save** God save   117 **stain** tincture

Parolles. There is none. Man, setting down before°
125   you, will undermine you and blow you up.°

Helena. Bless our poor virginity from underminers
and blowers-up! Is there no military policy how
virgins might blow up men?

Parolles. Virginity being blown down, man will quick-
130   lier be blown up;° marry,° in blowing him down
again, with the breach yourselves made you lose
your city. It is not politic in the commonwealth of
nature to preserve virginity. Loss of virginity is
rational increase, and there was never virgin got°
135   till virginity was first lost. That° you were made of
is metal° to make virgins. Virginity by being once
lost may be ten times found; by being ever kept
it is ever lost. 'Tis too cold a companion; away
with't!

140   *Helena.* I will stand for't a little, though therefore
I die a virgin.

Parolles. There's little can be said in't; 'tis against the
rule of nature. To speak on the part of virginity, is
to accuse your mothers, which is most infallible
145   disobedience. He that hangs himself is a virgin; virginity murders itself, and should be buried in high-
ways out of all sanctified limit,° as a desperate
offendress against nature. Virginity breeds mites,
much like a cheese, consumes itself to the very
150   paring, and so dies with feeding his own stomach.°
Besides, virginity is peevish, proud, idle, made of
self-love which is the most inhibited sin in the

---

124 **setting down before** laying siege to   125 **blow you up** (1) ex-
plode you (2) make you pregnant   130 **be blown up** be swollen, i.e.,
reach an orgasm   130 **marry** (a mild oath, "By the Virgin Mary")
134 **got** begotten   135 **That** that which   136 **metal** (1) substance
(2) coin (3) mettle, spirit   147 **sanctified limit** consecrated ground
150 **stomach** pride

canon.° Keep° it not; you cannot choose but lose
by't. Out with't! Within ten year it will make itself
ten, which is a goodly increase, and the principal   *155*
itself not much the worse. Away with't!

Helena. How might one do, sir, to lose it to her own
liking?

Parolles. Let me see. Marry, ill, to like him that ne'er it
likes. 'Tis a commodity will lose the gloss with   *160*
lying; the longer kept, the less worth. Off with't
while 'tis vendible; answer the time of request. Virginity, like an old courtier, wears her cap out of
fashion, richly suited, but unsuitable,° just like the
brooch and the toothpick, which wear not now.°   *165*
Your date is better in your pie and your porridge
than in your cheek; and your virginity, your old
virginity, is like one of our French withered pears:
it looks ill, it eats drily; marry, 'tis a withered pear;
it was formerly better; marry, yet 'tis a withered   *170*
pear. Will you anything with it?

Helena. Not my virginity yet!°
There shall your master have a thousand loves,
A mother, and a mistress, and a friend,
A phoenix,° captain, and an enemy,   *175*
A guide, a goddess, and a sovereign,
A counselor, a traitress, and a dear;
His humble ambition, proud humility;
His jarring, concord, and his discord, dulcet;
His faith, his sweet disaster;° with a world   *180*
Of pretty, fond, adoptious christendoms
That blinking Cupid gossips.° Now shall he—

152–53 **inhibited sin in the canon** prohibited sin in the Scripture
153 **Keep** hoard   164 **unsuitable** unfashionable   165 **wear not now**
are not now in fashion   172 **yet** (possibly there are missing some
ensuing lines in which Helena comments on Bertram's departure;
possibly the abrupt transition reveals that Helena's thoughts have
not been on Parolles' talk)   175 **phoenix** i.e., rarity (literally, a
fabulous bird)   180 **disaster** unfavorable star   181–82 **fond . . .
gossips** foolish, adopted names that blind ("blinking") Cupid gives
as godfather ("gossips")

I know not what he shall. God send him well!
The court's a learning place, and he is one—

185 *Parolles*. What one, i' faith?

Helena. That I wish well. 'Tis pity—

Parolles. What's pity?

Helena. That wishing well had not a body in't,
Which might be felt, that we, the poorer born,
190 Whose baser stars° do shut us up in wishes,
Might with effects of them follow our friends,
And show what we alone must think, which never
Returns us thanks.

Enter Page.

Page. Monsieur Parolles, my lord calls for you.

[*Exit*.]

195 *Parolles*. Little Helen, farewell. If I can remember
thee, I will think of thee at court.

Helena. Monsieur Parolles, you were born under a
charitable star.

Parolles. Under Mars, ay.

200 *Helena*. I especially think, under Mars.

Parolles. Why under Mars?

Helena. The wars hath so kept you under,° that you
must needs be born under Mars.

Parolles. When he was predominant.

205 *Helena*. When he was retrograde,° I think rather.

Parolles. Why think you so?

Helena. You go so much backward when you fight.

Parolles. That's for advantage.

Helena. So is running away, when fear proposes the

190 **baser stars** lower destinies   202 **under** in low fortune   205 **retrograde** moving backward (astrological term)

safety; but the composition° that your valor and fear 210
makes in you is a virtue of a good wing, and I like
the wear° well.

Parolles. I am so full of businesses, I cannot answer
thee acutely. I will return perfect courtier, in the
which my instruction shall serve to naturalize° 215
thee, so thou wilt be capable of a courtier's counsel,
and understand what advice shall thrust upon thee;
else thou diest in thine unthankfulness, and thine
ignorance makes thee away. Farewell. When thou
hast leisure, say thy prayers; when thou hast none, 220
remember thy friends. Get thee a good husband,
and use him as he uses thee. So, farewell.   [*Exit.*]

Helena. Our remedies oft in ourselves do lie,
Which we ascribe to heaven; the fated sky°
Gives us free scope; only doth backward pull   225
Our slow designs when we ourselves are dull.
What power is it which mounts my love so high,
That makes me see, and cannot feed mine eye?
The mightiest space in fortune nature brings
To join like likes, and kiss like native° things.   230
Impossible be strange attempts to those
That weigh their pains in sense, and do suppose
What hath been cannot be.° Who ever strove
To show her merit that did miss her love?
The King's disease—my project may deceive me,   235
But my intents are fixed, and will not leave me.
                                        Exit.

210 **composition** (1) union, mixture (2) truce, surrender   212 **wear** fashion (if "wing" has referred not only to Parolles' flight but to a flap on his clothing, "wear" puns—like the modern "fashion"—on habit and clothing)   215 **naturalize** familiarize   224 **fated sky** sky (heaven) that exerts influence   230 **native** closely related   231-33 **Impossible . . . cannot be** i.e., remarkable deeds are impossible to persons who cautiously calculate the efforts and who believe that unusual happenings cannot take place

[Scene 2. *Paris. The King's palace.*]

*Flourish° cornets. Enter the King of France with
letters, and divers Attendants.*

King. The Florentines and Senoys° are by th' ears,°
    Have fought with equal fortune, and continue
    A braving war.°

First Lord.   So 'tis reported, sir.

King. Nay, 'tis most credible. We here receive it
5   A certainty, vouched from our cousin° Austria,
    With caution, that the Florentine will move° us
    For speedy aid; wherein our dearest friend
    Prejudicates the business, and would seem
    To have us make denial.

First Lord.   His love and wisdom,
10   Approved° so to your Majesty, may plead
    For amplest credence.

King.   He hath armed our answer,
    And Florence is denied before he comes;
    Yet, for our gentlemen that mean to see
    The Tuscan service,° freely have they leave
    To stand on either part.°

15   *Second Lord.*   It well may serve
    A nursery° to our gentry, who are sick
    For breathing° and exploit.

1.2.s.d. **Flourish** musical notes heralding an important person
1 **Senoys** Sienese   1 **by th' ears** quarreling   3 **braving war** war of
challenges   5 **cousin** fellow sovereign   6 **move** petition   10 **Approved** proven   14 **The Tuscan service** the campaign in Tuscany
(N. Italy)   15 **stand on either part** serve on either side   16 **nursery**
training school   16–17 **sick/For breathing** eager for exercise

Enter Bertram, Lafew, and Parolles.

King.   What's he comes here?

First Lord. It is the Count Rousillon, my good lord,
 Young Bertram.

King.   Youth, thou bear'st thy father's face.
 Frank° nature, rather curious° than in haste,   20
 Hath well composed thee. Thy father's moral parts
 May'st thou inherit too! Welcome to Paris.

Bertram. My thanks and duty are your Majesty's.

King. I would I had that corporal soundness now,
 As when thy father and myself in friendship   25
 First tried our soldiership. He did look far
 Into the service of the time,° and was
 Discipled of the bravest. He lasted long,
 But on us both did haggish age steal on,
 And wore us out of act.° It much repairs me   30
 To talk of your good father; in his youth
 He had the wit which I can well observe
 Today in our young lords; but they may jest
 Till their own scorn return to them unnoted
 Ere they can hide their levity in° honor.   35
 So like a courtier, contempt nor bitterness
 Were in his pride or sharpness; if they were,
 His equal had awaked them, and his honor,
 Clock to itself, knew the true minute when
 Exception° bid him speak, and at this time   40
 His tongue obeyed his hand. Who° were below him
 He used as creatures of another place,°
 And bowed his eminent top to their low ranks,
 Making them proud of his humility,
 In their poor praise he humbled. Such a man   45
 Might be a copy to these younger times;

---

20 **Frank** bounteous   20 **curious** careful   26–27 **He did . . . time** he
had insight into war (?) he served long in wars (?)   30 **act** action
35 **hide . . . in** i.e., join . . . with (?)   40 **Exception** disapproval
41 **Who** those who   42 **another place** i.e., a higher rank

Which, followed well, would demonstrate them
now
But goers backward.

Bertram.   His good remembrance, sir,
Lies richer in your thoughts than on his tomb;
50   So in approof lives not his epitaph
As in your royal speech.°

King. Would I were with him! He would always say—
Methinks I hear him now; his plausive° words
He scattered not in ears, but grafted them,
55   To grow there, and to bear—"Let me not live,"
This his good melancholy oft began,
On the catastrophe and heel of pastime,°
When it was out°—"Let me not live," quoth he,
"After my flame lacks oil, to be the snuff°
60   Of younger spirits, whose apprehensive° senses
All but new things disdain; whose judgments are
Mere fathers of their garments; whose constancies
Expire before their fashions." This he wished.
I, after him, do after him° wish too,
65   Since I nor wax nor honey can bring home,
I quickly were dissolvèd from my hive
To give some laborers room.

Second Lord.   You're loved, sir;
They that least lend it you shall lack you first.

King. I fill a place, I know't. How long is't, Count,
70   Since the physician at your father's died?
He was much famed.

Bertram.   Some six months since, my lord.

King. If he were living, I would try him yet.

50–51 **So . . . speech** i.e., the validity of his epitaph is in no way
better confirmed than in your words   53 **plausive** laudable   57 **On
. . . pastime** at the end ("catastrophe," "heel") of pleasure   58 **out**
ended (perhaps punning on the idea "out at heel")   59 **snuff** burnt
wick that causes the lamp to smell and smolder, preventing the lower
("younger") wick from burning brightly   60 **apprehensive** percep-
tive, apt   64 **after him . . . after him** later than he . . . in accordance
with him

Lend me an arm. The rest have worn me out
With several applications.° Nature and sickness
Debate it at their leisure. Welcome, Count,   75
My son's no dearer.

Bertram.   Thank your Majesty.
                    Exit [the King with the rest]. Flourish.

[Scene 3. *Rousillon. The Count's palace.*]

Enter Countess, Steward, and Clown.

Countess. I will now hear. What say you of this
    gentlewoman?

Steward. Madam, the care I have had to even° your
    content I wish might be found in the calendar° of
    my past endeavors, for then we wound our mod-   5
    esty, and make foul the clearness of our deserv-
    ings, when of ourselves we publish them.

Countess. What does this knave here? Get you gone,
    sirrah.° The complaints I have heard of you I do
    not all believe; 'tis my slowness that I do not, for   10
    I know you lack not folly to commit them, and
    have ability enough to make such knaveries yours.

Clown. 'Tis not unknown to you, madam, I am a
    poor fellow.

Countess. Well, sir.   15

___

74 **several applications** various treatments   1.3.3 **even** make even,
satisfy   4 **calendar** record   9 **sirrah** (term of address used to an inferior)

Clown. No, madam, 'tis not so well that I am poor, though many of the rich are damned; but, if I may have your ladyship's good will to go to the world,° Isbel the woman and I will do° as we may.

20 *Countess.* Wilt thou needs be a beggar?

Clown. I do beg your good will in this case.

Countess. In what case?

Clown. In Isbel's case° and mine own. Service is no heritage,° and I think I shall never have the bless-
25 ing of God till I have issue o' my body; for they say barnes° are blessings.

Countess. Tell me thy reason why thou wilt marry.

Clown. My poor body, madam, requires it. I am driven on by the flesh, and he must needs go that
30 the devil drives.

Countess. Is this all your worship's reason?

Clown. Faith, madam, I have other holy reasons,° such as they are.

Countess. May the world know them?

35 *Clown.* I have been, madam, a wicked creature, as you and all flesh and blood are, and indeed I do marry that I may repent.

Countess. Thy marriage, sooner than thy wickedness.

Clown. I am out o' friends, madam, and I hope to
40 have friends for my wife's sake.

Countess. Such friends are thine enemies, knave.

Clown. Y'are shallow, madam, in great friends, for the knaves come to do that for me which I am

18 **go to the world** get married   19 **do** (punning on the bawdy meaning "have intercourse")   23 **case** (another bawdy pun, "pudendum")   23–24 **Service is no heritage** i.e., servants acquire no wealth
(proverbial)   26 **barnes** bairns, children   32 **holy reasons** (probably
there is a bawdy pun not only on "holy" but on "reasons," pronounced much like "raisings")

aweary of. He that ears° my land spares my team,
and gives me leave to in° the crop; if I be his   45
cuckold,° he's my drudge. He that comforts my
wife is the cherisher of my flesh and blood; he that
cherishes my flesh and blood loves my flesh and
blood; he that loves my flesh and blood is my
friend: ergo, he that kisses my wife is my friend.   50
If men could be contented to be what they are,
there were no fear in marriage; for young Charbon
the puritan and old Poysam° the papist, how-
some'er their hearts are severed in religion, their
heads are both one; they may jowl° horns to-   55
gether like any deer i' th' herd.

Countess. Wilt thou ever be a foul-mouthed and
calumnious knave?

Clown. A prophet I, madam, and I speak the truth
the next° way: 60

    For I the ballad will repeat,
      Which men full true shall find,
    Your marriage comes by destiny,
      Your cuckoo sings by kind.°

Countess. Get you gone, sir. I'll talk with you more   65
anon.

Steward. May it please you, madam, that he bid
Helen come to you. Of her I am to speak.

Countess. Sirrah, tell my gentlewoman I would speak
with her—Helen, I mean.   70

Clown. Was this fair face the cause, quoth she,
    Why the Grecians sackèd Troy?
    Fond° done, done fond,
    Was this King Priam's joy?

---

44 **ears** plows   45 **in** bring in   46 **cuckold** deceived husband (traditionally said to wear horns)   52–53 **Charbon . . . Poysam** Flesh-
eater . . . Fish-eater (from French *chair bonne* = good flesh; *poisson*
= fish)   55 **jowl** knock   60 **next** nearest   64 **by kind** according to
nature (the cuckoo allegedly sang to men that they were cuckolds)
73 **Fond** foolishly

75   With that she sighèd as she stood,
        With that she sighèd as she stood,
            And gave this sentence° then:
        Among nine bad if one be good,
        Among nine bad if one be good,
80   There's yet one good in ten.

Countess. What, one good in ten? You corrupt the
    song, sirrah.

Clown. One good woman in ten, madam, which is a
    purifying o' th' song. Would God would serve the
85 world so all the year! We'd find no fault with the
    tithe-woman,° if I were the parson. One in ten,
    quoth 'a!° And° we might have a good woman
    born but or every blazing star, or° at an earth-
    quake, 'twould mend the lottery well; a man may
90 draw his heart out, ere 'a pluck one.

Countess. You'll be gone, sir knave, and do as I com-
    mand you!

Clown. That man should be at woman's command,
    and yet no hurt done! Though honesty be no puri-
95 tan, yet it will do no hurt; it will wear the surplice
    of humility over the black gown of a big heart.°
    I am going, forsooth. The business is for Helen to
    come hither.   *Exit.*

Countess. Well, now.

100 *Steward.* I know, madam, you love your gentlewoman
    entirely.

Countess. Faith, I do. Her father bequeathed her to
    me, and she herself, without other advantage,° may
    lawfully make title to as much love as she finds.

---

77 **sentence** wise saying   86 **tithe-woman** tenth woman (sent as part
of the tithe, like a tithe-pig)   87 **quoth 'a** says he   87 **And** if
88 **or . . . or** either . . . or   95–96 **wear . . . heart** i.e., conform
outwardly, masking its pride (the Church of England required the
wearing of the surplice, but clerics inclined toward Calvinism asserted their independence by wearing beneath the surplice the black
Geneva gown)   103 **advantage** interest accruing to a sum of money

There is more owing her than is paid, and more 105
shall be paid her than she'll demand.

Steward. Madam, I was very late° more near her than
I think she wished me. Alone she was, and did
communicate to herself her own words to her own
ears. She thought, I dare vow for her, they touched 110
not any stranger sense.° Her matter was, she loved
your son. Fortune, she said, was no goddess, that
had put such difference betwixt their two estates;
Love no god, that would not extend his might only
where qualities were level; Diana no queen of vir- 115
gins, that would suffer her poor knight° surprised
without rescue in the first assault or ransom afterward. This she delivered in the most bitter touch
of sorrow that e'er I heard virgin exclaim in, which
I held my duty speedily to acquaint you withal, 120
sithence° in the loss that may happen it concerns
you something to know it.

Countess. You have discharged this honestly; keep it
to yourself. Many likelihoods informed me of this
before, which hung so tott'ring in the balance that 125
I could neither believe nor misdoubt. Pray you
leave me. Stall this° in your bosom, and I thank
you for your honest care. I will speak with you
further anon.   *Exit Steward.*

Enter Helena.

[*Aside*] Even so it was with me, when I was young; 130
If ever we are nature's, these° are ours; this thorn
Doth to our rose of youth rightly belong;
Our blood° to us, this to our blood is born.
It is the show and seal of nature's truth,
Where love's strong passion is impressed in youth. 135
By our remembrances of days foregone,

---

107 **late** lately   110–11 **touched not any stranger sense** reached
no stranger's ear   116 **knight** i.e., chaste follower of Diana
121 **sithence** since   127 **Stall this** keep this enclosed   131 **these**
sorrows (?) passions (?)   133 **blood** passion (?) disposition (?)

Such were our faults, or then we thought them
  none.
Her eye is sick on't; I observe her now.

Helena. What is your pleasure, madam?

Countess.   You know, Helen,
140 I am a mother to you.

Helena. Mine honorable mistress.

Countess.   Nay, a mother.
Why not a mother? When I said "a mother"
Methought you saw a serpent. What's in "mother"
That you start at it? I say I am your mother,
145 And put you in the catalogue of those
That were enwombèd mine. 'Tis often seen
Adoption strives with nature, and choice breeds
A native slip to us from foreign seeds.°
You ne'er oppressed me with a mother's groan,
150 Yet I express to you a mother's care.
God's mercy, maiden, does it curd thy blood
To say I am thy mother? What's the matter,
That this distempered° messenger of wet,
The many-colored Iris,° rounds thine eye?
Why, that you are my daughter?

155 *Helena.*   That I am not.°

Countess. I say I am your mother.

Helena.   Pardon, madam;
The Count Rousillon cannot be my brother.
I am from humble, he from honored name;
No note upon my parents, his all noble.
160 My master, my dear lord he is, and I
His servant live, and will his vassal die.
He must not be my brother.

147–48 **choice . . . seeds** i.e., a slip that is chosen for grafting from
foreign stock becomes native to us   153 **distempered** disturbed
154 **many-colored Iris** i.e., teardrop (Iris was goddess of the rainbow)
155 **That I am not** (Helena plays on the sense "daughter-in-law")

Countess.   Nor I your mother?

Helena. You are my mother, madam; would you
    were—
  So that my lord, your son, were not my brother—
  Indeed my mother! Or were you both our mothers   *165*
  I care no more for than I do for heaven,
  So I were not his sister. Can't no other°
  But, I your daughter, he must be my brother?

Countess. Yes, Helen, you might be my daughter-in-
    law.
  God shield° you mean it not! "Daughter" and
    "mother"   *170*
  So strive upon your pulse! What, pale again?
  My fear hath catched your fondness!° Now I see
  The myst'ry of your loneliness, and find
  Your salt tears' head.° Now to all sense 'tis gross:°
  You love my son! Invention is ashamed   *175*
  Against the proclamation of thy passion,
  To say thou dost not. Therefore tell me true;
  But tell me then, 'tis so; for look, thy cheeks
  Confess it, t' one to th' other, and thine eyes
  See it so grossly shown in thy behaviors,   *180*
  That in their kind° they speak it; only sin
  And hellish obstinacy tie thy tongue,
  That truth should be suspected. Speak, is't so?
  If it be so, you have wound a goodly clew;°
  If it be not, forswear't; howe'er, I charge thee,   *185*
  As heaven shall work in me for thine avail,
  To tell me truly.

Helena.   Good madam, pardon me!

Countess. Do you love my son?

Helena.   Your pardon, noble mistress!

Countess. Love you my son?

---

167 **Can't no other** can it not be otherwise 170 **shield** forbid
172 **fondness** foolishness 174 **head** source 174 **gross** obvious
181 **in their kind** according to their nature, i.e., with tears 184 **clew**
ball of string

Helena.   Do not you love him, madam?

190 *Countess.* Go not about; my love hath in't a bond
     Whereof the world takes note. Come, come, dis-
        close
     The state of your affection, for your passions
     Have to the full appeached.°

     Helena.   Then I confess,
     Here on my knee, before high heaven and you,
195 That before you, and next unto high heaven,
     I love your son.
     My friends° were poor but honest; so's my love.
     Be not offended, for it hurts not him
     That he is loved of me; I follow him not
200 By any token of presumptuous suit,
     Nor would I have him till I do deserve him;
     Yet never know how that desert should be.
     I know I love in vain, strive against hope;
     Yet, in this captious° and inteemable° sieve,
205 I still pour in the waters of my love,
     And lack not to lose still.° Thus, Indian-like,
     Religious in mine error, I adore
     The sun that looks upon his worshipper
     But knows of him no more. My dearest madam,
210 Let not your hate encounter with my love
     For loving where you do; but if yourself,
     Whose agèd honor cites° a virtuous youth,
     Did ever, in so true a flame of liking,
     Wish chastely, and love dearly that your Dian
215 Was both herself and Love, O, then give pity
     To her whose state is such that cannot choose
     But lend and give where she is sure to lose;
     That seeks not to find that° her search implies,
     But, riddle-like, lives° sweetly where she dies.

---

193 **appeached** accused   197 **friends** relatives   204 **captious** (1)
capacious (2) deceitful   204 **inteemable** incapable of pouring forth
(the sieve is capacious enough to accept all the love poured into it,
but is deceptive because it cannot pour forth love)   206 **lack not
to lose still** (1) fail not to go on losing (2) lack not a supply to go on
losing   212 **cites** demonstrates   218 **that** what   219 **lives** i.e., stays
in one place

Countess. Had you not lately an intent—speak truly—   *220*
 To go to Paris?

Helena.   Madam, I had.

Countess.   Wherefore? Tell true.

Helena. I will tell truth, by grace itself, I swear.
 You know my father left me some prescriptions
 Of rare and proved effects, such as his reading
 And manifest experience had collected   *225*
 For general sovereignty;° and that he willed me
 In heedfull'st reservation° to bestow them,
 As notes whose faculties inclusive were
 More than they were in note.° Amongst the rest,
 There is a remedy, approved,° set down,   *230*
 To cure the desperate languishings whereof
 The King is rendered lost.

Countess.   This was your motive
 For Paris, was it? Speak.

Helena. My lord your son made me to think of this;
 Else Paris, and the medicine, and the King,   *235*
 Had from the conversation of my thoughts
 Haply been absent then.

Countess.   But think you, Helen,
 If you should tender your supposèd aid,
 He would receive it? He and his physicians
 Are of a mind; he, that they cannot help him;   *240*
 They, that they cannot help. How shall they credit
 A poor unlearnèd virgin, when the schools,
 Emboweled of their doctrine,° have left off
 The danger to itself?

Helena.   There's something in't
 More than my father's skill, which was the great'st   *245*

---

226 **general sovereignty** universal excellence   227 **In heedfull'st
reservation** i.e., sparingly   228–29 **notes . . . in note** i.e., prescriptions
("notes") more powerful in fact than they were reported ("in note")
to be   230 **approved** tested   243 **Emboweled of their doctrine**
emptied of their knowledge

Of his profession, that his good receipt
Shall for my legacy be sanctified
By th' luckiest stars in heaven; and would your
    honor
But give me leave to try success,° I'd venture
250   The well-lost life of mine on his Grace's cure
By such a day, an hour.

Countess.   Dost thou believe't?

Helena. Ay, madam, knowingly.

Countess. Why, Helen, thou shalt have my leave and
    love,
Means and attendants, and my loving greetings
255   To those of mine in court. I'll stay at home
And pray God's blessing into thy attempt.
Be gone tomorrow; and be sure of this,
What I can help thee to, thou shalt not miss.

                                        Exeunt.

249 **try success** test the outcome

ACT 2

[Scene 1. *Paris. The King's palace.*]

Enter the King with divers young Lords taking leave for the Florentine war; Bertram and Parolles; [Attendants]. Flourish cornets.

King. Farewell, young lords! These warlike principles
  Do not throw from you; and you, my lords, fare-
    well!
  Share the advice betwixt you; if both gain all,
  The gift doth stretch itself as 'tis received,
  And is enough for both.

First Lord.   'Tis our hope, sir,   5
  After well-ent'red soldiers,° to return
  And find your Grace in health.

King. No, no, it cannot be; and yet my heart
  Will not confess he owes° the malady
  That doth my life besiege. Farewell, young lords!   *10*
  Whether I live or die, be you the sons

2.1.6 **After well-ent'red soldiers** after becoming experienced soldiers
9 owes owns

Of worthy Frenchmen: let higher Italy—
Those bated that inherit but the fall
Of the last monarchy°—see that you come
15 Not to woo honor, but to wed it, when
The bravest questant° shrinks: find what you seek,
That fame may cry you loud. I say, farewell.

First Lord. Health, at your bidding, serve your
Majesty!

King. Those girls of Italy, take heed of them.
20 They say our French lack language to deny
If they demand; beware of being captives
Before you serve.

Both Lords.   Our hearts receive your warnings.

King. Farewell. [*To Attendants*] Come hither to me.
[*Exit with Attendants.*]

First Lord. O my sweet lord, that you will stay behind
us!

Parolles. 'Tis not his fault, the spark.

25 *Second Lord.*   O, 'tis brave wars!

Parolles. Most admirable! I have seen those wars.

Bertram. I am commanded here,° and kept a coil° with
"Too young," and "the next year," and " 'tis too
early."

Parolles. And° thy mind stand to't, boy, steal away
bravely.

30 *Bertram.* I shall stay here the forehorse to a smock,°
Creaking my shoes on the plain masonry,
Till honor be bought up, and no sword worn
But one to dance with! By heaven, I'll steal away.

13–14 **Those . . . monarchy** except for those who gain by the fall of
the monarchy (?) except for those who continue in the decadent ways
of the past (?) 16 **questant** seeker 27 **commanded here** ordered
to stay here 27 **kept a coil** bothered 29 **And** if 30 **the forehorse
to a smock** i.e., in the service of women ("forehorse"=leader in a
team of horses)

First Lord. There's honor in the theft.

Parolles.   Commit it, Count.

Second Lord. I am your accessary; and so farewell.   *35*

Bertram. I grow to you, and our parting is a tortured body.

First Lord. Farewell, Captain.

Second Lord. Sweet Monsieur Parolles!

Parolles. Noble heroes, my sword and yours are kin.   *40*
Good sparks and lustrous, a word, good metals.°
You shall find in the regiment of the Spinii one
Captain Spurio,° with his cicatrice,° an emblem of
war, here on his sinister° cheek; it was this very
sword entrenched it. Say to him I live, and observe   *45*
his reports for me.

First Lord. We shall, noble Captain.   [*Exeunt Lords.*]

Parolles. Mars dote on you for his novices!° [*To
Bertram*] What will ye do?

Bertram. Stay° the King.   *50*

Parolles. Use a more spacious ceremony to the noble
lords; you have restrained yourself within the list°
of too cold an adieu. Be more expressive to them,
for they wear themselves in the cap of the time;
there do muster true gait, eat, speak, and move   *55*
under the influence of the most received° star; and
though the devil lead the measure,° such are to be
followed. After them, and take a more dilated°
farewell.

Bertram. And I will do so.   *60*

---

41 **metals** (with the additional sense of "mettles," spirits)   43 **Spurio**
(from Italian, "false")   43 **cicatrice** scar   44 **sinister** left   48 **Mars
. . . novices** may the god of war watch over you as his pupils
50 **Stay** support   52 **list** boundary (literally the selvage of cloth)
56 **received** fashionable   57 **measure** dance   58 **dilated** extended

Parolles. Worthy fellows, and like to prove most
  sinewy sword-men.   *Exeunt [Bertram and Parolles].*

          Enter [the King and] Lafew.

Lafew. [*Kneeling*] Pardon, my lord, for me and for
  my tidings.

King. I'll fee thee to stand up.°

Lafew. [*Rising*] Then here's a man stands that has
65   brought his pardon.
    I would you had kneeled, my lord, to ask me mercy,
    And that at my bidding you could so stand up.

King. I would I had, so I had broke thy pate°
    And asked thee mercy for't.

Lafew.   Good faith, across!°
70 But, my good lord, 'tis thus: will you be cured
    Of your infirmity?

King.   No.

Lafew.   O, will you eat
    No grapes, my royal fox?° Yes, but you will
    My noble grapes, and if my royal fox
    Could reach them. I have seen a medicine
75 That's able to breathe life into a stone,
    Quicken° a rock, and make you dance canary°
    With sprightly fire and motion, whose simple touch
    Is powerful to araise King Pippen,° nay,
    To give great Charlemain a pen in's hand,
    And write to her a love-line.

80 *King.*   What "her" is this?

---

64 **I'll fee thee to stand up** i.e., please arise ("fee" = reward)   68 **pate**
head   69 **across** clumsily (an unskilled tilter might break a lance
"across" instead of head-on)   72 **royal fox** (alluding to Aesop's fox
who said he did not want grapes, when he could not reach them;
Lafew suggests that the King says he does not want to be cured
because he thinks he cannot be cured)   76 **Quicken** endow with life
76 **canary** a lively dance   78 **Pippen** Pepin (died 768)

Lafew. Why, Doctor She! My lord, there's one ar-
    rived,
  If you will see her. Now, by my faith and honor,
  If seriously I may convey my thoughts
  In this my light deliverance,° I have spoke
  With one that, in her sex, her years, profession,°   85
  Wisdom and constancy, hath amazed me more
  Than I dare blame my weakness. Will you see her,
  For that is her demand, and know her business?
  That done, laugh well at me.

King.   Now, good Lafew,
  Bring in the admiration,° that we with thee   90
  May spend our wonder too, or take off thine
  By wond'ring how thou took'st it.

Lafew.   Nay, I'll fit° you,
  And not be all day neither.   [*Goes to door.*]

King. Thus he his special nothing ever prologues.

Lafew. Nay, come your ways.

             Enter Helena.

King.   This haste hath wings indeed. 95

Lafew. Nay, come your ways!
  This is his Majesty; say your mind to him.
  A traitor you do look like, but such traitors
  His Majesty seldom fears. I am Cressid's uncle,°
  That dare leave two together. Fare you well.   *Exit.* 100

King. Now, fair one, does your business follow us?

Helena. Ay, my good lord.
  Gerard de Narbon was my father;
  In what he did profess, well found.°

King.   I knew him.

---

84 **light deliverance** jesting utterance 85 **profession** claims 90 **admiration** wonder 92 **fit** satisfy 99 **Cressid's uncle** Pandarus (who
served as go-between for his niece and Troilus) 104 **well found**
found to be skilled

Helena. The rather will I spare my praises towards
105   him;
     Knowing him is enough. On's bed of death
     Many receipts he gave me, chiefly one,
     Which as the dearest issue of his practice
     And of his old experience th' only darling,
110   He bade me store up as a triple° eye,
     Safer than mine own two; more dear I have so,
     And, hearing your high Majesty is touched
     With that malignant cause wherein the honor
     Of my dear father's gift stands chief in power,
115   I come to tender° it and my appliance,°
     With all bound humbleness.

King.   We thank you, maiden,
     But may not be so credulous of cure,
     When our most learnèd doctors leave us, and
     The congregated College° have concluded
120   That laboring art° can never ransom nature
     From her inaidable estate. I say we must not
     So stain our judgment or corrupt our hope,
     To prostitute our past-cure malady
     To empirics,° or to dissever so
125   Our great self and our credit,° to esteem
     A senseless help, when help past sense we deem.

Helena. My duty then shall pay me for my pains.
     I will no more enforce mine office on you,
     Humbly entreating from your royal thoughts
130   A modest one to bear me back again.

King. I cannot give thee less, to be called grateful.
     Thou thought'st to help me, and such thanks I give
     As one near death to those that wish him live.
     But what at full I know, thou know'st no part,
135   I knowing all my peril, thou no art.

---

110 **triple** third, i.e., the remedy was as valuable as her eyes
115 **tender** offer 115 **appliance** (1) service (2) application, treatment
119 **congregated College** assembled College of Physicians 120 **art**
human skill 124 **empirics** quacks 125 **credit** reputation

Helena. What I can do can do no hurt to try,
   Since you set up your rest° 'gainst remedy:
   He that of greatest works is finisher,
   Oft does them by the weakest minister.
   So holy writ in babes hath judgment shown,   *140*
   When judges have been babes; great floods have
     flown
   From simple sources; and great seas have dried
   When miracles have by the great'st° been denied.
   Oft expectation fails, and most oft there
   Where most it promises, and oft it hits   *145*
   Where hope is coldest and despair most sits.

King. I must not hear thee; fare thee well, kind maid.
   Thy pains not used must by thyself be paid.
   Proffers not took reap thanks for their reward.

Helena. Inspirèd merit so by breath° is barred.   *150*
   It is not so with Him that all things knows,
   As 'tis with us that square our guess by shows;°
   But most it is presumption in us when
   The help of heaven we count the act of men.
   Dear sir, to my endeavors give consent;   *155*
   Of heaven, not me, make an experiment.
   I am not an impostor, that proclaim
   Myself against the level of mine aim,°
   But know I think, and think I know most sure,
   My art is not past power, nor you past cure.   *160*

King. Art thou so confident? Within what space
   Hop'st thou my cure?

Helena.   The greatest grace lending grace,
   Ere twice the horses of the sun shall bring
   Their fiery torcher his diurnal ring,°

---

137 **set up your rest** stake all (gambling term)   143 **the great'st** (if
Helena has been thinking of the Red Sea, "the great'st" = Pharaoh)
150 **breath** i.e., your words (contrast to God's breathing into Helena
is implicit in "inspirèd")   152 **square our guess by shows** make decisions by appearances   157–58 **that proclaim . . . aim** i.e., although I announce I will hit the target even before I take aim
164 **diurnal ring** daily circuit

165   Ere twice in murk and occidental damp°
      Moist Hesperus° hath quenched her sleepy lamp,
      Or four and twenty times the pilot's glass°
      Hath told the thievish minutes how they pass,
      What is infirm from your sound parts shall fly,
170   Health shall live free, and sickness freely die.

King. Upon thy certainty and confidence
      What dar'st thou venture?

Helena.   Tax° of impudence,
      A strumpet's boldness, a divulgèd shame,
      Traduced by odious ballads; my maiden's name
175   Seared° otherwise; ne° worse of worst, extended°
      With vilest torture, let my life be ended.

King. Methinks in thee some blessèd spirit doth speak
      His powerful sound within an organ weak;
      And what impossibility would slay
180   In common sense, sense saves another way.
      Thy life is dear, for all that life can rate
      Worth name of life in thee hath estimate:°
      Youth, beauty, wisdom, courage, all
      That happiness and prime° can happy call.
185   Thou this to hazard needs must intimate
      Skill infinite or monstrous desperate.
      Sweet practicer, thy physic° I will try,
      That ministers thine own death if I die.

Helena. If I break time, or flinch in property°
190   Of what I spoke, unpitied let me die,
      And well deserved. Not helping, death's my fee,
      But if I help what do you promise me?

King. Make thy demand.

Helena.   But will you make it even?°

165 **occidental damp** (alluding to the sun's alleged setting in the
ocean)   166 **Hesperus** the evening star   167 **glass** hourglass   172
Tax accusation   175 **Seared** branded   175 **ne** nor   175 **extended**
stretched (on the rack)   182 **estimate** value   184 **prime** springtime
(of life), i.e., youth   187 **physic** medicine   189 **flinch in property**
i.e., fail in any detail   193 **make it even** fulfill it

King. Ay, by my scepter and my hopes of heaven.

Helena. Then shalt thou give me with thy kingly hand   *195*
    What husband in thy power I will command:
    Exempted be from me the arrogance
    To choose from forth the royal blood of France
    My low and humble name to propagate
    With any branch or image of thy state;   *200*
    But such a one, thy vassal, whom I know
    Is free for me to ask, thee to bestow.

King. Hcre is my hand; the premises observed,
    Thy will by my performance shall be served;
    So make the choice of thy own time, for I,   *205*
    Thy resolved patient, on thee still rely.
    More should I question thee, and more I must,
    Though more to know could not be more to trust;
    From whence thou cam'st, how tended on—but rest
    Unquestioned, welcome, and undoubted blest.   *210*
    Give me some help here, ho! If thou proceed
    As high as word, my deed shall match thy deed.
               Flourish. Exit [King with Helena].

[Scene 2. *Rousillon. The Count's palace.*]

Enter Countess and Clown.

Countess. Come on, sir. I shall now put you to the height of° your breeding.

Clown. I will show myself highly fed and lowly taught. I know my business is but to the court.

2.2.1–2 **put you to the height of** test

5 *Countess.* To the court! Why, what place make you
special, when you put off that with such contempt?
"But to the court!"

 Clown. Truly, madam, if God have lent a man any
manners, he may easily put it off at court. He that
10 cannot make a leg,° put off's cap, kiss his hand, and
say nothing, has neither leg, hands, lip, nor cap;
and indeed such a fellow, to say precisely, were not
for the court. But for me, I have an answer will
serve all men.

15 *Countess.* Marry, that's a bountiful answer that fits
all questions.

 Clown. It is like a barber's chair that fits all buttocks:
the pin-buttock, the quatch-buttock,° the brawn-
buttock, or any buttock.

20 *Countess.* Will your answer serve fit to all questions?

 Clown. As fit as ten groats° is for the hand of an
attorney, as your French crown° for your taffety
punk,° as Tib's rush° for Tom's forefinger, as a
pancake for Shrove Tuesday,° a morris° for May-
25 day, as the nail to his hole, the cuckold to his horn,
as a scolding quean° to a wrangling knave, as the
nun's lip to the friar's mouth; nay, as the pudding°
to his skin.

 Countess. Have you, I say, an answer of such fitness
30 for all questions?

 Clown. From below your duke to beneath your constable, it will fit any question.

---

10 **make a leg** make obeisance (by drawing back one leg and bending
the other) 18 **quatch-buttock** fat behind 21 **ten groats** (a groat was
worth fourpence; ten groats was the usual attorney's fee) 22 **French
crown** (1) coin (2) bald or scabby head (caused by syphilis, "the
French disease") 22–23 **taffety punk** finely dressed prostitute
23 **rush** ring made of rush (used in mock weddings) 24 **Shrove
Tuesday** day preceding Ash Wednesday, hence a day of feasting
immediately before Lent 24 **morris** country dance 26 **quean**
prostitute 27 **pudding** sausage

Countess. It must be an answer of most monstrous size
that must fit all demands.

Clown. But a trifle neither,° in good faith, if the   35
learned should speak truth of it. Here it is, and all
that belongs to't. Ask me if I am a courtier; it shall
do you no harm to learn.

Countess. To be young again, if we could, I will be
a fool in question, hoping to be the wiser by your   40
answer. I pray you, sir, are you a courtier?

Clown. O Lord, sir!° There's a simple putting off.
More, more, a hundred of them.

Countess. Sir, I am a poor friend of yours, that loves
you.   45

Clown. O Lord, sir! Thick,° thick! Spare not me.

Countess. I think, sir, you can eat none of this homely
meat.

Clown. O Lord, sir! Nay, put me to't, I warrant you.

Countess. You were lately whipped, sir, as I think.   50

Clown. O Lord, sir! Spare not me.

Countess. Do you cry, "O Lord, sir!" at your whipping, and "spare not me"? Indeed, your "O Lord,
sir!" is very sequent to° your whipping; you would
answer very well to a whipping, if you were but   55
bound to't.°

Clown. I ne'er had worse luck in my life in my "O
Lord, sir!" I see things may serve long, but not
serve ever.

Countess. I play the noble housewife with the time,   60
To entertain it so merrily with a fool.

---

35 **neither** indeed (negating the Countess' conjecture)   42 **O Lord,
sir** (a phrase associated with courtiers)   46 **Thick** quickly   54 **is
very sequent to** i.e., would quickly follow   56 **bound to't** (1) bound
by oath to answer (2) tied to a whipping post

Clown. O Lord, sir! Why, there't serves well again.

Countess. An end, sir! To your business: give Helen this,
And urge her to a present° answer back.
65   Commend me to my kinsmen and my son.
This is not much.

Clown. Not much commendation to them?

Countess. Not much employment for you. You understand me?

70   *Clown.* Most fruitfully.° I am there before my legs.

Countess. Haste you again.   *Exeunt.*

·

[Scene 3. *Paris. The King's palace.*]

Enter Bertram, Lafew, and Parolles.

Lafew. They say miracles are past, and we have our philosophical persons, to make modern° and familiar, things supernatural and causeless. Hence is it that we make trifles of terrors, ensconcing° ourselves into seeming knowledge, when we should submit ourselves to an unknown fear.°

Parolles. Why, 'tis the rarest argument of° wonder that hath shot out in our latter times.

Bertram. And so 'tis.

64 **present** immediate   70 **fruitfully** (perhaps a bawdy punning reply, if "understand" means "have intercourse with")   2.3.2 **modern** commonplace   4 **ensconcing** fortifying   6 **unknown fear** i.e., inexplicable mystery   7 **argument of** subject for

Lafew. To be relinquished of the artists—°   10

Parolles. So I say—both of Galen and Paracelsus.°

Lafew. Of all the learned and authentic fellows—

Parolles. Right; so I say.

Lafew. That gave him out incurable—

Parolles. Why, there 'tis; so say I too.   15

Lafew. Not to be helped—

Parolles. Right, as 'twere a man assured of a—

Lafew. Uncertain life and sure death.

Parolles. Just; you say well. So would I have said.

Lafew. I may truly say it is a novelty to the world.   20

Parolles. It is indeed; if you will have it in showing, you shall read it in what-do-ye-call there?

Lafew. [*Reading*] "A showing of a heavenly effect in an earthly actor."

Parolles. That's it, I would have said the very same.   25

Lafew. Why, your dolphin is not lustier;° 'fore me,° I speak in respect—

Parolles. Nay, 'tis strange, 'tis very strange; that is the brief and the tedious of it, and he's of a most facinerious° spirit that will not acknowledge it to   30 be the—

Lafew. Very hand of heaven.

Parolles. Ay, so I say.

Lafew. In a most weak—

Parolles. And debile° minister; great power, great   35

10 **artists** physicians   11 **Galen . . . Paracelsus** (renowned physicians; the former was a Greek of the second century B.C., the latter a German of the sixteenth century)   26 **lustier** more vigorous   26 **'fore me** on my soul   30 **facinerious** villainous   35 **debile** weak

transcendence, which should indeed give us a
further use to be made than alone the recov'ry of
the King, as to be—

Lafew. Generally thankful.

Enter King, Helena, and Attendants.

40 *Parolles.* I would have said it. You say well. Here
comes the King.

Lafew. Lustig, as the Dutchman° says. I'll like a maid
the better whilst I have a tooth in my head. Why,
he's able to lead her a coranto.°

45 *Parolles.* Mor du vinager!° Is not this Helen?

Lafew. 'Fore God, I think so.

King. Go, call before me all the lords in court.
                                    [*Exit Attendant.*]
Sit, my preserver, by thy patient's side,
And with this healthful hand, whose banished sense
50 Thou hast repealed,° a second time receive
The confirmation of my promised gift,
Which but attends thy naming.

Enter three or four Lords.

Fair maid, send forth thine eye. This youthful parcel
Of noble bachelors stand at my bestowing,
55 O'er whom both sovereign power and father's voice
I have to use. Thy frank election° make;
Thou hast power to choose, and they none to
    forsake.

Helena. To each of you one fair and virtuous mistress
Fall, when Love please! Marry, to each but one!

60 *Lafew.* I'd give bay curtal and his furniture,°

---

42 **Dutchman** German   44 **coranto** lively dance   45 **Mor du vinager**
death of vinager (a meaningless pseudo-French oath)   50 **repealed**
recalled from banishment   56 **frank election** free choice   60 **bay
curtal and his furniture** my bay horse with the docked tail, and his
trappings

My mouth no more were broken° than these boys',
And writ° as little beard.

King.   Peruse them well:
Not one of those but had a noble father.

Helena. (She addresses her to a lord.) Gentlemen,
Heaven hath through me restored the King to
health.   65

All. We understand it, and thank heaven for you.

Helena. I am a simple maid, and therein wealthiest
That I protest I simply am a maid.
Please it your Majesty, I have done already.
The blushes in my cheeks thus whisper me,   70
"We blush that thou shouldst choose; but, be re-
fused,
Let the white death sit on thy cheek forever,
We'll ne'er come there again."

King.   Make choice and see,
Who shuns thy love shuns all his love in me.

Helena. Now, Dian, from thy altar do I fly,   75
And to imperial Love, that god most high,
Do my sighs stream. [*To First Lord*] Sir, will you
hear my suit?

First Lord. And grant it.

Helena.   Thanks, sir; all the rest is mute.

Lafew. I had rather be in this choice than throw ames-
ace° for my life.   80

Helena. [*To Second Lord*] The honor, sir, that flames
in your fair eyes,
Before I speak, too threat'ningly replies.
Love make your fortunes twenty times above
Her that so wishes and her humble love!

---

61 **broken** broken to the bit, i.e., tamed (?) missing some teeth (?)
62 **writ** claimed (?)   79–80 **ames-ace** two aces, the lowest throw in
dicing (the line is ironical, as one might say I would rather be in
this lottery than at death's door)

Second Lord. No better, if you please.

85 *Helena.*   My wish receive,
   Which great Love grant; and so, I take my leave.

Lafew. Do all they deny her?° And they were sons of
   mine, I'd have them whipped, or I would send them
   to th' Turk to make eunuchs of.

Helena. [*To Third Lord*] Be not afraid that I your
90   hand should take,
   I'll never do you wrong, for your own sake.
   Blessing upon your vows, and in your bed
   Find fairer fortune if you ever wed!

Lafew. These boys are boys of ice, they'll none have
95   her. Sure they are bastards to the English; the
   French ne'er got° 'em.

Helena. [*To Fourth Lord*] You are too young, too
   happy, and too good,
   To make yourself a son out of my blood.

Fourth Lord. Fair one, I think not so.

100 *Lafew.* There's one grape yet. I am sure thy father
   drunk wine.° But if thou be'st not an ass, I am a
   youth of fourteen; I have known thee already.

Helena. [*To Bertram*] I dare not say I take you, but
   I give
   Me and my service, ever whilst I live,
105   Into your guiding power. This is the man.

King. Why then, young Bertram, take her, she's thy
   wife.

Bertram. My wife, my liege? I shall beseech your
   Highness,
   In such a business give me leave to use
   The help of mine own eyes.

---

87 **deny her** (Lafew, at a distance, does not understand that Helena
denies the men) 96 **got** begot 101 **drunk wine** i.e., was manly

King.   Know'st thou not, Bertram,
What she has done for me?

Bertram.   Yes, my good lord;   *110*
But never hope to know why I should marry her.

King. Thou know'st she has raised me from my sickly
bed.

Bertram. But follows it, my lord, to bring me down
Must answer for your raising? I know her well;
She had her breeding° at my father's charge: *115*
A poor physician's daughter my wife! Disdain
Rather corrupt me ever!°

King. 'Tis only title thou disdain'st in her, the which
I can build up. Strange is it that our bloods,
Of color, weight, and heat, poured all together,   *120*
Would quite confound distinction, yet stands off
In differences so mighty. If she be
All that is virtuous, save what thou dislik'st—
A poor physician's daughter—thou dislik'st
Of virtue for the name. But do not so: *125*
From lowest place when virtuous things proceed,
The place is dignified by th' doer's deed.
Where great additions swell's° and virtue none,
It is a dropsied honor. Good alone
Is good, without a name; vileness is so: *130*
The property° by what it is should go,
Not by the title. She is young, wise, fair;
In these to nature she's immediate heir;
And these breed honor. That is honor's scorn
Which challenges itself as honor's born°   *135*
And is not like the sire. Honors thrive
When rather from our acts we them derive
Than our foregoers. The mere word's a slave,
Deboshed° on every tomb, on every grave

---

115 **breeding** upbringing   116–17 **Disdain . . . ever** may my disdain
of her ruin me forever   128 **additions swell's** titles inflate us
131 **property** quality (here, "good" or "vileness")   135 **challenges
. . . born** claims honor by descent   139 **Deboshed** debauched,
debased

140   A lying trophy, and as oft is dumb
        Where dust and damned oblivion is the tomb
        Of honored bones indeed. What should be said?
        If thou canst like this creature as a maid,
        I can create the rest. Virtue and she
145   Is her own dower; honor and wealth from me.

Bertram. I cannot love her, nor will strive to do't.

King. Thou wrong'st thyself, if thou shouldst strive to
    choose.

Helena. That you are well restored, my lord, I'm glad;
    Let the rest go.

150 *King.* My honor's at the stake,° which to defeat,
        I must produce my power. Here, take her hand,
        Proud, scornful boy, unworthy this good gift,
        That dost in vile misprision° shackle up
        My love and her desert; that canst not dream
155   We, poising us in her defective scale,
        Shall weigh thee to the beam;° that wilt not know,
        It is in us to plant thine honor where
        We please to have it grow. Check thy contempt;
        Obey our will, which travails in thy good;
160   Believe not thy disdain, but presently°
        Do thine own fortunes that obedient right
        Which both thy duty owes and our power claims;
        Or I will throw thee from my care forever
        Into the staggers° and the careless lapse
165   Of youth and ignorance; both my revenge and hate,
        Loosing upon thee in the name of justice,
        Without all terms of pity. Speak. Thine answer.

Bertram. Pardon, my gracious lord; for I submit
    My fancy° to your eyes. When I consider
170   What great creation and what dole° of honor

---

150 **at the stake** (the figure is from bearbaiting; a bear was tied to
a stake, and dogs were set upon him)   153 **misprision** contempt
(with pun on false imprisonment)   155–56 **We . . . beam** i.e., my
(royal "we") word added to Helena will outweigh your objection
160 **presently** immediately   164 **staggers** giddiness (disease of ani-
mals)   169 **fancy** love   170 **dole** portion

Flies where you bid it, I find that she, which late
Was in my nobler thoughts most base, is now
The praisèd of the King; who, so ennobled,
Is as 'twere born so.

King.   Take her by the hand,
And tell her she is thine; to whom I promise   *175*
A counterpoise, if not to thy estate,
A balance more replete.°

Bertram.   I take her hand.

King. Good fortune and the favor of the King
Smile upon this contract; whose ceremony
Shall seem expedient° on the now-born brief,°   *180*
And be performed tonight. The solemn feast
Shall more attend upon the coming space,
Expecting absent friends.° As thou lov'st her,
Thy love's to me religious; else, does err.
                    Exeunt. Parolles and Lafew stay
                    behind, commenting of this wedding.

Lafew. Do you hear, monsieur? A word with you.   *185*

Parolles. Your pleasure, sir?

Lafew. Your lord and master did well to make his
recantation.

Parolles. Recantation! My lord! My master!

Lafew. Ay; is it not a language I speak?   *190*

Parolles. A most harsh one, and not to be understood
without bloody succeeding.° My master!

Lafew. Are you companion to the Count Rousillon?

Parolles. To any count, to all counts; to what is man.°

176–77 **A counterpoise . . . replete** i.e., a reward that, if it does not
equal your estate, will overweigh it (?)   180 **expedient** swift   180
brief royal edict   181–83 **The solemn . . . friends** the ceremonious
("solemn") feast shall await ("attend") until absent friends arrive
192 **succeeding** consequences   194 **man** manly (but Lafew gives it
another sense, "servingman")

195 *Lafew*. To what is count's man; count's master is of another style.

Parolles. You are too old, sir; let it satisfy you, you are too old.

Lafew. I must tell thee, sirrah, I write man; to which
200 title age cannot bring thee.

Parolles. What I dare too well do, I dare not do.

Lafew. I did think thee, for two ordinaries,° to be a pretty wise fellow; thou didst make tolerable vent° of thy travel; it might pass. Yet the scarves° and the
205 bannerets about thee did manifoldly dissuade me from believing thee a vessel of too great a burden.° I have now found thee;° when I lose thee again I care not. Yet art thou good for nothing but taking up, and that thou'rt scarce worth.

210 *Parolles*. Hadst thou not the privilege of antiquity° upon thee—

Lafew. Do not plunge thyself too far in anger, lest thou hasten thy trial; which if—Lord have mercy on thee for a hen! So, my good window of lattice, fare
215 thee well; thy casement I need not open, for I look through thee. Give me thy hand.

Parolles. My lord, you give me most egregious indignity.

Lafew. Ay, with all my heart, and thou art worthy of it.

220 *Parolles*. I have not, my lord, deserved it.

Lafew. Yes, good faith, every dram of it, and I will not bate thee a scruple.°

Parolles. Well, I shall be wiser.

---

202 **ordinaries** tavern meals   203 **vent** free talk   204 **scarves** (military men wore scarves, usually over the shoulder; cp. the modern *fourragère*)   206 **burden** capacity   207 **found thee** found you out 210 **antiquity** old age   222 **bate thee a scruple** i.e., diminish by one drop what I have said of you

Lafew. Ev'n as soon as thou canst, for thou hast to pull at a smack o' th' contrary.° If ever thou be'st 225 bound in thy scarf and beaten, thou shall find what it is to be proud of thy bondage. I have a desire to hold my acquaintance with thee, or rather my knowledge, that I may say, in the default,° "He is a man I know." 230

Parolles. My lord, you do me most insupportable vexation.

Lafew. I would it were hell-pains for thy sake, and my poor doing eternal; for doing° I am past, as I will by thee, in what motion age will give me leave. 235
Exit.

Parolles. Well, thou hast a son shall take this disgrace off me; scurvy, old, filthy, scurvy lord! Well, I must be patient, there is no fettering of authority. I'll beat him, by my life, if I can meet him with any convenience,° and he were double and double a 240 lord. I'll have no more pity of his age than I would have of—I'll beat him, and if I could but meet him again.

Enter Lafew.

Lafew. Sirrah, your lord and master's married; there's news for you; you have a new mistress. 245

Parolles. I most unfeignedly beseech your lordship to make some reservation of your wrongs. He is my good lord; whom I serve above is my master.

Lafew. Who? God?

Parolles. Ay, sir. 250

Lafew. The devil it is that's thy master. Why dost thou garter up thy arms o' this fashion? Dost make hose of thy sleeves? Do other servants so? Thou

---

225 **pull . . . contrary** i.e., take a good taste of your folly   229 **in the default** when you fail   234 **doing** (perhaps with the bawdy meaning, "copulating")   240 **convenience** advantage

wert best set thy lower part where thy nose stands.
255 By mine honor, if I were but two hours younger I'd
beat thee. Methink'st thou art a general offense,
and every man should beat thee. I think thou wast
created for men to breathe° themselves upon thee.

Parolles. This is hard and undeserved measure, my
260 lord.

Lafew. Go to, sir. You were beaten in Italy for pick-
ing a kernel out of a pom'granate. You are a
vagabond and no true traveler. You are more saucy
with lords and honorable personages than the com-
265 mission of your birth and virtue gives you heraldry.
You are not worth another word, else I'd call you
knave. I leave you.   *Exit.*

Enter Bertram.

Parolles. Good, very good, it is so then. Good, very
good, let it be concealed awhile.

270 *Bertram.* Undone and forfeited to cares forever!

Parolles. What's the matter, sweetheart?

Bertram. Although before the solemn priest I have
sworn,
I will not bed her.

Parolles. What, what, sweetheart?

275 *Bertram.* O my Parolles, they have married me!
I'll to the Tuscan wars and never bed her.

Parolles. France is a dog-hole, and it no more merits
The tread of a man's foot; to th' wars!

Bertram. There's letters from my mother; what th'
import is,
280 I know not yet.

Parolles. Ay, that would be known. To th' wars, my
boy, to th' wars!

258 **breathe** exercise

He wears his honor in a box unseen,
That hugs his kicky-wicky° here at home,
Spending his manly marrow in her arms,
Which should sustain the bound and high curvet°   285
Of Mars's fiery steed. To other regions!
France is a stable, we that dwell in't jades;°
Therefore to th' war!

Bertram. It shall be so. I'll send her to my house,
Acquaint my mother with my hate to her,   290
And wherefore I am fled; write to the King
That which I durst not speak. His present gift
Shall furnish me to those Italian fields
Where noble fellows strike. Wars is no strife
To the dark house and the detested wife.   295

Parolles. Will this capriccio° hold in thee, art sure?

Bertram. Go with me to my chamber and advise me.
I'll send her straight away. Tomorrow
I'll to the wars, she to her single sorrow.

Parolles. Why, these balls bound; there's noise in it.
'Tis hard;   300
A young man married is a man that's marred.
Therefore away, and leave her bravely; go.
The King has done you wrong; but hush 'tis so.
                                        Exit [*with Bertram*].

283 **kicky-wicky** woman (but apparently an obscene term, perhaps from French *quelque chose*, "something," a euphemism for pudendum)   285 **curvet** prancing   287 **jades** nags   296 **capriccio** caprice (an affected Italian word)

[Scene 4. *Paris. The King's Palace.*]

Enter Helena and Clown.

Helena. My mother greets me kindly. Is she well?°

Clown. She is not well, but yet she has her health; she's very merry, but yet she is not well. But thanks be given she's very well and wants nothing i' th' world; but yet she is not well.

Helena. If she be very well what does she ail that she's not very well?

Clown. Truly, she's very well indeed, but for two things.

10 *Helena.* What two things?

Clown. One, that she's not in heaven, whither God send her quickly; the other, that she's in earth, from whence God send her quickly.

Enter Parolles.

Parolles. Bless you, my fortunate lady!

15 *Helena.* I hope, sir, I have your good will to have mine own good fortune.

Parolles. You had my prayers to lead them on, and to keep them on have them still. O, my knave, how does my old lady?

20 *Clown.* So that you had her wrinkles and I her money, I would she did as you say.

Parolles. Why, I say nothing.

2.4.1 **well** (in his reply, the Clown plays on the Elizabethan euphemism in which the dead are said to be well, i.e., well-off, being in heaven)

Clown. Marry, you are the wiser man; for many a
man's tongue shakes out his master's undoing. To
say nothing, to do nothing, to know nothing, and   25
to have nothing, is to be a great part of your
title°—which is within a very little of nothing.

Parolles. Away, th'art a knave.

Clown. You should have said, sir, "Before a knave
th'art a knave"; that's "Before me,° th'art a   30
knave." This had been truth, sir.

Parolles. Go to, thou art a witty fool; I have found
thee.

Clown. Did you find me in° yourself, sir, or were you
taught to find me? The search, sir, was profitable;   35
and much fool may you find in you, even to the
world's pleasure and the increase of laughter.

Parolles. A good knave, i' faith, and well fed.
Madam, my lord will go away tonight,
A very serious business calls on him.   40
The great prerogative and rite of love,
Which as your due time claims, he does acknowl-
edge,
But puts it off to a compelled restraint;
Whose want, and whose delay, is strewed with
sweets,
Which they distil now in the curbèd time,°   45
To make the coming hour o'erflow with joy,
And pleasure drown the brim.

Helena.   What's his will else?

Parolles. That you will take your instant leave o' th'
King,
And make this haste as your own good proceed-
ing,°

27 **title** possession   30 **Before me** (punning on the sense "on my
soul")   34 **in** by   45 **curbèd time** delay (?) time spent in the con-
fining still (?)   49 **as your own good proceeding** as if it originated
from you

50   Strength'ned with what apology you think
     May make it probable need.

Helena.   What more commands he?

Parolles. That, having this obtained, you presently
     Attend his further pleasure.

Helena. In everything I wait upon his will.

55   *Parolles.* I shall report it so.   *Exit Parolles.*

Helena. I pray you. Come, sirrah.   *Exit [with Clown].*

[Scene 5. *Paris. The King's palace.*]

Enter Lafew and Bertram.

Lafew. But I hope your lordship thinks not him a
     soldier.

Bertram. Yes, my lord, and of very valiant approof.°

Lafew. You have it from his own deliverance.°

5   *Bertram.* And by other warranted testimony.

Lafew. Then my dial goes not true; I took this lark
     for a bunting.°

Bertram. I do assure you, my lord, he is very great in
     knowledge, and accordingly valiant.

2.5.3 **very valiant approof** great proven valor   4 **deliverance** speech
6–7 **took this lark for a bunting** i.e., underestimated him

Lafew. I have then sinned against his experience and   10
transgressed against his valor; and my state that
way is dangerous, since I cannot yet find in my
heart to repent. Here he comes. I pray you make
us friends; I will pursue the amity.

Enter Parolles.

Parolles. [*To Bertram*] These things shall be done, sir.   15

Lafew. Pray you, sir, who's his tailor?

Parolles. Sir?

Lafew. O, I know him well. Ay sir, he, sir, 's a good
workman, a very good tailor.

Bertram. [*Aside to Parolles*] Is she gone to the King?   20

Parolles. She is.

Bertram. Will she away tonight?

Parolles. As you'll have her.

Bertram. I have writ my letters, casketed my treasure,
Given order for our horses; and tonight,   25
When I should take possession of the bride,
End ere I do begin.

Lafew. [*Aside*] A good traveler is something at the
latter end of a dinner, but one that lies three thirds
and uses a known truth to pass a thousand noth-   30
ings with, should be once heard and thrice beaten.
[*Aloud*] God save you, Captain.

Bertram. Is there any unkindness between my lord
and you, monsieur?

Parolles. I know not how I have deserved to run into   35
my lord's displeasure.

Lafew. You have made shift° to run into't, boots and
spurs and all, like him that leaped into the custard;

---

37 **made shift** managed

and out of it you'll run again rather than suffer
40 question for your residence.°

Bertram. It may be you have mistaken him, my lord.

Lafew. And shall do so ever, though I took him at's
prayers. Fare you well, my lord, and believe this of
me, there can be no kernel in this light nut; the
45 soul of this man is his clothes. Trust him not in
matter of heavy consequence; I have kept of them
tame° and know their natures. Farewell, monsieur;
I have spoken better of you than you have or will
to deserve at my hand, but we must do good against
50 evil.   [*Exit.*]

Parolles. An idle° lord, I swear.

Bertram. I think not so.

Parolles. Why, do you not know him?

Bertram. Yes, I do know him well, and common
speech
55 Gives him a worthy pass.° Here comes my clog.

Enter Helena.

Helena. I have, sir, as I was commanded from you,
Spoke with the King, and have procured his leave
For present parting; only he desires
Some private speech with you.

Bertram.   I shall obey his will.
60 You must not marvel, Helen, at my course,
Which holds not color with the time,° nor does
The ministration and requirèd office
On my particular. Prepared I was not
For such a business; therefore am I found
65 So much unsettled. This drives me to entreat you
That presently you take your way for home,
And rather muse than ask why I entreat you,

39–40 **suffer question for your residence** put up with questions on
why you are there   46–47 **kept of them tame** had some of them as pets
51 **idle** foolish   55 **pass** reputation   61 **holds not color with the
time** does not match the situation

For my respects° are better than they seem,
And my appointments° have in them a need
Greater than shows itself at the first view   70
To you that know them not. [*Gives a letter.*] This
    to my mother.
'Twill be two days ere I shall see you, so
I leave you to your wisdom.

Helena.   Sir, I can nothing say
But that I am your most obedient servant.

Bertram. Come, come; no more of that.

Helena.   And ever shall   75
With true observance° seek to eke out that
Wherein toward me my homely stars° have failed
To equal my great fortune.

Bertram.   Let that go:
My haste is very great. Farewell; hie home.

Helena. Pray sir, your pardon.

Bertram.   Well, what would you say?   80

Helena. I am not worthy of the wealth I owe,°
Nor dare I say 'tis mine—and yet it is;
But like a timorous thief most fain would steal
What law does vouch mine own.

Bertram.   What would you have?

Helena. Something, and scarce so much: nothing, in-
    deed.   85
I would not tell you what I would, my lord.
Faith, yes—
Strangers and foes do sunder and not kiss.

Bertram. I pray you, stay not, but in haste to horse.

Helena. I shall not break your bidding, good my
    lord.   90
Where are my other men? Monsieur, farewell.
                                        Exit.

68 **respects** reasons 69 **appointments** purposes 76 **observance**
dutiful service 77 **homely stars** fate of low birth 81 **owe** own

Bertram. Go thou toward home, where I will never come
Whilst I can shake my sword or hear the drum.
Away, and for our flight.

Parolles.   Bravely, coragio!°

                                [*Exeunt.*]

94 **coragio** courage (Italian)

ACT 3

[Scene 1. *Florence. The Duke's palace.*]

*Flourish. Enter the Duke of Florence, the two
Frenchmen, with a troop of Soldiers.*

Duke. So that from point to point now have you
    heard
  The fundamental reasons of this war,
  Whose great decision hath much blood let forth,
  And more thirsts after.

First Lord.   Holy seems the quarrel
  Upon your Grace's part; black and fearful   5
  On the opposer.

Duke. Therefore we marvel much our cousin France
  Would in so just a business shut his bosom
  Against our borrowing prayers.

Second Lord.   Good my lord,
  The reasons of our state I cannot yield,°   10

3.1.10 **yield** produce

55

But like a common and an outward man
That the great figure of a council frames
By self-unable motion;° therefore dare not
Say what I think of it, since I have found
15   Myself in my incertain grounds to fail
As often as I guessed.

Duke.   Be it his pleasure.

First Lord. But I am sure the younger of our nature,
That surfeit on° their ease, will day by day
Come here for physic.

Duke.   Welcome shall they be;
20   And all the honors that can fly from us
Shall on them settle. You know your places well;
When better fall, for your avails they fell:°
Tomorrow to the field!   *Flourish; [exeunt].*

[Scene 2. *Rousillon. The Count's palace.*]

Enter Countess and Clown.

Countess. It hath happened all as I would have had it, save that he comes not along with her.

Clown. By my troth,° I take my young lord to be a very melancholy man.

5   *Countess.* By what observance, I pray you?

13 **self-unable motion** impotent guess   18 **surfeit on** grow sick from
22 **When . . . fell** when better places fall vacant, for you they will
have fallen   3.2.3 **troth** truth

Clown. Why, he will look upon his boot and sing,
  mend the ruff and sing, ask questions and sing,
  pick his teeth and sing. I know a man that had this
  trick of melancholy sold a goodly manor for a song.

Countess. Let me see what he writes, and when he   10
  means to come.   [*Reads a letter.*]

Clown. I have no mind to Isbel, since I was at court.
  Our old lings° and our Isbels o' th' country are
  nothing like your old ling and your Isbels o' th'
  court. The brains of my Cupid's knocked out, and   15
  I begin to love as an old man loves money, with
  no stomach.°

Countess. What have we here?

Clown. E'en that you have there.   *Exit.*

Countess. [*Reads*] *a letter.* "I have sent you a   20
  daughter-in-law. She hath recovered the King, and
  undone me. I have wedded her, not bedded her,
  and sworn to make the 'not'° eternal. You shall
  hear I am run away; know it before the report
  come. If there be breadth enough in the world, I   25
  will hold a long distance. My duty to you.
                    Your unfortunate son,
                              Bertram."

This is not well, rash and unbridled boy,
To fly the favors of so good a king,   30
To pluck his indignation on thy head
By the misprizing° of a maid too virtuous
For the contempt of empire.

                    Enter Clown.

Clown. O madam, yonder is heavy news within, between two soldiers and my young lady.   35

Countess. What is the matter?

Clown. Nay, there is some comfort in the news, some

13 **lings** salt cod (but also with the sense of "lecherous men")
17 **stomach** appetite   23 **not** (with pun on "knot," the symbol of
marriage)   32 **misprizing** despising

comfort; your son will not be killed so soon as I
thought he would.

40 *Countess.* Why should he be killed?

Clown. So say I, madam, if he run away, as I hear
he does. The danger is in standing to't;° that's the
loss of men, though it be the getting of children.
Here they come will tell you more. For my part,
45 I only hear your son was run away.

    Enter Helena and two [French] Gentlemen.

First Lord. Save you, good madam.

Helena. Madam, my lord is gone, forever gone.

Second Lord. Do not say so.

Countess. Think upon patience. Pray you, gentlemen,
50 I have felt so many quirks of joy and grief,
    That the first face of neither, on the start,
    Can woman me° unto't. Where is my son, I pray
      you?

Second Lord. Madam, he's gone to serve the Duke
      of Florence.
    We met him thitherward, for thence we came,
55 And, after some dispatch in hand at court,
    Thither we bend again.

Helena. Look on his letter, madam, here's my pass-
      port.°
    [*Reads*] "When thou canst get the ring upon my
    finger, which never shall come off, and show me a
60 child begotten of thy body that I am father to,
    then call me husband; but in such a 'then' I write
    a 'never.' " This is a dreadful sentence.

Countess. Brought you this letter, gentlemen?

---

42 **standing to't** (1) standing one's ground (2) having sexual intercourse 52 **woman me** make me weep 57 **passport** license to
wander as a beggar

First Lord. Ay, madam, and for the contents' sake are
   sorry for our pains.   65

Countess. I prithee, lady, have a better cheer.
   If thou engrossest° all the griefs are thine,
   Thou robb'st me of a moiety.° He was my son,
   But I do wash his name out of my blood
   And thou art all my child. Towards Florence is he?   70

Second Lord. Ay, madam.

Countess.   And to be a soldier?

Second Lord. Such is his noble purpose, and, be-
   lieve't,
   The Duke will lay upon him all the honor
   That good convenience° claims.

Countess.   Return you thither?

First Lord. Ay, madam, with the swiftest wing of
   speed.   75

Helena. [*Reads*] "Till I have no wife, I have nothing
   in France."
   'Tis bitter.

Countess.   Find you that there?

Helena.   Ay, madam.

First Lord. 'Tis but the boldness of his hand, haply,°
   which his heart was not consenting to.   80

Countess. Nothing in France, until he have no wife!
   There's nothing here that is too good for him
   But only she, and she deserves a lord
   That twenty such rude boys might tend upon
   And call her, hourly, mistress. Who was with him?   85

First Lord. A servant only, and a gentleman which
   I have sometime known.

Countess. Parolles, was it not?

67 **thou engrossest** you monopolize   68 **moiety** share   74 **convenience** propriety   79 **haply** perhaps

First Lord. Ay, my good lady, he.

Countess. A very tainted fellow, and full of wicked-
90   ness.
    My son corrupts a well-derivèd nature
    With his inducement.°

First Lord.   Indeed, good lady,
    The fellow has a deal of that too much,
    Which holds° him much to have.

95 *Countess.* Y'are welcome, gentlemen.
    I will entreat you, when you see my son,
    To tell him that his sword can never win
    The honor that he loses; more I'll entreat you
    Written to bear along.

Second Lord.   We serve you, madam,
100   In that and all your worthiest affairs.

Countess. Not so, but as we change our courtesies.°
    Will you draw near?   *Exit [with Lords and Clown].*

Helena. "Till I have no wife, I have nothing in
    France."
105   Nothing in France until he has no wife!
    Thou shalt have none, Rousillon,° none in France;
    Then hast thou all again. Poor lord! Is't I
    That chase thee from thy country and expose
    Those tender limbs of thine to the event°
110   Of the none-sparing war? And is it I
    That drive thee from the sportive court, where thou
    Wast shot at with fair eyes, to be the mark
    Of smoky muskets? O you leaden messengers,
    That ride upon the violent speed of fire,
115   Fly with false aim, move the still-piecing° air
    That sings with piercing; do not touch my lord!
    Whoever shoots at him, I set him there.
    Whoever charges on his forward breast,

92 **his inducement** i.e., Parolles' influence   94 **holds** profits   101
Not . . . courtesies no, you may serve me only if I may serve you
(a courteous reply)   106 **Rousillon** Bertram, Count of Rousillon
109 **event** outcome   115 **still-piecing** ever-repairing

I am the caitiff° that do hold him to't.
And though I kill him not I am the cause   *120*
His death was so effected. Better 'twere
I met the ravin° lion when he roared
With sharp constraint of hunger; better 'twere
That all the miseries which nature owes°
Were mine at once. No; come thou home, Rousil-
    lon,   *125*
Whence honor but of danger wins a scar,
As oft it loses all.° I will be gone;
My being here it is that holds thee hence.
Shall I stay here to do't? No, no, although
The air of paradise did fan the house   *130*
And angels officed° all. I will be gone,
That pitiful rumor may report my flight
To consolate thine ear. Come night, end day;
For with the dark, poor thief, I'll steal away.   *Exit.*

[Scene 3. *Florence.*]

Flourish. Enter the Duke of Florence, Bertram,
    Drum and Trumpets, Soldiers, Parolles.

Duke. The general of our horse thou art, and we,
    Great in our hope, lay° our best love and credence
    Upon thy promising fortune.

---

119 **caitiff** wretch   122 **ravin** ravenous   124 **owes** owns, has   126–
27 **Whence . . . all** from where honor at best gains from danger a
scar, and may lose everything   131 **officed** served   3.3.2 **lay**
wager

Bertram.   Sir, it is
  A charge too heavy for my strength; but yet
5 We'll strive to bear it for your worthy sake
  To th' extreme edge of hazard.

Duke.   Then go thou forth,
  And fortune play upon thy prosperous helm,°
  As thy auspicious mistress!

Bertram.   This very day,
  Great Mars, I put myself into thy file!
10 Make me but like my thoughts and I shall prove
  A lover of thy drum, hater of love.   *Exeunt omnes.*

[Scene 4. *Rousillon. The Count's palace.*]

Enter Countess and Steward.

Countess. Alas! And would you take the letter of her?
  Might you not know she would do as she has done,
  By sending me a letter? Read it again.

[*Steward reads the*] *letter.* "I am Saint Jaques' pilgrim,°
    thither gone.
5 Ambitious love hath so in me offended
  That barefoot plod I the cold ground upon,
  With sainted vow my faults to have amended.
  Write, write, that from the bloody course of war
  My dearest master, your dear son, may hie.°
10 Bless him at home in peace, whilst I from far
  His name with zealous fervor sanctify.

7 **helm** helmet 3.4.4 **Saint Jaques' pilgrim** making a pilgrimage
to St. James's shrine (at Compostela, in Spain; "Jaques" is disyllabic:
Jăkis) 9 **hie** hurry

His taken° labors bid him me forgive;
I, his despiteful Juno,° sent him forth
From courtly friends with camping foes to live,
Where death and danger dogs the heels of worth.   15
He is too good and fair for death and me,
Whom I myself embrace to set him° free."

[*Countess*.] Ah, what sharp stings are in her mild-
est words!
Rinaldo, you did never lack advice° so much
As letting her pass so; had I spoke with her,   20
I could have well diverted her intents,
Which thus she hath prevented.

Steward.   Pardon me, madam.
If I had given you this at overnight,°
She might have been o'erta'en; and yet she writes,
Pursuit would be but vain.

Countess.   What angel shall   25
Bless this unworthy husband? He cannot thrive,
Unless her prayers, whom heaven delights to hear
And loves to grant, reprieve him from the wrath
Of greatest justice. Write, write, Rinaldo,
To this unworthy husband of his wife;   30
Let every word weigh heavy of her worth
That he does weigh too light. My greatest grief,
Though little he do feel it, set down sharply.
Dispatch the most convenient messenger.
When haply he shall hear that she is gone,   35
He will return; and hope I may that she,
Hearing so much, will speed her foot again,
Led hither by pure love. Which of them both
Is dearest to me, I have no skill in sense
To make distinction. Provide this messenger.   40
My heart is heavy and mine age is weak;
Grief would have tears, and sorrow bids me speak.
                                        Exeunt.

12 **taken** undertaken   13 **despiteful Juno** (alluding to Juno's per-
secution of Hercules, on whom she imposed the legendary twelve
labors)   17 **Whom . . . him** i.e., Death . . . Bertram   19 **advice**
discretion   23 **at overnight** last night

[Scene 5. *Outside Florence.*]

A tucket° afar off. Enter old Widow of Florence,
her daughter [Diana], and Mariana, with other
citizens.

Widow. Nay come, for if they do approach the city,
we shall lose all the sight.

Diana. They say the French count has done most
honorable service.

5 *Widow.* It is reported that he has taken their great'st
commander, and that with his own hand he slew
the Duke's brother. [*Tucket.*] We have lost our
labor; they are gone a contrary way. Hark! You
may know by their trumpets.

10 *Mariana.* Come, let's return again, and suffice ourselves with the report of it. Well, Diana, take heed
of this French earl. The honor of a maid is her
name, and no legacy is so rich as honesty.°

Widow. I have told my neighbor how you have been
15 solicited by a gentleman his companion.

Mariana. I know that knave, hang him, one Parolles;
a filthy officer he is in those suggestions for the
young earl. Beware of them, Diana: their promises,
enticements, oaths, tokens, and all these engines°
20 of lust, are not the things they go under;° many a
maid hath been seduced by them. And the misery
is, example, that so terrible shows in the wrack of
maidenhood, cannot for all that dissuade succes-

3.5.s.d. **tucket** trumpet call heralding the approach of an important
person   13 **honesty** chastity   19 **engines** devices   20 **go under** mas-
querade as

sion,° but that they are limed° with the twigs that
threatens them. I hope I need not to advise you   25
further, but I hope your own grace will keep you
where you are, though there were no further danger
known but the modesty which is so lost.

Diana. You shall not need to fear me.

    Enter Helena, [disguised as a pilgrim].

Widow. I hope so. Look, here comes a pilgrim. I   30
know she will lie° at my house; thither they send
one another. I'll question her. God save you, pilgrim! Whither are you bound?

Helena. To Saint Jaques le Grand.
    Where do the palmers° lodge, I do beseech you?   35

Widow. At the Saint Francis here beside the port.°

Helena. Is this the way?

Widow. Ay, marry, is't. *(A march afar.)* Hark you!
    They come this way.
If you will tarry, holy pilgrim,
But till the troops come by,   40
I will conduct you where you shall be lodged;
The rather for I think I know your hostess
As ample° as myself.

Helena.   Is it yourself?

Widow. If you shall please so, pilgrim.

Helena. I thank you, and will stay upon your leisure.°   45

Widow. You came, I think, from France?

Helena.   I did so.

Widow. Here you shall see a countryman of yours
    That has done worthy service.

23–24 **dissuade succession** prevent others from following   24 **limed**
caught (as by birdlime, a sticky substance smeared on twigs to trap
birds)   31 **lie** lodge   35 **palmers** pilgrims   36 **port** city gate   43
ample well   45 **stay upon your leisure** wait until convenient for you

Helena.   His name, I pray you.

Diana. The Count Rousillon. Know you such a one?

50 *Helena.* But by the ear, that hears most nobly of him;
   His face I know not.

Diana.   Whatsome'er he is,
   He's bravely taken° here. He stole from France,
   As 'tis reported, for the King had married him
   Against his liking. Think you it is so?

55 *Helena.* Ay, surely, mere° the truth. I know his lady.

Diana. There is a gentleman that serves the Count
   Reports but coarsely of her.

Helena.   What's his name?

Diana. Monsieur Parolles.

Helena.   O, I believe with him,
   In argument of praise, or to the worth
60 Of the great Count himself, she is too mean
   To have her name repeated; all her deserving
   Is a reservèd honesty,° and that
   I have not heard examined.

Diana.   Alas, poor lady!
   'Tis a hard bondage to become the wife
65 Of a detesting lord.

Widow. I warrant, good creature, wheresoe'er she is,
   Her heart weighs sadly. This young maid might do
       her
   A shrewd turn,° if she pleased.

Helena.   How do you mean?
   Maybe the amorous Count solicits her
   In the unlawful purpose.

70 *Widow.*   He does indeed,

___

52 **bravely taken** well esteemed   55 **mere** absolutely   62 **reservèd
honesty** preserved chastity   68 **shrewd turn** nasty deed (with sexual
implication in "turn")

And brokes° with all that can in such a suit
Corrupt the tender honor of a maid;
But she is armed for him, and keeps her guard
In honestest defense.

Mariana.   The gods forbid else!

> *Drum and colors. Enter Bertram, Parolles, and*
> *the whole army.*

Widow. So, now they come.   75
That is Antonio, the Duke's eldest son;
That, Escalus.

Helena.   Which is the Frenchman?

Diana.   He—
That with the plume; 'tis a most gallant fellow.
I would he loved his wife. If he were honester
He were much goodlier. Is't not a handsome gentle-
man?   80

Helena. I like him well.

Diana. 'Tis pity he is not honest. Yond's that same
knave
That leads him to these places. Were I his lady
I would poison that vile rascal.

Helena.   Which is he?

Diana. That jackanapes with scarves. Why is he
melancholy?   85

Helena. Perchance he's hurt i' th' battle.

Parolles. Lose our drum! Well.

Mariana. He's shrewdly° vexed at something. Look,
he has spied us.

Widow. Marry, hang you!   90

Mariana. And your curtsy, for a ring-carrier!°
> *Exit [Bertram, with Parolles and the army].*

---

71 **brokes** bargains   88 **shrewdly** bitterly   91 **ring-carrier** bawd

Widow. The troop is past. Come, pilgrim, I will bring
            you
        Where you shall host;° of enjoined° penitents
        There's four or five, to great Saint Jaques bound,
        Already at my house.

95 *Helena.*   I humbly thank you.
        Please it this matron and this gentle maid
        To eat with us tonight, the charge and thanking
        Shall be for me; and, to requite you further,
        I will bestow some precepts of° this virgin
        Worthy the note.

100 *Both.*   We'll take your offer kindly.
                                                    Exeunt.

[Scene 6. *The Florentine camp.*]

*Enter Bertram and the [two] Frenchmen, as at
            first.*

First Lord. Nay, good my lord, put him to't;° let him
    have his way.

Second Lord. If your lordship find him not a hilding,°
    hold me no more in your respect.

5 *First Lord.* On my life, my lord, a bubble.

Bertram. Do you think I am so far deceived in him?

First Lord. Believe it, my lord, in mine own direct

93 **host** lodge   93 **enjoined** bound by oath   99 **of** on   3.6.1 **put
him to't** test him   3 **hilding** worthless fellow

knowledge, without any malice, but to speak of him
as my kinsman,° he's a most notable coward, an
infinite and endless liar, an hourly promise-breaker,   10
the owner of no one good quality worthy your lordship's entertainment.°

Second Lord. It were fit you knew him, lest reposing
too far in his virtue which he hath not, he might at
some great and trusty business in a main danger   15
fail you.

Bertram. I would I knew in what particular action to
try him.

Second Lord. None better than to let him fetch off his
drum,° which you hear him so confidently under-   20
take to do.

First Lord. I, with a troop of Florentines, will suddenly surprise him; such I will have whom I am
sure he knows not from the enemy. We will bind
and hoodwink° him so, that he shall suppose no   25
other but that he is carried into the leaguer° of the
adversaries when we bring him to our own tents.
Be but your lordship present at his examination;
if he do not for the promise of his life and in the
highest compulsion of base fear offer to betray you   30
and deliver all the intelligence° in his power against
you, and that with the divine forfeit of his soul
upon oath, never trust my judgment in anything.

Second Lord. O, for the love of laughter, let him fetch
his drum. He says he has a stratagem for't. When   35
your lordship sees the bottom of his success in't,
and to what metal this counterfeit lump of ore will
be melted, if you give him not John Drum's enter-
tainment° your inclining cannot be removed. Here
he comes.   40

9 **as my kinsman** i.e., impartially   12 **entertainment** maintenance
19–20 **fetch off his drum** recapture his drum (the loss of the drum
was a military disgrace)   25 **hoodwink** blindfold   26 **leaguer** camp
31 **intelligence** information   38–39 **John Drum's entertainment**
manhandling

Enter Parolles.

First Lord. O, for the love of laughter, hinder not the
honor of his design; let him fetch off his drum in
any hand.

Bertram. How now, monsieur! This drum sticks sorely
45   in your disposition.

Second Lord. A pox° on't, let it go, 'tis but a drum.

Parolles. "But a drum!" Is't "but a drum"? A drum
so lost! There was excellent command: to charge
in with our horse upon our own wings, and to rend
50   our own soldiers!

Second Lord. That was not to be blamed in the command of the service; it was a disaster of war that
Caesar himself could not have prevented if he had
been there to command.

55   **Bertram.** Well, we cannot greatly condemn our success;° some dishonor we had in the loss of that
drum, but it is not to be recovered.

Parolles. It might have been recovered.

Bertram. It might, but it is not now.

60   **Parolles.** It is to be recovered. But that the merit of
service is seldom attributed to the true and exact
performer, I would have that drum or another, or
hic jacet.°

Bertram. Why, if you have a stomach,° to't, monsieur.
65   If you think your mystery° in stratagem can bring
this instrument of honor again into his native quarter, be magnanimous in the enterprise, and go on;
I will grace the attempt for a worthy exploit. If you
speed° well in it, the Duke shall both speak of it
70   and extend to you what further becomes his great-

---

46 **pox** plague (literally, syphilis)   55–56 **success** outcome, fortune
(either good or bad)   63 **hic jacet** here lies (Latin, beginning an
epitaph)   64 **stomach** appetite   65 **mystery** art, skill   69 **speed**
prosper

ness, even to the utmost syllable of your worthiness.

Parolles. By the hand of a soldier, I will undertake it.

Bertram. But you must not now slumber in it.

Parolles. I'll about it this evening, and I will presently   *75*
pen down my dilemmas,° encourage myself in my
certainty, put myself into my mortal preparation;°
and by midnight look to hear further from me.

Bertram. May I be bold to acquaint his Grace you
are gone about it?   *80*

Parolles. I know not what the success will be, my
lord, but the attempt I vow.

Bertram. I know, th'art valiant; and to the possibility° of thy soldiership will subscribe for thee. Farewell.   *85*

Parolles. I love not many words.   *Exit.*

First Lord. No more than a fish loves water. Is not
this a strange fellow, my lord, that so confidently
seems to undertake this business, which he knows
is not to be done, damns himself to do, and dares   *90*
better be damned than to do't.

Second Lord. You do not know him, my lord, as we
do. Certain it is that he will steal himself into a
man's favor and for a week escape a great deal of
discoveries, but when you find him out you have   *95*
him ever after.

Bertram. Why, do you think he will make no deed at
all of this that so seriously he does address himself
unto?

First Lord. None in the world, but return with an in-   *100*
vention, and clap upon you two or three probable
lies; but we have almost embossed him.° You shall

76 **dilemmas** arguments   77 **my mortal preparation** preparation for
my death (?) my weapons for killing (?)   83–84 **possibility** capacity
102 **embossed him** exhausted him (hunting term)

see his fall tonight, for indeed he is not for your
lordship's respect.

105 *Second Lord.* We'll make you some sport with the fox
ere we case° him. He was first smoked° by the old
lord Lafew. When his disguise and he is parted, tell
me what a sprat° you shall find him; which you
shall see this very night.

110 *First Lord.* I must go look my twigs; he shall be
caught.

Bertram. Your brother, he shall go along with me.

First Lord. As't please your lordship: I'll leave you.

Exit.

Bertram. Now will I lead you to the house and show
you
The lass I spoke of.

115 *Second Lord.*   But you say she's honest.

Bertram. That's all the fault. I spoke with her but
once,
And found her wondrous cold, but I sent to her,
By this same coxcomb that we have i' th' wind,°
Tokens and letters which she did re-send,
120 And this is all I have done. She's a fair creature;
Will you go see her?

Second Lord.   With all my heart, my lord.

Exeunt.

---

106 **case** skin   106 **smoked** exposed (like a fox smoked out)   108
sprat small fish   118 **have i' th' wind** are hunting

[Scene 7. *Florence. The Widow's house.*]

Enter Helena and Widow.

Helena. If you misdoubt me that I am not she,
　I know not how I shall assure you further,
　But I shall lose the grounds I work upon.°

Widow. Though my estate be fall'n, I was well born,
　Nothing acquainted with these businesses,　　　　　　　5
　And would not put my reputation now
　In any staining act.

Helena.　　　　　　　Nor would I wish you.
　First give me trust the Count he is my husband,
　And what to your sworn counsel I have spoken°
　Is so from word to word; and then you cannot,　　　　10
　By the good aid that I of you shall borrow,
　Err in bestowing it.

Widow.　　　　　　I should believe you,
　For you have showed me that which well approves
　Y'are great in fortune.

Helena.　　　　　　　　Take this purse of gold,
　And let me buy your friendly help thus far,　　　　　15
　Which I will over-pay and pay again
　When I have found it. The Count he woos your
　　daughter,
　Lays down his wanton siege before her beauty,
　Resolved to carry° her; let her in fine° consent
　As we'll direct her how 'tis best to bear it.　　　　20
　Now his important° blood will nought deny
　That she'll demand; a ring the County° wears,

3.7.3 **But . . . upon** i.e., unless ("But") I reveal myself to Bertram
9 **to . . . spoken** I have confided to you, upon your oath of secrecy
19 **carry** conquer   19 **in fine** finally   21 **important** importunate,
pressing   22 **County** Count

        That downward hath succeeded in his house
        From son to son some four or five descents
25   Since the first father wore it. This ring he holds
        In most rich choice; yet, in his idle fire,
        To buy his will° it would not seem too dear,
        Howe'er repented after.

Widow.   Now I see
        The bottom of your purpose.

30 *Helena.* You see it lawful then. It is no more
        But that your daughter, ere she seems as won,
        Desires this ring; appoints him an encounter;
        In fine, delivers me to fill the time,
        Herself most chastely absent. After,
35   To marry her° I'll add three thousand crowns
        To what is passed already.

Widow.   I have yielded.
        Instruct my daughter how she shall persever°
        That time and place with this deceit so lawful
        May prove coherent.° Every night he comes
40   With musics of all sorts, and songs composed
        To her unworthiness. It nothing steads° us
        To chide him from our eaves, for he persists
        As if his life lay on't.

Helena.   Why then tonight
        Let us assay our plot, which, if it speed,°
45   Is wicked meaning° in a lawful deed,
        And lawful meaning in a lawful act,
        Where both not sin, and yet a sinful fact.
        But let's about it.   [*Exeunt.*]

27 **will** lust   35 **To marry her** i.e., as a dowry to help her marry
37 **persever** (accent on second syllable)   39 **coherent** in accordance
41 **steads** helps   44 **speed** prosper   45 **meaning** intention (the point
of this passage is that Bertram's intention is wicked, though his deed
—copulating with his wife—will be lawful; Helena's intention and
her act will be good, and the deed will not be a sin though in
Bertram's mind he will be sinning)

ACT 4

[Scene 1. *Outside the Florentine camp*.]

*Enter one of the Frenchmen, with five or six
other Soldiers in ambush.*

First Lord. He can come no other way but by this
hedge-corner. When you sally upon him, speak
what terrible language you will; though you understand it not yourselves, no matter; for we must not
seem to understand him, unless someone among us   5
whom we must produce for an interpreter.

First Soldier. Good captain, let me be th' interpreter.

First Lord. Art not acquainted with him? Knows he
not thy voice?

First Soldier. No sir, I warrant you.   10

First Lord. But what linsey-woolsey° hast thou to
speak to us again?

4.1.11 **linsey-woolsey** nonsense (literally a coarse fabric of linen
and wool)

First Soldier. E'en such as you speak to me.

First Lord. He must think us some band of strangers°
15 i' th' adversary's entertainment. Now he hath a
smack of all neighboring languages; therefore we
must everyone be a man of his own fancy, not to
know what we speak one to another; so we seem
to know is to know straight our purpose; choughs'°
20 language, gabble enough and good enough. As for
you, interpreter, you must seem very politic. But
couch, ho! Here he comes to beguile two hours in
a sleep, and then to return and swear the lies he
forges.

Enter Parolles.

25 *Parolles.* Ten o'clock. Within these three hours 'twill
be time enough to go home. What shall I say I have
done? It must be a very plausive° invention that
carries it. They begin to smoke me, and disgraces
have of late knocked too often at my door. I find
30 my tongue is too foolhardy, but my heart hath the
fear of Mars before it and of his creatures, not
daring the reports of my tongue.

First Lord. [*Aside*] This is the first truth that e'er
thine own tongue was guilty of.

35 *Parolles.* What the devil should move me to undertake the recovery of this drum, being not ignorant
of the impossibility, and knowing I had no such
purpose? I must give myself some hurts, and say
I got them in exploit. Yet slight ones will not carry
40 it. They will say, "Came you off with so little?"
And great ones I dare not give. Wherefore, what's
the instance? Tongue, I must put you into a butter-
woman's° mouth, and buy myself another of Bajazet's mule° if you prattle me into these perils.

---

14 **strangers** foreigners   19 **choughs'** jackdaws'   27 **plausive** plausible   42–43 **butter-woman's** i.e., shrill-voiced woman's   43–44 **Bajazet's mule** (mules were proverbial for muteness, but "Bajazet" is
inexplicable)

First Lord. [*Aside*] Is it possible he should know what   45
he is, and be that he is?

Parolles. I would the cutting of my garments would
serve the turn, or the breaking of my Spanish sword.

First Lord. [*Aside*] We cannot afford you so.°

Parolles. Or the baring of my beard, and to say it was   50
in stratagem.

First Lord. [*Aside*] 'Twould not do.

Parolles. Or to drown my clothes, and say I was
stripped.

First Lord. [*Aside*] Hardly serve.   55

Parolles. Though I swore I leaped from the window
of the citadel—

First Lord. [*Aside*] How deep?

Parolles. Thirty fathom.

First Lord. [*Aside*] Three great oaths would scarce   60
make that be believed.

Parolles. I would I had any drum of the enemy's; I
would swear I recovered it.

First Lord. [*Aside*] You shall hear one anon.°

Parolles. A drum now of the enemy's—   65
                              Alarum° within.

First Lord. Throca movousus, cargo, cargo, cargo.

All. Cargo, cargo, cargo, villianda par corbo, cargo.

Parolles. O, ransom, ransom! Do not hide mine eyes.
                              [*They blindfold him.*]

Interpreter. Boskos thromuldo boskos.

Parolles. I know you are the Muskos' regiment,   70
And I shall lose my life for want of language.

49 **afford you so** let you off thus   64 **anon** soon   65s.d. **Alarum**
call to arms

If there be here German, or Dane, low Dutch,
Italian, or French, let him speak to me,
I'll discover° that which shall undo the Florentine.

75 *Interpreter. Boskos vauvado.* I understand thee, and
can speak thy tongue. *Kerelybonto.* Sir, betake thee
to thy faith, for seventeen poniards are at thy
bosom.

Parolles. O!

80 *Interpreter.* O, pray, pray, pray! *Manka revania
dulche.*

First Lord. Oscorbidulchos volivorco.

Interpreter. The General is content to spare thee yet,
And, hoodwinked as thou art, will lead thee on
85   To gather from thee. Haply thou mayst inform
Something to save thy life.

Parolles.   O, let me live!
And all the secrets of our camp I'll show,
Their force, their purposes; nay, I'll speak that
Which you will wonder at.

Interpreter.   But wilt thou faithfully?

Parolles. If I do not, damn me.

90 *Interpreter.*   *Acordo linta.*
Come on, thou art granted space.
                         Exit [*with Parolles guarded*].

     A short alarum within.°

First Lord. Go, tell the Count Rousillon and my
     brother
We have caught the woodcock° and will keep him
     muffled
Till we do hear from them.

---

74 **discover** reveal   91s.d. **A short alarum within** (perhaps Parolles
is taken off to a ruffle of drums)   93 **woodcock** stupid bird

Soldier.   Captain, I will.

First Lord. 'A° will betray us all unto ourselves; in-   95
   form on that.

Soldier. So I will, sir.

First Lord. Till then, I'll keep him dark, and safely
   locked.   *Exit [with the others].*

[Scene 2. *Florence. The Widow's house.*]

Enter Bertram and the maid called Diana.

Bertram. They told me that your name was Fontibell.

Diana. No, my good lord, Diana.

Bertram.   Titled goddess;
   And worth it, with addition.° But, fair soul,
   In your fine frame hath love no quality?
   If the quick fire of youth light not your mind   5
   You are no maiden but a monument.
   When you are dead you should be such a one
   As you are now; for you are cold and stern,
   And now you should be as your mother was
   When your sweet self was got.   10

Diana. She then was honest.

Bertram.   So should you be.

Diana.   No.

95 'A he   4.2.3 **addition** further distinguished title

My mother did but duty; such, my lord,
As you owe to your wife.

Bertram.   No more o' that!
I prithee, do not strive against my vows;
15   I was compelled to her, but I love thee
By love's own sweet constraint, and will forever
Do thee all rights of service.

Diana.   Ay, so you serve us
Till we serve you; but when you have our roses,
You barely leave our thorns to prick ourselves,
And mock us with our bareness.

20   *Bertram.*   How have I sworn!

Diana. 'Tis not the many oaths that makes the truth,
But the plain single vow that is vowed true.
What is not holy, that we swear not by,
But take the High'st to witness; then, pray you, tell
me:
25   If I should swear by Jove's great attributes
I loved you dearly, would you believe my oaths
When I did love you ill?° This has no holding,
To swear by Him whom I protest to love
That I will work against Him. Therefore your oaths
30   Are words and poor conditions but unsealed,°
At least in my opinion.

Bertram.   Change it, change it;
Be not so holy-cruel. Love is holy,
And my integrity ne'er knew the crafts
That you do charge men with. Stand no more off,
35   But give thyself unto my sick desires,
Who then recovers. Say thou art mine, and ever
My love as it begins shall so persever.

Diana. I see that men make rope's in such a scarre,°
That we'll forsake ourselves. Give me that ring.

---

27 **ill** not well, not at all   30 **but unsealed** merely invalid   38 **I see
. . . scarre** (possibly "scarre" means "splice" and thus "snare," but
the text is probably corrupt)

Bertram. I'll lend it thee, my dear, but have no power   40
  To give it from me.

Diana.   Will you not, my lord?

Bertram. It is an honor 'longing to our house,
  Bequeathèd down from many ancestors,
  Which were the greatest obloquy i' th' world
  In me to lose.

Diana.   Mine honor's such a ring;   45
  My chastity's the jewel of our house,
  Bequeathèd down from many ancestors,
  Which were the greatest obloquy i' th' world
  In me to lose. Thus your own proper° wisdom
  Brings in the champion Honor on my part   50
  Against your vain assault.

Bertram.   Here, take my ring.
  My house, mine honor, yea, my life be thine,
  And I'll be bid by thee.

Diana. When midnight comes, knock at my chamber-
      window:
  I'll order take my mother shall not hear.   55
  Now will I charge you in the band° of truth,
  When you have conquered my yet maiden bed,
  Remain there but an hour, nor speak to me.
  My reasons are most strong and you shall know
      them
  When back again this ring shall be delivered;   60
  And on your finger in the night I'll put
  Another ring, that what in time proceeds
  May token to the future our past deeds.
  Adieu till then; then fail not. You have won
  A wife of me, though there my hope be done.   65

Bertram. A heaven on earth I have won by wooing
      thee.   [*Exit.*]

Diana. For which live long to thank both heaven and
      me!

49 **proper** personal   56 **band** bond

You may so in the end.
My mother told me just how he would woo,
70 As if she sat in's heart. She says all men
Have the like oaths. He had sworn to marry me
When his wife's dead; therefore I'll lie with him
When I am buried. Since Frenchmen are so braid,°
Marry that will, I live and die a maid.
75 Only, in this disguise, I think't no sin
To cozen° him that would unjustly win.   *Exit.*

[Scene 3. *The Florentine camp.*]

*Enter the two French Captains, and some
two or three Soldiers.*

First Lord. You have not given him his mother's
letter?

Second Lord. I have delivered it an hour since. There is
something in't that stings his nature, for on the
5 reading it he changed almost into another man.

First Lord. He has much worthy blame laid upon him
for shaking off so good a wife and so sweet a lady.

Second Lord. Especially he hath incurred the ever-
lasting displeasure of the King, who had even
10 tuned his bounty to sing happiness to him. I will
tell you a thing, but you shall let it dwell darkly
with you.

73 **braid** deceitful (?)   76 **cozen** deceive

First Lord. When you have spoken it, 'tis dead, and I
am the grave of it.

Second Lord. He hath perverted a young gentlewoman   15
here in Florence, of a most chaste renown, and this
night he fleshes his will in the spoil of her honor; he
hath given her his monumental° ring, and thinks
himself made in the unchaste composition.°

First Lord. Now, God delay our rebellion! As we are   20
ourselves, what things are we!

Second Lord. Merely° our own traitors. And as in the
common course of all treasons we still see them
reveal themselves till they attain to their abhorred
ends, so he that in this action contrives against his   25
own nobility, in his proper° stream o'erflows° himself.

First Lord. Is it not meant damnable in us to be
trumpeters of our unlawful intents? We shall not
then have his company tonight?   30

Second Lord. Not till after midnight, for he is dieted°
to his hour.

First Lord. That approaches apace. I would gladly
have him see his company anatomized,° that he
might take a measure of his own judgments, wherein   35
so curiously he had set this counterfeit.°

Second Lord. We will not meddle with him till he°
come, for his presence must be the whip of the
other.

First Lord. In the meantime, what hear you of these   40
wars?

Second Lord. I hear there is an overture of peace.

4.3.18 **monumental** serving as a memento   19 **composition** bargain   22 **Merely** utterly   26 **proper** own   26 **o'erflows** (1) betrays
in talk (2) drowns   31 **dieted** restricted   34 **company anatomized**
companion (i.e., Parolles) minutely analyzed   35–36 **wherein . . .
counterfeit** in which he has so elaborately set this false jewel
37 **him . . . he** i.e., Parolles . . . Bertram

First Lord. Nay, I assure you, a peace concluded.

Second Lord. What will Count Rousillon do then?
45   Will he travel higher, or return again into France?

First Lord. I perceive by this demand you are not
   altogether of his council.

Second Lord. Let it be forbid, sir; so should I be a
   great deal of his act.

50 *First Lord.* Sir, his wife some two months since fled
   from his house. Her pretense° is a pilgrimage to
   Saint Jaques le Grand; which holy undertaking with
   most austere sanctimony° she accomplished; and,
   there residing, the tenderness of her nature became
55   as a prey to her grief; in fine, made a groan of her
   last breath, and now she sings in heaven.

Second Lord. How is this justified?°

First Lord. The stronger part of it by her own letters,
   which makes her story true even to the point of her
60   death. Her death itself, which could not be her
   office to say is come, was faithfully confirmed by the
   rector° of the place.

Second Lord. Hath the Count all this intelligence?°

First Lord. Ay, and the particular confirmations, point
65   from point, to the full arming of the verity.

Second Lord. I am heartily sorry that he'll be glad of
   this.

First Lord. How mightily sometimes we make us comforts of our losses!

70 *Second Lord.* And how mightily some other times we
   drown our gain in tears! The great dignity that his
   valor hath here acquired for him shall at home be
   encount'red with a shame as ample.

---

51 **pretense** intention   53 **sanctimony** holiness   57 **justified** made
certain   62 **rector** ruler (?) priest (?)   63 **intelligence** news

First Lord. The web of our life is of a mingled yarn, good and ill together; our virtues would be proud 75 if our faults whipped them not, and our crimes would despair if they were not cherished by our virtues.

Enter a Messenger.

How now! Where's your master?

Servant. He met the Duke in the street, sir, of whom 80 he hath taken a solemn leave. His lordship will next morning for France. The Duke hath offered him letters of commendations to the King.

Second Lord. They shall be no more than needful there, if they were more than they can commend.° 85

First Lord. They cannot be too sweet for the King's tartness.

Enter Bertram.

Here's his lordship now. How now, my lord? Is't not after midnight?

Bertram. I have tonight dispatched sixteen businesses, 90 a month's length apiece. By an abstract of success:° I have congied with° the Duke, done my adieu with his nearest, buried a wife, mourned for her, writ to my lady mother I am returning, entertained my convoy,° and between these main parcels of dis- 95 patch° effected many nicer° needs; the last was the greatest, but that I have not ended yet.

Second Lord. If the business be of any difficulty, and this morning your departure hence, it requires haste of your lordship. 100

84–85 **They shall . . . commend** i.e., the recommendations to the King will not be more than needed, even if they commend Bertram excessively (?)   91 **abstract of success** summary of my successes (?) list, in sequence (?)   92 **congied with** taken leave of   94–95 **entertained my convoy** hired my transportation   95–96 **parcels of dispatch** things to be settled   96 **nicer** (1) more trivial (2) lascivious (alluding to his affair with Diana)

Bertram. I mean the business is not ended, as fearing
to hear of it hereafter. But shall we have this dialogue between the Fool and the Soldier? Come,
bring forth this counterfeit module° has deceived me
105 like a double-meaning prophesier.

Second Lord. Bring him forth. [*Exeunt Soldiers.*] Has
sat i' th' stocks all night, poor gallant° knave.

Bertram. No matter, his heels have deserved it, in
usurping his spurs so long. How does he carry him-
110 self?

Second Lord. I have told your lordship already; the
stocks carry him. But to answer you as you would
be understood, he weeps like a wench that had shed
her milk. He hath confessed himself to Morgan,
115 whom he supposes to be a friar, from the time of
his remembrance to this very instant disaster of his
setting i' th' stocks. And what think you he hath
confessed?

Bertram. Nothing of me, has 'a?

120 *Second Lord.* His confession is taken, and it shall be
read to his face. If your lordship be in't, as I believe
you are, you must have the patience to hear it.

    Enter Parolles [*guarded*], *with his Interpreter.*

Bertram. A plague upon him! Muffled!° He can say
nothing of me.

125 *First Lord.* [*Aside to Bertram*] Hush, hush! Hoodman
comes!° [*Aloud*] *Portotartarossa.*

Interpreter. He calls for the tortures. What will you
say without 'em?

Parolles. I will confess what I know without con-
130 straint. If ye pinch me like a pasty I can say no
more.

104 **module** image   107 **gallant** finely dressed   123 **Muffled** blindfolded   125–26 **Hoodman comes** the blind man comes (customary
call in the game blindman's buff)

Interpreter. Bosko chimurcho.

First Lord. Boblibindo chicurmurco.

Interpreter. You are a merciful general. Our General
bids you answer to what I shall ask you out of a   *135*
note.

Parolles. And truly, as I hope to live.

Interpreter. "First demand of him how many horse
the Duke is strong." What say you to that?

Parolles. Five or six thousand, but very weak and   *140*
unserviceable. The troops are all scattered and the
commanders very poor rogues, upon my reputation
and credit, and as I hope to live.

Interpreter. Shall I set down your answer so?

Parolles. Do. I'll take the sacrament on't, how and   *145*
which way you will.

Bertram. [*Aside*] All's one to him. What a past-saving
slave is this!

First Lord. [*Aside to Bertram*] Y'are deceived, my
lord; this is Monsieur Parolles, the gallant mili-   *150*
tarist—that was his own phrase—that had the
whole theoric of war in the knot of his scarf, and
the practice in the chape° of his dagger.

Second Lord. [*Aside*] I will never trust a man again
for keeping his sword clean, nor believe he can   *155*
have everything in him by wearing his apparel
neatly.

Interpreter. Well, that's set down.

Parolles. "Five or six thousand horse," I said—I will
say true—"or thereabouts" set down, for I'll speak   *160*
truth.

First Lord. [*Aside*] He's very near the truth in this.

153 **chape** metal plate on a scabbard covering the point

Bertram. [*Aside*] But I con° him no thanks for't, in the nature he delivers it.

165 *Parolles.* "Poor rogues," I pray you say.

Interpreter. Well, that's set down.

Parolles. I humbly thank you, sir; a truth's a truth; the rogues are marvelous poor.

Interpreter. "Demand of him of what strength they are
170 a-foot."   What   say   you   to   that?

Parolles. By my troth, sir, if I were to live this present hour, I will tell true. Let me see: Spurio, a hundred and fifty; Sebastian, so many; Corambus, so many; Jaques, so many; Guiltian, Cosmo, Lodowick, and
175 Gratii, two hundred fifty each; mine own company, Chitopher, Vaumond, Bentii, two hundred fifty each; so that the muster-file, rotten and sound, upon my life, amounts not to fifteen thousand poll,° half of the which dare not shake the snow from off
180 their cassocks° lest they shake themselves to pieces.

Bertram. [*Aside*] What shall be done to him?

First Lord. [*To Bertram*] Nothing, but let him have thanks. [*To Interpreter*] Demand of him my condition, and what credit I have with the Duke.

185 *Interpreter.* Well, that's set down. "You shall demand of him whether one Captain Dumaine be i' th' camp, a Frenchman; what his reputation is with the Duke, what his valor, honesty, and expertness in wars; or whether he thinks it were not possible
190 with well-weighing sums of gold to corrupt him to a revolt." What say you to this? What do you know of it?

Parolles. I beseech you, let me answer to the particular of the inter'gatories. Demand them singly.

195 *Interpreter.* Do you know this Captain Dumaine?

163 **con** give (literally, learn) 178 **poll** head 180 **cassocks** soldiers' cloaks

Parolles. I know him; 'a was a botcher's° prentice in
   Paris, from whence he was whipped for getting the
   shrieve's fool° with child, a dumb innocent that
   could not say him nay.

Bertram. [*Aside to Dumaine*] Nay, by your leave, hold 200
   your hands, though I know his brains are forfeit to
   the next tile that falls.°

Interpreter. Well, is this captain in the Duke of Florence's camp?

Parolles. Upon my knowledge he is, and lousy.   205

First Lord. [*Aside*] Nay, look not so upon me; we
   shall hear of your lordship anon.

Interpreter. What is his reputation with the Duke?

Parolles. The Duke knows him for no other but a poor
   officer of mine, and writ to me this other day to 210
   turn him out o' th' band. I think I have his letter
   in my pocket.

Interpreter. Marry, we'll search.

Parolles. In good sadness,° I do not know; either it
   is there or it is upon a file with the Duke's other 215
   letters in my tent.

Interpreter. Here 'tis; here's a paper; shall I read it
   to you?

Parolles. I do not know if it be it or no.

Bertram. [*Aside*] Our interpreter does it well.   220

First Lord. [*Aside*] Excellently.

Interpreter. "Dian, the Count's a fool, and full of
   gold."

Parolles. That is not the Duke's letter, sir; that is an

---

196 **botcher's** mender's (e.g., tailor's or cobbler's)   198 **shrieve's
fool** idiot girl placed under a sheriff's charge   202 **tile that falls**
i.e., accident   214 **sadness** seriousness

advertisement° to a proper maid in Florence, one
225   Diana, to take heed of the allurement of one Count
Rousillon, a foolish idle boy, but for all that very
ruttish.° I pray you, sir, put it up again.

Interpreter. Nay, I'll read it first, by your favor.

Parolles. My meaning in't, I protest, was very honest
230   in the behalf of the maid; for I knew the young
Count to be a dangerous and lascivious boy, who
is a whale to virginity, and devours up all the fry°
it finds.

Bertram. [*Aside*] Damnable both-sides rogue!

235 *Interpreter.* ([*Reads a*] *letter.*) "When he swears
        oaths, bid him drop gold, and take it;
After he scores, he never pays the score.
Half won is match well made; match and well make
    it;°
He ne'er pays after-debts, take it before.
And say a soldier, Dian, told thee this:
240   Men are to mell° with, boys are not to kiss:
For count of this, the Count's a fool, I know it,
Who pays before, but not when he does owe it.
       Thine, as he vowed to thee in thine ear,
                        Parolles."

245 *Bertram.* [*Aside*] He shall be whipped through the
    army with this rhyme in's forehead.

Second Lord. [*Aside*] This is your devoted friend, sir,
· the manifold linguist, and the armipotent° soldier.

Bertram. [*Aside*] I could endure anything before but
250   a cat, and now he's a cat to me.

Interpreter. I perceive, sir, by your General's looks,
we shall be fain to hang you.

---

224 advertisement advice **227 ruttish** lustful **232 fry** small fish
237 Half . . . make it i.e., you are halfway to success if you bargain
well; so bargain well, and you will prosper (?) **240 mell** mingle
248 armipotent mighty in arms (a huffing word, like "manifold")

Parolles. My life, sir, in any case! Not that I am afraid to die, but that my offenses being many I would repent out the remainder of nature. Let me 255 live, sir, in a dungeon, i' th' stocks, or anywhere, so I may live.

Interpreter. We'll see what may be done, so you confess freely. Therefore once more to this Captain Dumaine: you have answered to his reputation with 260 the Duke and to his valor: what is his honesty?

Parolles. He will steal, sir, an egg out of a cloister; for rapes and ravishments he parallels Nessus.° He professes not keeping of oaths, in breaking 'em he is stronger than Hercules. He will lie, sir, with such 265 volubility that you would think truth were a fool; drunkenness is his best virtue, for he will be swine-drunk, and in his sleep he does little harm, save to his bedclothes about him; but they know his conditions° and lay him in straw. I have but little more 270 to say, sir, of his honesty—he has everything that an honest man should not have; what an honest man should have, he has nothing.

First Lord. [*Aside*] I begin to love him for this.

Bertram. [*Aside*] For this description of thine honesty? 275 A pox upon him for me, he's more and more a cat.

Interpreter. What say you to his expertness in war?

Parolles. Faith, sir, has led the drum before the English tragedians°—to belie him I will not—and more of his soldiership I know not, except in that coun- 280 try he had the honor to be the officer at a place there called Mile-end,° to instruct for the doubling of files.° I would do the man what honor I can, but of this I am not certain.

263 **Nessus** centaur who attempted to rape Deianira, Hercules' wife 269–70 **conditions** traits 278–79 **led . . . tragedians** i.e., been a low drummer, leading strolling actors rather than soldiers 282 **Mile-end** (because the citizen militia drilled at Mile-end, the place was a byname for military incompetence) 282–83 **doubling of files** drill maneuver in which pairs of men separate

285 *First Lord.* [*Aside*] He hath out-villained villainy so
far that the rarity redeems him.

Bertram. [*Aside*] A pox on him! He's a cat still.

Interpreter. His qualities being at this poor price, I
need not to ask you if gold will corrupt him to
290 revolt.

Parolles. Sir, for a cardecue° he will sell the fee-
simple° of his salvation, the inheritance of it, and
cut th' entail° from all remainders, and a perpetual
succession for it perpetually.

295 *Interpreter.* What's his brother, the other Captain
Dumaine?

Second Lord. [*Aside*] Why does he ask him of me?

Interpreter. What's he?

Parolles. E'en a crow o' th' same nest; not altogether
300 so great as the first in goodness, but greater a great
deal in evil. He excels his brother for a coward, yet
his brother is reputed one of the best that is. In a
retreat he outruns any lackey; marry, in coming on
he has the cramp.

305 *Interpreter.* If your life be saved will you undertake
to betray the Florentine?

Parolles. Ay, and the captain of his horse, Count
Rousillon.

Interpreter. I'll whisper with the General, and know
310 his pleasure.

Parolles. [*Aside*] I'll no more drumming. A plague of
all drums! Only to seem to deserve well, and to
beguile the supposition of that lascivious young boy,
the Count, have I run into this danger. Yet who
315 would have suspected an ambush where I was
taken?

291 **cardecue** *quart d'écu* (French coin of little value)   291–92 **fee-
simple** absolute possession   293 **entail** right of succession

Interpreter. There is no remedy, sir, but you must
die. The General says you that have so traitorously
discovered the secrets of your army and made such
pestiferous reports of men very nobly held, can   320
serve the world for no honest use; therefore you
must die. Come, headsman, off with his head.

Parolles. O Lord, sir, let me live, or let me see my
death!

Interpreter. That shall you, and take your leave of all   325
your friends.   [*Unmuffles Parolles.*]
So, look about you. Know you any here?

Bertram. Good morrow, noble Captain.

Second Lord. God bless you, Captain Parolles.

First Lord. God save you, noble Captain.   330

Second Lord. Captain, what greeting will you to my
Lord Lafew? I am for France.

First Lord. Good Captain, will you give me a copy of
the sonnet you writ to Diana in behalf of the Count
Rousillon? And I were not a very coward I'd com-   335
pel it of you, but fare you well.
                    Exeunt [*Bertram and Lords*].

Interpreter. You are undone, Captain, all but your
scarf; that has a knot on't yet.

Parolles. Who cannot be crushed with a plot?

Interpreter. If you could find out a country where but   340
women were that had received so much shame, you
might begin an impudent nation. Fare ye well, sir.
I am for France too; we shall speak of you there.
                    Exit [*with other Soldiers*].

Parolles. Yet am I thankful. If my heart were great
'Twould burst at this. Captain I'll be no more,   345
But I will eat and drink and sleep as soft
As captain shall. Simply the thing I am
Shall make me live. Who knows himself a braggart,

350

Let him fear this; for it will come to pass
That every braggart shall be found an ass.
Rust, sword; cool, blushes; and Parolles live
Safest in shame! Being fooled, by fool'ry thrive!
There's place and means for every man alive.
I'll after them.   *Exit.*

[Scene 4. *Florence. The Widow's house.*]

Enter Helena, Widow, and Diana.

Helena. That you may well perceive I have not
      wronged you,
   One of the greatest in the Christian world
   Shall be my surety; 'fore whose throne 'tis needful,
   Ere I can perfect mine intents, to kneel.
5   Time was, I did him a desirèd office,
   Dear almost as his life, which gratitude
   Through flinty Tartar's bosom would peep forth,
   And answer thanks. I duly am informed
   His Grace is at Marseilles, to which place
10   We have convenient convoy.° You must know
   I am supposèd dead. The army breaking,°
   My husband hies him home, where, heaven aiding,
   And by the leave of my good lord the King,
   We'll be before our welcome.

Widow.   Gentle madam,
15   You never had a servant to whose trust
   Your business was more welcome.

4.4.10 **convoy** transportation   11 **breaking** disbanding

Helena.   Nor you, mistress,
  Ever a friend whose thoughts more truly labor
  To recompense your love. Doubt not but heaven
  Hath brought me up to be your daughter's dower,
  As it hath fated her to be my motive°   20
  And helper to a husband. But, O strange men,
  That can such sweet use make of what they hate,
  When saucy° trusting of the cozened° thoughts
  Defiles the pitchy night! So lust doth play
  With what it loathes for that which is away.   25
  But more of this hereafter. You, Diana,
  Under my poor instructions yet must suffer
  Something in my behalf.

Diana.   Let death and honesty°
  Go with your impositions,° I am yours
  Upon your will to suffer.

Helena.   Yet, I pray you;   30
  But with the word° the time will bring on summer,
  When briars shall have leaves as well as thorns,
  And be as sweet as sharp. We must away;
  Our wagon is prepared, and time revives us.
  All's well that ends well; still the fine's the crown.°   35
  Whate'er the course, the end is the renown.
                                        Exeunt.

---

20 **motive** means (?)   23 **saucy** lascivious   23 **cozened** deceived
28 **death and honesty** an honest death   29 **impositions** tasks imposed
on me   31 **with the word** soon (?) as the proverb says (?)   35 **the
fine's the crown** the end is the crown (cf. the Latin proverb
Finis coronat opus, "the end crowns the work")

[Scene 5. *Rousillon. The Count's palace.*]

Enter Clown, Old Lady [i.e., Countess], and Lafew.

Lafew. No, no, no, your son was misled with a snipped taffeta° fellow there, whose villainous saffron° would have made all the unbaked and doughy youth of a nation in his color. Your daughter-in-law
5 had been alive at this hour, and your son here at home, more advanced by the King than by that red-tailed humble-bee I speak of.

Countess. I would I had not known him; it was the death of the most virtuous gentlewoman that ever
10 nature had praise for creating. If she had partaken of my flesh and cost me the dearest groans of a mother, I could not have owed her a more rooted love.

Lafew. 'Twas a good lady, 'twas a good lady. We
15 may pick a thousand sallets° ere we light on such another herb.

Clown. Indeed, sir, she was the sweet-marjoram of the sallet, or rather, the herb of grace.°

Lafew. They are not° herbs, you knave, they are nose-
20 herbs.

Clown. I am no great Nebuchadnezzar, sir; I have not much skill in grace.°

4.5.1–2 **snipped taffeta** cloth slashed to show the colors beneath
2 **saffron** yellow dye (used to dye starch—for ruffs—and also dough)
15 **sallets** salads   18 **herb of grace** rue   19 **not** (pun on "knot"=
flower bed, leading to the contrasting "nose-herbs"=fragrant but not
tasty herbs)   22 **grace** (pun on "grass," following the allusion to
the King of Babylon who in Daniel 4:28–37 is said to have insanely
eaten grass)

Lafew. Whether° dost thou profess thyself, a knave or
a fool?

Clown. A fool, sir, at a woman's service, and a knave   25
at a man's.

Lafew. Your distinction?

Clown. I would cozen the man of his wife and do his
service.

Lafew. So you were a knave at his service indeed.   30

Clown. And I would give his wife my bauble,° sir,
to do her service.

Lafew. I will subscribe for thee; thou art both knave
and fool.

Clown. At your service.   35

Lafew. No, no, no.

Clown. Why, sir, if I cannot serve you, I can serve
as great a prince as you are.

Lafew. Who's that? A Frenchman?

Clown. Faith, sir, 'a has an English name, but his   40
fisnomy° is more hotter in France than there.

Lafew. What prince is that?

Clown. The Black Prince,° sir, alias the prince of
darkness, alias the devil.

Lafew. Hold thee, there's my purse. I give thee not   45
this to suggest thee from° thy master thou talk'st of;
serve him still.

Clown. I am a woodland fellow, sir, that always loved
a great fire, and the master I speak of ever keeps a
good fire. But sure he is the prince of the world; let   50
his nobility remain in's court. I am for the house

23 **Whether** which   31 **bauble** fool's stick (bawdy innuendo)   41
fisnomy physiognomy   43 **Black Prince** (1) son of Edward III, foe of
the French (2) devil   46 **suggest thee from** tempt you away from

with the narrow gate,° which I take to be too little
for pomp to enter; some that humble themselves
may, but the many will be too chill and tender, and
55 they'll be for the flow'ry way that leads to the broad
gate and the great fire.

Lafew. Go thy ways; I begin to be aweary of thee,
and I tell thee so before, because I would not fall
out with thee. Go thy ways; let my horses be well
60 looked to, without any tricks.

Clown. If I put any tricks upon 'em, sir, they shall
be jades' tricks,° which are their own right by the
law of nature.   *Exit.*

Lafew. A shrewd° knave and an unhappy.

65 *Countess.* So 'a is. My lord that's gone made himself
much sport out of him; by his authority he remains
here, which he thinks is a patent for his sauciness;
and indeed he has no pace, but runs where he will.

Lafew. I like him well, 'tis not amiss. And I was about
70 to tell you, since I heard of the good lady's death
and that my lord your son was upon his return
home, I moved the King my master to speak in the
behalf of my daughter; which, in the minority of
them both, his Majesty out of a self-gracious re-
75 membrance did first propose. His Highness hath
promised me to do it—and to stop up the displeasure he hath conceived against your son there
is no fitter matter. How does your ladyship like it?

Countess. With very much content, my lord, and I
80 wish it happily effected.

Lafew. His Highness comes post° from Marseilles, of
as able body as when he numbered thirty. 'A will
be here tomorrow, or I am deceived by him that in
such intelligence hath seldom failed.

51–52 **house with the narrow gate** heaven (with bawdy reference to
vulva?)   62 **jades' tricks** mischievous doings (like those of undesir-
able horses)   64 **shrewd** bitter   81 **post** by rapid relays of horses

Countess. It rejoices me that I hope I shall see him   *85*
ere I die. I have letters that my son will be here
tonight. I shall beseech your lordship to remain with
me till they meet together.

Lafew. Madam, I was thinking with what manners I
might safely be admitted.   *90*

Countess. You need but plead your honorable privilege.

Lafew. Lady, of that I have made a bold charter;° but
I thank my God it holds yet.

Enter Clown.

Clown. O madam, yonder's my lord your son with a   *95*
patch of velvet on's face; whether there be a scar
under't or no, the velvet knows, but 'tis a goodly
patch of velvet.° His left cheek is a cheek of two
pile and a half, but his right cheek is worn bare.

Lafew. A scar nobly got, or a noble scar, is a good   *100*
liv'ry° of honor; so belike is that.

Clown. But it is your carbonadoed° face.

Lafew. Let us go see your son, I pray you. I long to
talk with the young noble soldier.

Clown. Faith, there's a dozen of 'em with delicate   *105*
fine hats and most courteous feathers which bow
the head and nod at every man.   *Exeunt.*

---

93 **charter** claim 98 **patch of velvet** bandage (but it might cover an
honorable scar or dishonorable signs of syphilis) 101 **liv'ry** badge
of noble service 102 **carbonadoed** slashed (with incisions to drain
venereal ulcers)

ACT 5

[Scene 1. *Marseilles*.]

Enter Helena, Widow, and Diana, with two
Attendants.

Helena. But this exceeding posting° day and night
Must wear your spirits low; we cannot help it.
But since you have made the days and nights as
one,
To wear your gentle limbs in my affairs,
Be bold° you do so grow in my requital°
As nothing can unroot you.

      Enter a Gentleman, a stranger.

                             In happy time!°
This man may help me to his Majesty's ear,
If he would spend his power. God save you, sir.

Gentleman. And you.

5.1.1 **exceeding posting** excessive haste 5 **bold** assured 5 **re-quital** debt 6 **In happy time** just at the right moment

Helena. Sir, I have seen you in the court of France.   10

Gentleman. I have been sometimes there.

Helena. I do presume, sir, that you are not fall'n
From the report that goes upon your goodness,
And therefore, goaded with most sharp occasions
Which lay nice manners by, I put you to   15
The use of your own virtues, for the which
I shall continue thankful.

Gentleman.   What's your will?

Helena. That it will please you
To give this poor petition to the King,
And aid me with that store of power you have   20
To come into his presence.

Gentleman. The King's not here.

Helena.   Not here, sir?

Gentleman.   Not indeed.
He hence removed last night, and with more haste
Than is his use.

Widow.   Lord, how we lose our pains!

Helena. All's well that ends well yct,   25
Though time seem so adverse and means unfit.
I do beseech you, whither is he gone?

Gentleman. Marry, as I take it, to Rousillon,
Whither I am going.

Helena.   I do beseech you, sir,
Since you are like to see the King before me,   30
Commend the paper to his gracious hand,
Which I presume shall render you no blame
But rather make you thank your pains for it.
I will come after you with what good speed
Our means will make us means.

Gentleman.   This I'll do for you.   35

Helena. And you shall find yourself to be well
    thanked,
Whate'er falls° more. We must to horse again.
Go, go, provide.   [*Exeunt*.]

[Scene 2. *Rousillon. The Count's palace*.]

Enter Clown and Parolles.

Parolles. Good Master Lavatch,° give my Lord
    Lafew this letter. I have ere now, sir, been better
    known to you, when I have held familiarity with
    fresher clothes; but I am now, sir, muddied in for-
5   tune's mood,° and smell somewhat strong of her
    strong displeasure.

Clown. Truly, fortune's displeasure is but sluttish if
    it smell so strongly as thou speak'st of. I will hence-
    forth eat no fish of fortune's butt'ring. Prithee,
10   allow the wind.°

Parolles. Nay, you need not to stop your nose, sir;
    I spake but by a metaphor.

Clown. Indeed, sir, if your metaphor stink, I will stop
    my nose, or against any man's metaphor. Prithee,
15   get thee further.

Parolles. Pray you, sir, deliver me this paper.

Clown. Foh! Prithee, stand away. A paper from for-

37 **falls** befalls 5.2.1 **Lavatch** (apparently from French *la vache*=
the cow, or *lavage*=slop) 5 **mood** displeasure (with pun on "mud")
10 **allow the wind** let me have the windward side

tune's close-stool,° to give to a nobleman! Look, here he comes himself.

Enter Lafew.

Here is a pur° of fortune's, sir, or of fortune's 20
cat, but not a musk-cat,° that has fall'n into the
unclean fishpond of her displeasure, and, as he
says, is muddied withal. Pray you, sir, use the carp
as you may, for he looks like a poor, decayed, ingenious,° foolish, rascally knave. I do pity his dis- 25
tress in my similes of comfort, and leave him to
your lordship.

[*Exit.*]

Parolles. My lord, I am a man whom fortune hath
cruelly scratched.

Lafew. And what would you have me to do? 'Tis too 30
late to pare her nails now. Wherein have you
played the knave with fortune that she should
scratch you, who of herself is a good lady and
would not have knaves thrive long under? There's
a cardecue° for you. Let the justices make you and 35
fortune friends;° I am for other business.

Parolles. I beseech your honor to hear me one single
word.

Lafew. You beg a single penny more. Come, you shall
ha't; save your word. 40

Parolles. My name, my good lord, is Parolles.

Lafew. You beg more than "word" then. Cox my
passion!° Give me your hand. How does your
drum?

---

18 **close-stool** toilet   20 **pur** (1) dung (2) cat's sound (3) knave in
a card game (Lafew picks up this last meaning when he speaks)
21 **musk-cat** musk deer (which yields perfume)   24–25 **ingenious**
stupid (as though written "un-genius")   35 **cardecue** French coin
35–36 **Let . . . friends** i.e., appeal to the justices for alms   42–43
Cox my passion (mild oath, from "God's my passion," i.e., by God's
suffering)

45 *Parolles.* O my good lord, you were the first that
        found me.°

    Lafew. Was I, in sooth? And I was the first that lost
        thee.

    Parolles. It lies in you, my lord, to bring me in some
50   grace, for you did bring me out.

    Lafew. Out upon thee, knave! Dost thou put upon
        me at once both the office of God and the devil?
        One brings thee in grace and the other brings thee
        out. [*Trumpets sound.*] The King's coming; I know
55   by his trumpets. Sirrah, inquire further after me.
        I had talk of you last night; though you are a fool
        and a knave you shall eat. Go to, follow.

    Parolles. I praise God for you.   [*Exeunt.*]

    [Scene 3. *Rousillon. The Count's palace.*]

    *Flourish. Enter King, Old Lady [i.e., Countess],
    Lafew, the two French Lords, with Attendants.*

    King. We lost a jewel of her, and our esteem°
        Was made much poorer by it; but your son,
        As mad in folly, lacked the sense to know
        Her estimation home.°

    Countess.   'Tis past, my liege,

46 **found me** found me out   5.3.1 **esteem** value, i.e., reputation
4 **home** fully

And I beseech your Majesty to make it   5
Natural rebellion done i' th' blade° of youth,
When oil and fire, too strong for reason's force,
O'erbears it and burns on.

King.   My honored lady,
I have forgiven and forgotten all,
Though my revenges were high bent upon him   10
And watched the time to shoot.

Lafew.   This I must say—
But first I beg my pardon—the young lord
Did to his Majesty, his mother, and his lady
Offense of mighty note, but to himself
The greatest wrong of all. He lost a wife   15
Whose beauty did astonish the survey
Of richest eyes; whose words all ears took captive;
Whose dear perfection hearts that scorned to serve
Humbly called mistress.

King.   Praising what is lost
Makes the remembrance dear. Well, call him
    hither;   20
We are reconciled, and the first view shall kill
All repetition.° Let him not ask our pardon;
The nature of his great offense is dead,
And deeper than oblivion we do bury
Th' incensing relics° of it. Let him approach,   25
A stranger, no offender; and inform him
So 'tis our will he should.

Gentleman.   I shall, my liege.   [*Exit.*]

King. What says he to your daughter? Have you
    spoke?

Lafew. All that he is hath reference° to your High-
    ness.

6 **blade** green shoot (editors distressed by the mixed metaphor produced by "fire" emend to "blaze") 22 **repetition** i.e., mention of
what is past 25 **incensing relics** reminders that (would) anger 29
hath reference is submitted

King. Then shall we have a match. I have letters sent
30   me,
         That sets him high in fame.

                    Enter Bertram.

Lafew.   He looks well on't.

King. I am not a day of season,
         For thou mayst see a sunshine and a hail
         In me at once. But to the brightest beams
35   Distracted clouds give way; so stand thou forth;
         The time is fair again.

Bertram.   My high-repented blames,°
         Dear sovereign pardon to me.

King.   All is whole.
         Not one word more of the consumèd time.
         Let's take the instant by the forward top;°
40   For we are old, and on our quick'st decrees
         Th' inaudible and noiseless foot of Time
         Steals ere we can effect them. You remember
         The daughter of this lord?

Bertram. Admiringly, my liege. At first
45   I stuck my choice upon her, ere my heart
         Durst make too bold a herald of my tongue;
         Where, the impression of mine eye infixing,
         Contempt his scornful perspective° did lend me,
         Which warped the line of every other favor,°
50   Scorned a fair color or expressed it stol'n,
         Extended or contracted all proportions
         To a most hideous object. Thence it came
         That she whom all men praised and whom myself,
         Since I have lost, have loved, was in mine eye
         The dust that did offend it.

55 *King.*   Well excused.
         That thou didst love her, strikes some scores away

---

36 **blames** blameworthy deeds   39 **take . . . top** seize Time by the
forelock   48 **perspective** optical instrument that distorts (accented
on first syllable)   49 **favor** face

From the great compt;° but love that comes too
    late,
Like a remorseful° pardon slowly carried,
To the great sender turns a sour offense,
Crying "That's good that's gone." Our rash faults   60
Make trivial price of serious things we have,
Not knowing them, until we know their grave.
Oft our displeasures, to ourselves unjust,
Destroy our friends and after weep their dust;
Our own love waking cries to see what's done,   65
While shameful hate sleeps out the afternoon.
Be this sweet Helen's knell, and now forget her.
Send forth your amorous token for fair Maudlin.
The main consents are had, and here we'll stay
To see our widower's second marriage-day,   70
Which better than the first, O dear heaven, bless!
Or, ere they meet, in me, O nature, cesse!°

Lafew. Come on, my son, in whom my house's name
    Must be digested;° give a favor° from you
    To sparkle in the spirits of my daughter,   75
    That she may quickly come.   [*Bertram gives a ring.*]
        By my old beard,
    And ev'ry hair that's on't, Helen that's dead
    Was a sweet creature; such a ring as this,
    The last that e'er I took her leave at court,
    I saw upon her finger.

Bertram.   Hers it was not.   80

King. Now pray you let me see it; for mine eye,
    While I was speaking, oft was fastened to't.
    This ring was mine, and when I gave it Helen
    I bade her, if her fortunes ever stood
    Necessitied to help, that by this token   85
    I would relieve her. Had you that craft to reave°
        her
    Of what should stead° her most?

---

57 **compt** account   58 **remorseful** compassionate   72 **cesse** cease
74 **digested** swallowed up (?) assimilated (?)   74 **favor** token
86 **reave** deprive   87 **stead** help

Bertram.   My gracious sovereign,
  Howe'er it pleases you to take it so,
  The ring was never hers.

Countess.   Son, on my life,
90 I have seen her wear it, and she reckoned it
  At her life's rate.

Lafew.   I am sure I saw her wear it.

Bertram. You are deceived, my lord; she never saw it.
  In Florence was it from a casement thrown me,
  Wrapped in a paper which contained the name
95 Of her that threw it. Noble she was, and thought
  I stood ingaged;° but when I had subscribed
  To mine own fortune° and informed her fully
  I could not answer in that course of honor
  As she had made the overture, she ceased
100 In heavy satisfaction° and would never
  Receive the ring again.

King.   Plutus° himself,
  That knows the tinct and multiplying med'cine,°
  Hath not in nature's mystery more science°
  Than I have in this ring. 'Twas mine, 'twas Helen's,
105 Whoever gave it you; then if you know
  That you are well acquainted with yourself,
  Confess 'twas hers, and by what rough enforcement
  You got it from her. She called the saints to surety
  That she would never put it from her finger
110 Unless she gave it to yourself in bed,
  Where you have never come, or sent it us
  Upon her great disaster.

Bertram.   She never saw it.

King. Thou speak'st it falsely, as I love mine honor,
  And mak'st conjectural fears to come into me

96 **ingaged** not pledged (to another woman) 96–97 **subscribed/To
mine own fortune** admitted my condition, i.e., that I was married
100 **heavy satisfaction** sorrowful acceptance 101 **Plutus** god of
wealth 102 **tinct and multiplying med'cine** elixir that transmutes
base metals to gold and multiplies gold 103 **science** knowledge

Which I would fain shut out. If it should prove   *115*
That thou art so inhuman—'twill not prove so,
And yet I know not—thou didst hate her deadly,
And she is dead, which nothing but to close
Her eyes myself could win me to believe,
More than to see this ring. Take him away.   *120*
My fore-past proofs, howe'er the matter fall,
Shall tax my fears of little vanity,
Having vainly feared too little.° Away with him,
We'll sift this matter further.

Bertram.   If you shall prove
This ring was ever hers, you shall as easy   *125*
Prove that I husbanded her bed in Florence,
Where yet she never was.   [*Exit guarded.*]

King. I am wrapped in dismal thinkings.

          Enter a Gentleman, [*the stranger*].

Gentleman.   Gracious sovereign,
Whether I have been to blame or no, I know not:
Here's a petition from a Florentine   *130*
Who hath for four or five removes° come short
To tender it herself. I undertook it,
Vanquished thereto by the fair grace and speech
Of the poor suppliant, who, by this, I know
Is here attending; her business looks in her   *135*
With an importing° visage, and she told me,
In a sweet verbal brief, it did concern
Your Highness with herself.

[*King rèads*] *a letter.* "Upon his many protestations
to marry me when his wife was dead, I blush to *140*
say it, he won me. Now is the Count Rousillon a
widower, his vows are forfeited to me, and my
honor's paid to him. He stole from Florence, taking
no leave, and I follow him to his country for justice.

121–23 **My fore-past . . . too little** the evidence already established,
however the affair turns out, will rebuke ("tax") my lightweight
("of little vanity") fears; I have unreasonably feared too little
131 **removes** stopping places (changes of residence) on the King's
journey   136 **importing** significant

145   Grant it me, O King! In you it best lies; otherwise a
        seducer flourishes and a poor maid is undone.
                                    Diana Capilet."

Lafew. I will buy me a son-in-law in a fair, and toll
        for° this. I'll none of him.

150 *King.* The heavens have thought well on thee, Lafew,
        To bring forth this discov'ry. Seek these suitors.
                        [*Exeunt Attendants.*]
        Go, speedily and bring again the Count.
        I am afeard the life of Helen, lady,
        Was foully snatched.

Countess.   .   Now, justice on the doers!

                Enter Bertram, [*guarded*].

155 *King.* I wonder, sir, since wives are monsters to you,
        And that you fly them as you swear them lordship,
        Yet you desire to marry.

                Enter Widow [*and*] *Diana.*

                            What woman's that?

Diana. I am, my lord, a wretched Florentine,
        Derivèd from the ancient Capilet.
160   My suit, as I do understand, you know,
        And therefore know how far I may be pitied.

Widow. I am her mother, sir, whose age and honor
        Both suffer under this complaint we bring,
        And both shall cease, without your remedy.°

King. Come hither, Count—do you know these
165   women?

Bertram. My lord, I neither can nor will deny
        But that I know them. Do they charge me further?

Diana. Why do you look so strange upon your wife?

148–49 **toll for** put up for sale   164 **both . . . remedy** both my life
("age") and honor will die unless you give us relief (by having
Bertram marry Diana)

Bertram. She's none of mine, my lord.

Diana.   If you shall marry,
  You give away this hand, and that is mine;   170
  You give away heaven's vows, and those are mine;
  You give away myself, which is known mine;
  For I by vow am so embodied yours
  That she which marries you must marry me,
  Either both or none.   175

Lafew. Your reputation comes too short for my
  daughter; you are no husband for her.

Bertram. My lord, this is a fond° and desp'rate crea-
  ture,
  Whom sometime I have laughed with. Let your
  Highness
  Lay a more noble thought upon mine honor,   180
  Than for to think that I would sink it here.

King. Sir, for my thoughts, you have them ill to
  friend
  Till your deeds gain them; fairer prove your honor
  Than in my thought it lies.

Diana.   Good my lord,
  Ask him upon his oath if he does think   185
  He had not my virginity.

King. What say'st thou to her?

Bertram.   She's impudent, my lord,
  And was a common gamester° to the camp.

Diana. He does me wrong, my lord; if I were so,
  He might have bought me at a common price.   190
  Do not believe him. O, behold this ring,
  Whose high respect and rich validity
  Did lack a parallel; yet for all that
  He gave it to a commoner o' th' camp,
  If I be one.

Countess.   He blushes, and 'tis hit!   195

178 **fond** foolish   188 **gamester** prostitute

Of six preceding ancestors, that gem,
Conferred by testament to th' sequent issue,°
Hath it been owed° and worn. This is his wife,
That ring's a thousand proofs.

King.   Methought you said
200   You saw one here in court could witness it.

Diana. I did, my lord, but loath am to produce
So bad an instrument. His name's Parolles.

Lafew. I saw the man today, if man he be.

King. Find him and bring him hither.
                              [*Exit an Attendant.*]

Bertram.   What of him?
205   He's quoted for° a most perfidious slave,
With all the spots o' th' world taxed and deboshed,°
Whose nature sickens but to speak a truth.
Am I or that or this for what he'll utter,
That will speak anything?

King.   She hath that ring of yours.

210   *Bertram.* I think she has. Certain it is I liked her,
And boarded her i' th' wanton way of youth.
She knew her distance, and did angle for me,
Madding my eagerness with her restraint,
As all impediments in fancy's° course
215   Are motives of more fancy; and in fine
Her inf'nite cunning with her modern° grace
Subdued me to her rate. She got the ring,
And I had that which any inferior might
At market-price have bought.

Diana.   I must be patient:
220   You that have turned off a first so noble wife,
May justly diet° me. I pray you yet—
Since you lack virtue I will lose a husband—

197 **sequent issue** next heir   198 **owed** owned   205 **quoted for**
known as   206 **taxed and deboshed** censured as debauched   214
fancy's love's   216 **modern** commonplace   221 **diet** restrain yourself from

Send for your ring, I will return it home,
And give me mine again.

Bertram.   I have it not.

King. What ring was yours, I pray you?

Diana.   Sir, much like   225
The same upon your finger.

King. Know you this ring? This ring was his of late.

Diana. And this was it I gave him, being abed.

King. The story then goes false you threw it him
Out of a casement?

Diana.   I have spoke the truth.   230

Enter Parolles.

Bertram. My lord, I do confess, the ring was hers.

King. You boggle shrewdly;° every feather starts you.
Is this the man you speak of?

Diana.   Ay, my lord.

King. Tell me, sirrah, but tell me true, I charge you,
Not fearing the displeasure of your master,   235
Which on your just proceeding I'll keep off—
By him and by this woman here what know you?

Parolles. So please your Majesty, my master hath been
an honorable gentleman. Tricks he hath had in him,
which gentlemen have.   240

King. Come, come, to th' purpose: did he love this
woman?

Parolles. Faith, sir, he did love her; but how?

King. How, I pray you?

Parolles. He did love her, sir, as a gentleman loves a 245
woman.°

---

232 **boggle shrewdly** startle excessively   246 **woman** (in contrast to
a highborn lady)

King. How is that?

Parolles. He loved her, sir, and loved her not.°

King. As thou art a knave and no knave. What an
250 equivocal companion° is this!

Parolles. I am a poor man, and at your Majesty's
command.

Lafew. He's a good drum, my lord, but a naughty°
orator.

255 *Diana.* Do you know he promised me marriage?

Parolles. Faith, I know more than I'll speak.

King. But wilt thou not speak all thou know'st?

Parolles. Yes, so please your Majesty. I did go between them as I said; but more than that, he loved
260 her, for indeed he was mad for her and talked of
Satan and of Limbo and of Furies and I know not
what; yet I was in that credit with them at that time
that I knew of their going to bed and of other mo-
tions, as promising her marriage, and things which
265 would derive me ill will to speak of; therefore I will
not speak what I know.

King. Thou hast spoken all already, unless thou canst
say they are married. But thou art too fine° in thy
evidence; therefore stand aside.
This ring, you say, was yours?

270 *Diana.*   Ay, my good lord.

King. Where did you buy it? Or who gave it you?

Diana. It was not given me, nor I did not buy it.

King. Who lent it you?

Diana.   It was not lent me neither.

---

248 **not** (perhaps punning on "knot" = maidenhead)   250 **equivocal
companion** equivocating fellow ("companion" is contemptuous)
253 **naughty** (1) worthless, worth naught (2) wicked   268 **fine** subtle

King. Where did you find it then?

Diana.   I found it not.

King. If it were yours by none of all these ways,   275
  How could you give it him?

Diana.   I never gave it him.

Lafew. This woman's an easy glove, my lord; she goes
  off and on at pleasure.

King. This ring was mine; I gave it his first wife.

Diana. It might be yours or hers for aught I know.   280

King. Take her away; I do not like her now.
  To prison with her. And away with him.
  Unless thou tell'st me where thou hadst this ring
  Thou diest within this hour.

Diana.   I'll never tell you.

King. Take her away.

Diana.   I'll put in bail, my liege.   285

King. I think thee now some common customer.°

Diana. By Jove, if ever I knew man, 'twas you.

King. Wherefore hast thou accused him all this while?

Diana. Because he's guilty and he is not guilty:
  He knows I am no maid, and he'll swear to't: 290
  I'll swear I am a maid and he knows not.
  Great King, I am no strumpet; by my life
  I am either maid or else this old man's wife.

King. She does abuse our ears. To prison with her!

Diana. Good mother, fetch my bail.   [*Exit Widow.*]
      Stay, royal sir,   295
  The jeweler that owes the ring is sent for
  And he shall surety me. But for this lord
  Who hath abused me as he knows himself,

286 **customer** prostitute

Though yet he never harmed me, here I quit° him.
300 He knows himself my bed he hath defiled,
And at that time he got his wife with child.
Dead though she be, she feels her young one kick.
So there's my riddle: one that's dead is quick.°
And now behold the meaning.

Enter Helena and Widow.

King.   Is there no exorcist°
305 Beguiles the truer office of mine eyes?
Is't real that I see?

Helena.   No, my good lord,
'Tis but the shadow of a wife you see,
The name and not the thing.

Bertram.   Both, both. O, pardon!

Helena. O, my good lord, when I was like° this maid,
310 I found you wondrous kind. There is your ring,
And, look you, here's your letter. This it says:
"When from my finger you can get this ring,
And is by me with child," &c. This is done.
Will you be mine, now you are doubly won?

Bertram. If she, my liege, can make me know this
315   clearly,
I'll love her dearly, ever, ever dearly.

Helena. If it appear not plain and prove untrue,
Deadly divorce step between me and you!
O, my dear mother, do I see you living?

320 *Lafew.* Mine eyes smell onions, I shall weep anon.
[*To Parolles*] Good Tom Drum, lend me a handker-
cher. So, I thank thee. Wait on me home, I'll make
sport with thee. Let thy curtsies alone, they are
scurvy ones.

325 *King.* Let us from point to point this story know,
To make the even truth in pleasure flow.

299 **quit** acquit   303 **quick** (1) alive (2) pregnant   304 **exorcist**
summoner of spirits   309 **like** i.e., substitute for

[*To Diana*] If thou be'st yet a fresh uncroppèd
    flower,
Choose thou thy husband, and I'll pay thy dower,
For I can guess that by thy honest aid
Thou kept'st a wife herself, thyself a maid.   *330*
Of that and all the progress more and less
Resolvedly° more leisure shall express.
All yet seems well, and if it end so meet,
The bitter past, more welcome is the sweet.

Flourish.

[*Epilogue*]

The King's a beggar° now the play is done.
All is well ended if this suit be won,
That you express content; which we will pay
With strife° to please you, day exceeding day.
Ours be your patience then, and yours our parts,°   *5*
Your gentle hands lend us, and take our hearts.

Exeunt omnes.

FINIS

332 **Resolvedly** so that doubt is removed   Epilogue 1 **beggar** i.e.,
for applause 4 **strife** striving 5 **Ours . . . parts** i.e., we will
silently listen, as you have done, and you are now the performers

Textual Note

A bookseller's reference in 1603 to "love's labor won" suggests that there was by that date a published version of a play so entitled. No copies survive. Some scholars identify this title with *All's Well*, but whatever the validity of the identification, the only authoritative text for *All's Well* is that of the First Folio (1623). Exactly what sort of text for this play the Folio's editors worked from is not certain, but probably it was either Shakespeare's finished manuscript or a scribe's copy of the manuscript. The play seems complete; it is not, for example, notably short, like *Timon of Athens*, and although it has some loose ends, they do not bulk large, as they do in *Timon*, which must be incomplete. There are, of course, puzzling words and lines, possibly as a result of a scribe's failure to transcribe accurately, and there are signs that a little tidying up remained to be done. For example, there is some inconsistency in the assignment of speeches to the two French lords, and some of their speeches are puzzlingly designated "G" and "E"—possibly the initials of actors for whom the speeches were written. And in a stage direction at 3.5 there is given the name "Violenta," yet no such character speaks or is addressed. Possibly Violenta was Shakespeare's first thought of a name for the widow's daughter, who is later called Diana, or possibly Violenta is a character that Shakespeare at first believed he would use in

the scene but (as he worked further into the scene) decided
was of no use. In a way, these minor confusions are reas-
suring; they suggest we have the play as Shakespeare wrote
it, rather than a neat stage version that perhaps omits some
of his material.

The Signet text modernizes spelling and punctuation,
expands abbreviations, straightens out some confusion in
the assignment of lines to the First and Second Lords, regu-
larizes speech prefixes (e.g., the Folio's "Mother," "Mo.,"
"Coun[tess]," "La[dy]," etc., all are given as "Countess"),
and regularly gives in the stage directions "Bertram" (for the
Folio's "Count," or "Count Rosse," etc.) and "Helena"
(because the Folio's first stage direction and first reference
to her in dialogue call her so, though the Folio later calls her
"Helen"). The act divisions are translated from Latin into
English. The Folio does not divide the play into scenes,
giving only "Actus Primus. Scoena Prima," but the conven-
tional and convenient scene divisions of the Globe text have
been given here. These additions and others (locales and
necessary stage directions not found in the Folio) have been
placed in square brackets. The position of an authentic stage
direction has occasionally been slightly altered when necessary, and some passages that are printed as prose in the Folio
are printed as verse here. Other substantial departures from
the Folio are listed below, the present reading given first, in
italic type, followed by the original reading, in roman.

1.1.134 *got* goe   155 *ten* two   165 *wear* were

1.3.19 *I* w   115 *Diana no queen* Queene   173 *loneliness* louelinesse
179 *t'one to th'other* 'ton tooth to th'other   204 *inteemable* in-
temible   237 *Haply* Happily

2.1.43 *with his cicatrice, an emblem* his sicatrice, with an Embleme
64 *fee* see   146 *sits* shifts   157 *impostor* Impostrue   194 *heaven*
helpe

2.2.63 *An* And

2.3.95 *her* heere   126 *when* whence   131 *it is* is is   295 *detested*
detected

2.5.27 *End* And   29 *one* on   52 *think not* thinke

3.1.23 *the* th the

3.2.9 *sold* hold   19 *E'en* In   115 *still-piecing* still-peering

3.5.s.d. *her daughter Diana* her daughter, Violenta   34 *le* la
66 *warrant* write

3.6.36 *his* this   37 *ore* ours

3.7.19 *Resolved* Resolue

4.1.91 *art* are

4.3.86–89 *They . . . midnight* [Folio gives to Bertram]   126 *Hush,
hush* [Folio gives to Bertram]   148 *All's . . . him* [Folio gives to
Parolles]   208 *lordship* Lord

4.4.9 *Marseilles* Marcella   16 *you* your

4.5.40 *name* maine   81 *Marseilles* Marcellus

5.1.6.s.d. *Gentleman, a stranger* gentle Astringer

5.2.26 *similes* smiles

5.3.122 *tax* taze   155 *since* sir   157s.d. *Widow* [*and*] *Diana* Wid-
dow, Diana, and Parolles   216 *inf'nite cunning* insuite comming

Epilogue 4 *strife* strift

The Source of
All's Well That Ends Well

All's Well is derived from the ninth story of the third day of Boccaccio's *Decameron* (written 1348–58), presumably in William Painter's translation in *The Palace of Pleasure*. (Nothing is gained by assuming that Shakespeare used a French translation of Boccaccio.) As even a casual reading of story and play will show, Shakespeare made substantial additions, and a few deletions, altering a well-told but scarcely brilliant or weighty little tale into a play of considerable subtlety and density.

Painter's translation appeared in the first edition (1566) of *The Palace,* but the version given below is the revision in the third edition (1575), which, because later, Shakespeare is more likely to have had at hand. In any case, the alterations are slight and there are no differences important to the student of Shakespeare. Spelling and punctuation have been modernized, and two errors in pronouns have been corrected.

WILLIAM PAINTER

From The Palace of Pleasure

THE THIRTY-EIGHTH NOVEL

Giletta, a physician's daughter of Narbon, healed the French King of a fistula, for reward whereof she demanded Beltramo, Count of Rossiglione, to husband. The Count being married against his will, for despite fled to Florence and loved another. Giletta, his wife, by policy found means to lie with her husband, in place of his lover, and was begotten with child of two sons; which known to her husband, he received her again, and afterwards he lived in great honor and felicity.

In France there was a gentleman called Isnardo, the Count of Rossiglione, who, because he was sickly and diseased, kept always in his house a physician, named Master Gerardo of Narbona. This Count had only one son called Beltramo, a very young child, amiable and fair; with whom there was nourished and brought up many other children of his age, amongs whom one of the daughters of the said physician, named Giletta, who fervently fell in love with Beltramo, more than was meet for a maiden of her age. This Beltramo, when his father was dead, and left under the royal custody of the King, was sent to Paris, for whose departure the maiden was very pensive. A little while after, her father being likewise dead, she was desirous to go to Paris, only to see the young

Count, if for that purpose she could get any good occasion. But being diligently looked unto by her kinsfolk (because she was rich and fatherless) she could see no convenient way for her intended journey; and being now marriageable, the love she bare to the Count was never out of her remembrance, and refused many husbands with whom her kinsfolk would have matched her, without making them privy to the cause of her refusal. Now it chanced that she burned more in love with Beltramo than ever she did before, because she heard tell that he was grown to the state of a goodly young gentleman. She heard by report that the French King had a swelling upon his breast which by reason of ill cure was grown to be a fistula, which did put him to marvelous pain and grief, and that there was no physician to be found (although many were proved) that could heal it, but rather did impair the grief and made it worse and worse. Wherefore the King, like one in despair, would take no more counsel or help. Whereof the young maiden was wonderful glad, thinking to have by this means not only a lawful occasion to go to Paris, but if the disease were such (as she supposed) easily to bring to pass that she might have the Count Beltramo to her husband. Whereupon with such knowledge as she had learned at her father's hands beforetime, she made a powder of certain herbs, which she thought meet for that disease, and rode to Paris. And the first thing she went about when she came thither was to see the Count Beltramo. And then she repaired to the King, praying his Grace to vouchsafe to show her his grief. The King, perceiving her to be a fair young maiden and a comely, would not hide it, but opened the same unto her. So soon as she saw it she put him in comfort that she was able to heal him, saying, "Sir, if it may please your Grace, I trust in God, without any great pain unto your Highness, within eight days to make you whole of this disease." The King, hearing her say so, began to mock her, saying, "How is it possible for thee, being a young woman, to do that which the best renowned physicians in the world cannot?" He thanked her for her goodwill and made her a direct answer, that he was determined no more to follow the counsel of any physician. Whereunto the maiden answered, "Sir, you despise my knowledge because I am young and a woman, but I assure you that I do not minister physic by profession but by the aid and help of God; and with the cunning of Master Gerardo of Narbona, who was my father and a physician of great fame so long as he lived." The King, hearing these words, said to himself, "This woman, aperadventure, is sent unto me of God, and therefore why should I disdain to prove her cunning, for so much as she promiseth to heal me within a little space without any offense or grief unto me?" And being determined to prove her, he said, "Damsel, if thou dost not heal me, but make me to break my determination, what wilt thou shall follow thereof?" "Sir," said the maiden, "let me be kept in what guard and keeping you list, and if I do not heal you within these eight days let me be burned; but if I do heal your Grace, what recompense shall I have then?" To whom the King answered, "Because thou art a maiden and unmarried, if thou heal me according to thy promise, I will bestow thee upon some gentleman that shall be of right good worship and estimation." To whom she answered, "Sir, I am very well content that you bestow me in marriage; but I beseech your Grace let me have such a husband as I myself shall demand, without presumption to any of your children or other of your blood." Which request the King incontinently granted. The young maiden began to minister her physic, and in short space before her appointed time she had throughly cured the King. And when the King perceived himself whole, said unto her, "Thou hast well deserved a husband, Giletta, even such a one as thyself shalt choose." "I have then, my lord," quoth she, "deserved the County Beltramo of Rossiglione, whom I have loved from my youth." The King was very loath to grant him unto her, but for that he had made a promise, which he was loath to break, he caused him to be called forth, and said unto him: "Sir County, knowing full well that you are a gentleman of great honor, our pleasure is that you return home to your own house, to order your estate according to your degree; and that you take with you a damsel which I have appointed to be your wife." To whom the County gave his humble thanks and demanded what she was. "It is she," quoth the King, "that with her medicines hath healed me." The Count knew her well, and had already seen her, although she was fair, yet knowing her not to be of a stock convenable to his nobility, scornfully said unto the King, "Will you then, sir, give me a physician to wife? It is not the pleasure of God that ever I should in that wise bestow myself." To whom the King said, "Wilt thou then that we should break our faith, which we to recover health, have given to the damsel, who for a reward asked thee to husband?" "Sir," quoth Beltramo, "you may take from me all that I have and give my person to whom you please because I am your subject; but I assure you I shall never be contented with that marriage." "Well, you shall have her," said the King, "for the maiden is fair and wise and loveth you most entirely, thinking verily you shall lead a more joyful life with her than with a lady of a greater house." The County therewithal held his peace, and the King made great preparation for the marriage. And when the appointed day was come, the Count in the presence of the King (although it were against his will) married the maiden, who loved him better than her own self. Which done, the Count, determining before what he would do, prayed license to return to his country to consummate the marriage. And when he was on horseback he went not thither, but took his journey into Tuscane, where, understanding that the Florentines and Senoys were at wars, he determined to take the Florentines' part, and was willingly received and honorably entertained and was made captain of a certain number of men, continuing in their service a long time. The new-married gentlewoman, scarce contented with his unkindness, hoping by her well-doing to cause him to return into his country, went to Rossiglione, where she was received of all his subjects for their lady. And perceiving that through the Count's absence all things were spoiled and out of order, she, like a sage lady, with great diligence and care disposed his things in order again, whereof the subjects rejoiced very much, bearing to her their hearty love and affection, greatly blaming the Count because he could not content himself with her. This notable gentlewoman, having restored all the country again to their ancient liberties, sent word to the Count, her husband, by two knights to signify unto him that if it were for her sake that he had abandoned his country, upon return of answer she to do him pleasure would depart from thence. To whom he churlishly replied, "Let her do what she list. For I do purpose to dwell with her when she shall have this ring (meaning a ring which he wore) upon her finger, and a son in her arms begotten by me." He greatly loved that ring and kept it very carefully and never took it from his finger for a certain virtue that he knew it had. The knights, hearing the hard condition of two things impossible, and seeing that by them he could not be removed from his determination, returned again to the lady, telling her his answer, who very sorrowful, after she had a good while bethought her, purposed to find means to attain the two things, that thereby she might recover her husband. And having advised herself what to do, she assembled the noblest and chiefest of her country, declaring unto them in lamentable wise what she had already done to win the love of the Count, showing them also what followed thereof. And in the end said unto them that she was loath the Count for her sake should dwell in perpetual exile; therefore she determined to spend the rest of her time in pilgrimages and devotion for preservation of her soul, praying them to take the charge and government of the country and that they would let the Count understand that she had forsaken his house and was removed far from thence, with purpose never to return to Rossiglione again.

Many tears were shed by the people as she was speaking those words, and divers supplications were made unto her to alter her opinion, but all in vain. Wherefore commending them all unto God she took her way, with her maid and one of her kinsmen, in the habit of a pilgrim, well furnished with silver and precious jewels, telling no man whither she went, and never rested till she came to Florence, where, arriving by fortune at a poor widow's house, she contented herself with the state of a poor pilgrim, desirous to hear news of her lord whom by fortune she saw the next day passing by the house (where she lay) on horseback with his company. And although she knew him well enough, yet she demanded of the good wife of the house what he was, who answered that he was a strange gentleman called the Count Beltramo of Rossiglione, a courteous knight and well beloved in the city, and that he was marvelously in love with a neighbor of hers that was a gentlewoman, very poor and of small substance, nevertheless of right honest life and good report, and by reason of her poverty was yet unmarried and dwelt with her mother, that was a wise and honest lady. The Countess, well noting these words, and by little and little debating every particular point thereof, comprehending the effect of those news, concluded what to do, and when she had well understanded which was the house and the name of the lady and of her daughter that was beloved of the Count, upon a day repaired to the house secretly, in the habit of a pilgrim, where finding the mother and daughter in poor estate amongs their family, after she had saluted them told the mother that she had to say unto her. The gentlewoman rising up courteously entertained her, and being entered alone in a chamber they sat down, and the Countess began to speak unto her in this wise. "Madam, methink that ye be one upon whom fortune doth frown, so well as upon me; but if you please, you may both comfort me and yourself." The lady answered that there was nothing in the world whereof she was more desirous than of honest comfort. The Countess proceeding in her talk said unto her, "I have need now of your fidelity and trust, whereupon if I do stay and you deceive me you shall both undo me and yourself." "Tell me then what it is, hardly," said the gentle-woman, "for you shall never be deceived of me." Then the Countess began to recite her her whole estate of love, telling her what she was and what had chanced to that present day, in such perfit order as the gentlewoman believing her, because she had partly heard report before, began to have compassion upon her, and after that the Countess had rehearsed the whole circumstance, she continued her pur-pose, saying, "Now you have heard amongs other my trou-bles what two things they be which behooveth me to have if I do recover my husband, which I know none can help me to obtain but only you, if it be true that I hear, which is that the Count my husband is far in love with your daughter." To whom the gentlewoman said, "Madam, if the Count love my daughter, I know not, albeit the likelihood is great; but what am I able to do in that which you desire?" "Madam," answered the Countess, "I will tell you, but first I will declare what I mean to do for you if my purpose be brought to effect. I see your fair daughter of good age, ready to marry, but, as I understand, the cause why she is unmarried is the lack of substance to bestow her. Wherefore I purpose for recompense of the pleasure which you shall do for me to give so much ready money to marry her honorably, as you shall think sufficient." The Countess' offer was very well liked of the lady, because she was poor; yet having a noble heart she said unto her, "Madam, tell me wherein I may do you service; and if it be a thing honest, I will gladly perform it, and the same being brought to pass do as it shall please you." Then said the Countess, "I think it requisite that by some one whom you trust you give knowledge to the Count my husband that your daughter is and shall be at his com-mandment. And to the intent she may be well assured that he loveth her indeed above any other, she must pray him to send her a ring that he weareth upon his finger, which ring as she knoweth he loveth very dearly. And when he sendeth the ring, you shall give it unto me, and afterwards send him word that your daughter is ready to accomplish his pleasure, and then you shall cause him secretly to come hither, and place me by him (instead of your daughter); peradventure God will give me the grace that I may be with child, and so having this ring on my finger and the child in mine arms begotten by him I may recover him, and by your means continue with him as a wife ought to do with her husband." This thing seemed difficult unto the gentlewoman, fearing that there would follow reproach unto her daughter. Notwithstanding, considering what an honest part it were to be a mean that the good lady might recover her husband, and that she might do it for a good purpose, having affiance in her honest affection, not only promised the Countess to bring this to pass but in few days with great subtilty, following the order wherein she was instructed, she had gotten the ring, although it was the Count's ill will, and took order that the Countess instead of her daughter did lie with him. And at the first meeting, so effectuously desired by the Count, God so disposed the matter that the Countess was begotten with child, of two goodly sons, and her delivery chanced at the due time. Whereupon the gentlewoman not only contented the Countess at that time with the company of her husband but at many other times so secretly as it was never known, the Count not thinking that he had lien with his wife, but with her whom he loved, to whom at his uprising in the morning he used many courteous and amiable words and gave divers fair and precious jewels which the Countess kept most carefully; and when she perceived herself with child she determined no more to trouble the gentlewoman but said unto her, "Madam, thanks be to God and you I have the thing that I desire, and even so it is time to recompense your desert, that afterwards I may depart. The gentlewoman said unto her that if she had done any pleasure agreeable to her mind she was right glad thereof, which she did not for hope of reward but because it appertained to her by well doing so to do. Whereunto the Countess said, "Your saying pleaseth me well, and for my part I do not purpose to give unto you the thing you shall demand in reward but for consideration of your well doing, which duty forceth me to do." The gentlewoman then constrained with necessity demanded of her with great bashfulness an hundred pounds to marry her daughter. The Countess perceiving the shamefastness of the gentlewoman, and her courteous demand, gave her five hundred pounds and so many fair and costly jewels as almost amounted to like valor. For which the gentlewoman, more than contented, gave most hearty thanks to the Countess, who departed from the gentlewoman and returned to her lodging. The gentlewoman, to take occasion from the Count of any farther repair or sending to her house, took her daughter with her and went into the country to her friends. The Count Beltramo within few days after, being revoked home to his own house by his subjects (hearing that the Countess was departed from thence), returned. The Countess knowing that her husband was gone from Florence and returned home was very glad, continuing in Florence till the time of her childbed, being brought abed of two sons which were very like unto their father, and caused them carefully to be nursed and brought up, and when she saw time she took her journey (unknown to any) and arrived at Monpellier, and resting herself there for certain days, hearing news of the Count, and where he was, and that upon the day of All Saints he purposed to make a great feast and assembly of ladies and knights, in her pilgrim's weed she repaired thither. And knowing that they were all assembled at the palace of the Count ready to sit down at the table, she passed through the people, without change of apparel, with her two sons in her arms. And when she was come up into the hall, even to the place where the Count sat, falling down prostrate at his feet, weeping, saying unto him, "My lord, I am thy poor

infortunate wife, who to th' intent thou mightest return and
dwell in thine own house, have been a great while begging
about the world. Therefore I now beseech thee, for the honor
of God, that thou wilt observe the conditions which the two
knights that I sent unto thee did command me to do; for
behold, here in mine arms not only one son begotten by thee
but twain, and likewise thy ring. It is now time then (if thou
keep promise) that I should be received as thy wife." The
Count, hearing this, was greatly astoned, and knew the ring
and the children also, they were so like him. "But tell me,"
quoth he, "how is this come to pass?" The Countess, to the
great admiration of the Count and of all those that were in
presence, rehearsed unto them in order all that which had
been done, and the whole discourse thereof. For which cause
the Count, knowing the things she had spoken to be true (and
perceiving her constant mind and good wit and the two fair
young boys to keep his promise made, and to please his subjects and the ladies that made suit unto him to accept her
from that time forth as his lawful wife and to honor her),
abjected his obstinate rigor, causing her to rise up, and
embraced and kissed her, acknowledging her again for his
lawful wife. And after he had appareled her according to her
estate, to the great pleasure and contentation of those that
were there and of all his other friends, not only that day but
many others, he kept great cheer, and from that time forth he
loved and honored her as his dear spouse and wife.

Commentaries

SAMUEL JOHNSON

From The Plays of William Shakespeare

[Note to 5.2.56–57: "though you are a fool and a knave you shall eat"] Parolles has many of the lineaments of Falstaff and seems to be the character which Shakespeare delighted to draw, a fellow that had more wit than virtue. Though justice required that he should be detected and exposed, yet his "vices sit so fit in him" that he is not at last suffered to starve.

[Note to 5.3.21–22: "the first view shall kill/All repetition"] Shakespeare is now hastening to the end of the play, finds his matter sufficient to fill up his remaining scenes, and therefore, as on other such occasions, contracts his dialogue and precipitates his action. Decency required that Bertram's double crime of cruelty and disobedience, joined likewise with some hypocrisy, should raise more resentment; and that though his mother might easily forgive him, his king should more pertinaciously vindicate his own authority and Helen's merit. Of all this Shakespeare could not be ignorant, but Shakespeare wanted to conclude his play.

From *The Plays of William Shakespeare* (1765).

[General comment] This play has many delightful scenes, though not sufficiently probable, and some happy characters, though not new, nor produced by any deep knowledge of human nature. Parolles is a boaster and a coward, such as has always been the sport of the stage, but perhaps never raised more laughter or contempt than in the hands of Shakespeare.

I cannot reconcile my heart to Bertram; a man noble without generosity, and young without truth; who marries Helen as a coward and leaves her as a profligate; when she is dead by his unkindness, sneaks home to a second marriage, is accused by a woman whom he has wronged, defends himself by falsehood, and is dismissed to happiness.

M. C. BRADBROOK

From Shakespeare and Elizabethan Poetry

Hovering uncertainly in date between early and late nineties, *All's Well That Ends Well* is a play which is of its age rather than for all time.* It might have as subtitle "Two plays in one," for the reason of its neglect—and the reason why in spite of the title, all did not end well, and it is not a successful play—is that a personal and an impersonal theme are here in conflict. It began by being a "moral play," a grave discussion of the question of what constituted true nobility, and the relation of birth to merit. This was *the* great topic of the courtesy books, and in a court that included such a high proportion of self-made men as Elizabeth's did, the question was not without practical consequences. Such questions were the equivalent of a political discussion today. But in *All's Well* the "social problem"—to give it the modern term—of high birth, exemplified in Bertram, and native merit, exemplified in Hellen,†

From *Shakespeare and Elizabethan Poetry*. London: Chatto & Windus, 1951, pp. 162–70. Reprinted by permission of Chatto & Windus, Ltd.

*In the following pages I have summarized my article "Virtue is the true Nobility," *R.E.S.*, N.S., vol. I, 4 (1950). Those who are interested will find there a more extended account of the background of courtesy literature, and in particular the relation of civil nobility to Christian nobility as it is treated by the writers of courtesy books, and books of nobility.

†Her name is so spelt throughout the folio text. There is only one occasion on which the meter requires Helena. Shakespeare evidently took great care over his proper names; consider the way in which the diminutives Harry and Kate are used (like Jane Austen, he seems to think only the best people worthy to be called Henry): the beauty of his new forms, Desdemona and Cordelia. James Joyce erected a considerable biographic speculation upon Shakespeare's aversion from the name Richard.

is bisected by a human problem of unrequited love. The structural center of the play is the King's speech on nobility, by which he justifies Hellen's marriage: the poetic center is Hellen's confession of her love to the Countess. Few readers would deny that this speech is different in kind from anything else in the play:

> I know I love in vain; strive against hope;
> Yet in this captious and intemable sieve
> I still pour in the waters of my love,
> And lack not to lose still. Thus Indian-like,
> Religious in mine error, I adore
> The sun that looks upon his worshipper
> But knows of him no more.   (1.3.203–9)

This is the voice of Juliet.

> My bounty is as boundless as the sea,
> My love as deep; the more I give to thee
> The more I have, for both are infinite.   (2.2.133–35)

Seen through Hellen's eyes, Bertram is handsome, brave, the glass of fashion and the mold of form; seen through older and wiser eyes, he is a degenerate son, an undutiful subject, a dishonorable seducer. The two images blend in the action as he sinks from irresponsibility to deceit, but makes a name for himself in the wars. He ends in an abject position: no other hero receives the open condemnation that Bertram does. Modern taste may disrelish Claudio, Bassanio or Orsino; but Shakespeare does not ratify it.

Here all the harsh words are spoken upon the stage: all but Hellen condemn Bertram. After suffering rebukes from his elders, his contemporaries, and even his inferiors, he ends unable to plead any excuses,* in danger of the law. The characters of the Countess and Lafeu were invented by Shakespeare, and the King's role much expanded, in order that judgment might be passed on Bertram. By these three, who have an equal share of blood and merit and are therefore impartial judges, he is compared with Hellen throughout the play, to his increasing disadvantage.† In the end she alone can restore the honors he has lost.

Bertram is very young, perhaps seventeen or eighteen at most, left without a father's direction and highly conscious of his position. He is handsome, courageous, winning in manners; but also an inveterate liar. Yet the Elizabethan code of honor supposed a gentleman to be absolutely incapable of a lie. To give the lie was the deadliest of insults, not to be wiped out but in blood. Honor was irretrievably lost only by lies or cowardice; a gentleman, as Touchstone remembered, swore by his troth, as a knight by his honor. Crimes of violence were less dishonorable: the convicted liar was finished socially. Bassanio, though he thinks of a lie at the end, to get himself out of an awkward situation, does not utter it.

Bertram's fall is due to ill company: Parolles, or Words, another character of Shakespeare's own invention, is perceived in the end by Bertram himself to be the Lie incarnate, a fact which everyone else has known from the beginning.‡

---

*E.g., 4.2.11–30 where Diana rebukes him: 4.3.1–39 where the young Lords criticize him. Parolles' sonnet to Diana, "Dian, the Count's a fool," contains some nasty hometruths. In the last scene the King and Lafeu are quite uncompromising. Bertram's word is no longer of the slightest value (5.3.182–84).

†The Countess is convinced of Hellen's virtue in the first scene (1.1.40–48), but not so fully of Bertram's. She loves Hellen as her own child (1.3.100–1, 144–46) and after Bertram's flight disclaims him for her son and takes Hellen as her only child (3.2.69–70). Lafeu's view of Bertram is never very high (2.3.100–2). In 4.5. he and the Countess unite in praise of Hellen's memory and at the beginning of 5.3. the King laments her and accuses Bertram's "mad folly" in which he is heartily seconded by Lafeu, who joins his condemnation with still more praise of Hellen.

‡E.g., the Countess (3.2.90–92), Hellen (1.1.105–7). Parolles is meant to be representative of the evils of the court, which are much stressed in the opening scenes. It is no longer the fount of good manners, exclusively, as it had been in *Two Gentlemen of Verona.*

He is that principal danger of noble youth, the flatterer and misleader, the base companion against whom all books of behavior issued lengthy warning. The relation of Bertram and Parolles resembles that which everyone except Prince Hal takes to exist between himself and Falstaff. Parolles claims to be both courtier and soldier but his courtship is entirely speech, as his soldiership is entirely dress. Even the clown calls him knave and fool to his face; he is ready to play the pander, and at the end he crawls to the protection of old Lafeu, the first to detect and, with provocative insults, to "uncase" him.

The model of a perfect courtier is set before the young man by the King, in a "mirror" or portrait of his father.

His father's "morall parts" are what the King wishes for Bertram; their physical likeness has already been commented on. The elder Rousillon was a soldier first of all, but also a courtier.

> ... in his youth
> He had the wit, which I can well observe
> To day in our young Lords, but they may iest
> Till their owne scorne returne to them unnoted
> Ere they can hide their levitie in honour:
> So like a Courtier, contempt nor bitternesse
> Were in his pride, or sharpnesse: if they were
> His equall had awakd them, and his honour
> Clocke to it selfe, knew the true minute when
> Exception bid him speake: and at this time
> His tongue obeyd his hand. Who were below him
> He us'd as creatures of another place,
> And bow'd his eminent top to their low ranks. . . .
>
> (1.2.31–43)

Such is Bertram's inheritance of conduct, and he had a duty to live up to it. Hellen's miraculous cure of the King, which is proffered by her and accepted by him and the court as an

act of Heaven,* makes her a candidate for nobility, though
she is only the daughter of a poor gentleman belonging to the
least dignified of the professions.† The recognized causes
for ennobling the simple were headed by "virtue public,"
that is, some great public service. Sir Thomas Elyot had
declared that nobility is "only the prayse and surname of
virtue" and set forth the eleven moral virtues as the model
for his Governor. Desert for virtue is Hellen's claim, and
this, all but Bertram allow her.

By making his social climber a woman Shakespeare took
a good deal of the sting out of the situation. The question of
blood and descent versus native worth was an ancient subject of debate on the stage; indeed the first secular play to
survive, *Fulgens and Lucres,* deals with precisely this
matter. Here the lady's verdict was given for the worthy
commoner against the degenerate nobleman. Though noble
descent was prized as giving a disposition to virtue, and the
opportunity of good education and good examples, yet "one
standard commonplace on nobility took shape; that lineage
was not enough, but that the son of a noble house should
increase and not degrade the glory of his ancestors."‡

Hellen has been conscious throughout of her humble station, and has urged the Countess that though she loves
Bertram she would not have him till she should deserve him
(1.3.201). Before and after marriage she thinks of Bertram

---

*The formal couplets in which Hellen, after making ready to retire, sud-
denly returns and announces herself as a minister of Heaven mark the porten-
tousness of the occasion. See Hardin Craig, *Shakespeare's Bad Poetry*
(*Shakespeare Survey,* I; Cambridge, 1948). The automatic writing down of
such passages as "first draft fossils" is not justified. Hellen's "miracle" is discussed at length by Lafeu (2.3.1–44); it is "a showing of a heavenly effect in
an earthly actor," as Hellen confirms (2.3.65) to the court.

†For those younger sons of the nobility who were obliged to take to the professions, Law was considered the noblest study; the profession of arms was of
course the oldest and most honorable, but it notoriously failed to supply means
of livelihood. The physician was concerned with base matters, and approximated
too nearly to the barber-surgeon and the apothecary to receive much honor.

‡John E. Mason, *Gentlefolk in the Making* (Philadelphia, 1935), p. 8. This
book is the most comprehensive account known to me of the doctrine of
gentility.

as her "master" as well as her lord, a title Parolles will not give him. It was within the power of the King to confer honor where he chose; and Hellen had already been ennobled in a superior way by being marked out as the instrument of Heaven towards the King's recovery.

When therefore she is offered her choice of a husband, none save Bertram think of refusing her. The "lottery" is like a reversal of Portia's caskets, for here the lady makes her choice, sure to win. In bestowing a wife upon his ward, the King was certainly doing no more than Elizabeth or any other monarch might do. Yet Bertram's cry, "A poor physician's daughter my wife!" would not sound so outrageous to an Elizabethan ear as it does today, for marriage out of one's degree was a debasing of the blood which blemished successive generations. The King, in his great central speech, whose formality is marked by the couplet form, replies and sets out to Bertram the causes why he should not disdain merit. This speech contains the germ of the play—or one of the two plays which together make up this story.

> Tis only title thou disdainst in her, which
> I can build up: strange is it that our bloods
> Of colour, weight and heat, pour'd all together
> Would quite confound distinction: yet stands off
> In differences so mighty. If she bee
> All that is vertuous (saue what thou dislik'st,
> A poor Phisitians daughter), thou dislikst
> Of vertue for the name: but do not soe:
> From lowest place, whence vertuous things proceed,
> The place is dignified by th' doers' deede.
> Whence great additions, swells, and vertue none,
> It is a dropsied honour. Good alone
> Is good without a name: Vileness is so:
> The propertie, by what it is, should goe,
> Not by the title. She is young, wise, faire,
> In these to Nature shee's immediate heire:

And these breed honour: that is honour's scorne,
Which challenges it selfe as honour's borne,
And is not like the sire: Honours thrive
When rather from our acts we them derive
Then our forgoers: the meere words, a slave
Deboshed on every tombe, on every grave:
A lying Trophee, and as oft is dumbe
Where dust, and damn'd oblivion is the Tombe
Of honour'd bones indeed . . .   (2.3.118 ff)

This is doctrine of a kind which ought to convince Bertram. It is only after he has objected, "I cannot love her, nor will strive to do it," that the King exercises his power to compel submission.

The customary formula when presenting young people to each other in such circumstances was, "Can you like of this man?" "Can you like of this maid?"; in other words, can you make a harmonious marriage? Love was not expected. If Bertram is thought to show peculiar delicacy in demanding passion as the basis of marriage, he removes all such notions at the end of the play by his alacrity in accepting Lafeu's daughter, a match which the King had planned since their childhood. In the original story, Beltramo protests his unwillingness but he does not defy the King, nor does he recant as Bertram so abjectly does under the King's threats, protesting that he now sees Hellen to be ennobled by the royal choice. The King's fury, far more reasonable than old Capulet's when Juliet exercises a right of rejection, depends on his and everyone else's conviction that Hellen is "vertuous" and the special favorite of Heaven. Not only his king but his mother accepts it. That Bertram should misprize her is not in keeping with the decorum of the play. This is not *Romeo and Juliet;* it is written upon quite different premises, the social premises which that play so pointedly omits. And Bertram has no precontract; for his vamped-up excuse in the fifth act that he was really in love with Mademoiselle Lafeu is patently one of his fibs. He dislikes Hellen on social, not personal grounds. He is being willful; and in running away after the marriage ceremony, he is evading obligations which are imposed by the Church as well as the State, as Diana does not fail to recall to him (4.2.12–13).

His rejection of Hellen must be seen then not in isolation but as linked with his choice of Parolles. The first dialogue of Hellen and Parolles, the Liar and Virtue as she herself designates them, must be seen as the encounter of Bertram's good and evil angels, who, if this were a morality play, would contend for his soul in open debate.*

The exposure of Parolles' cowardice and lies precedes but foreshadows the exposure of Bertram. The last scene, which is Shakespeare's improvement of his source, is a "judgment," like those which conclude so many of Chapman's comedies. The most extraordinary stratagems are practiced by Diana and Hellen to extract Truth from the Accused. The jewels which are bandied about have symbolic significance; they stand for a contract and an estate of life. The King's gem derived from him to Hellen, and Bertram neither knows nor cares what it is. His own monumental ring symbolizes all he has thrown away.

> an honour longing to our house
> Bequeathed down from manie Ancestors,
> Which were the greatest obloquie i' th' world
> In me to lose   (4.2.42–45)

This jewel, with which he had taunted Hellen, is found at the end to be in her keeping. Hellen too is a "Jewell" (5.3.1)

---

*Parolles, it should be noted, is a character entirely of Shakespeare's own invention. His alterations of his source (ultimately Boccaccio, *Il Decamerone*, 3.9) are highly significant, tending to greater humility and dependence on Hellen's part—in the original she has a fortune—and greater perfidy, weakness and youthfulness on Bertram's. I do not wish to suggest that *All's Well* is a morality disguised, but it is a moral play which, like *The Merchant of Venice*, depends on a central theme of ethical significance.

which Bertram has thrown away. In this scene the King appears as the fount of justice, as earlier he had been the fount of honor; he deprives Bertram of all honor (182–84) and the rapidity with which he jumps to thoughts of murder is prompted as much by his affection for Hellen as his well-merited distrust of her lord. Lafeu and the Countess also recall Hellen's memory with sorrow. The likeness with the later play of *Measure for Measure,** which was evidently modeled in part on *All's Well,* is particularly strong in this judgment scene, with charge and countercharge piled up in bewildering succession till they are resolved as if by magic in the appearance of the central figure. The ingenuities of Hellen, like those of the Duke, are not to modern taste but their purpose is conversion.

Bertram's conversion must be reckoned among Hellen's miracles. It is notable that on the fulfillment of the bargain she turns to seek, not her husband, but the King. What is achieved is public recognition of her right, which he concedes her. She has been acknowledged by her lord; that her personal happiness is simply irrelevant, and the ending neither hypocritical nor cynical, can be granted only if the play is seen as a moral debate on the subject: Wherein consists true honor and nobility?

This is a grave subject—more lofty than that of *Romeo and Juliet,* for example. But such a subject needed to remain upon the level of debate. An Elizabethan audience might have been quite willing to see it worked out as a species

---

**Measure for Measure* has in common the rejection of a devoted bride for insufficiency and a marriage compelled by the ruler; the substitution of one woman for another; the false self-accusation of the chaste woman followed by denial from the culprit and culminating in his exposure through the arrival of an absent person. The similarity between the themes is also noticeable: both plays deal with what Bacon called "Great Place," the problems of authority, and both are moral plays; that is to say, they are concerned with general truths explicitly handled, though handled in human terms. But *Measure for Measure* seems to me to belong to a much later period; the close resemblances in plot, far from suggesting that the two plays were written close together, imply that Shakespeare returned to his earlier material when he returned to a similar theme.

of morality play, without taking the personal aspect into account. What is now called "the love interest" is generally overweighted in the modern view of Shakespearean comedy. His audience would be well accustomed to see a love-intrigue provide the spring of the action without providing any of the interest or body of the play, as it does in the comedies of Jonson or Chapman, where it is like the love interest in a detective story, strictly subordinate to the disguisings. But here the nature of the story makes it extremely difficult to insulate the marriage as a social and religious contract.

Two incompatible "species" are mingled because the personal aspect awakened to life. The play is a genuine hybrid, one of the few examples of Shakespeare's failure to master and control his form. Bertram is magnificently drawn: his petulance, his weakness, his cublike sulkiness, his crude and youthful pride of rank. His charm has to be accepted because Hellen loves him, but there is little other evidence for it. Hellen's love, as expressed in her three great speeches, is a devotion so absolute that all thought of self is obliterated; yet her action cannot but make her appear, however much more modestly to an Elizabethan than to us, a claimant, and a stickler for her bond.* The parallels between her love speeches and the sonnets (especially xxxv, lxvii, lxxxii, lxxxiv, xcv, xcvi), something in common between the lineaments of Bertram and those of Adonis, Bassanio, and Proteus, suggest that the theme of high birth versus native merit, first approached impersonally, had touched off reactions which could not properly be related to the story as it originally stood. The figure of Bertram, so radically changed

---

*Hellen's three great speeches (1.1.85–111, 1.3.193–219, 3.2.103–34) have a number of parallels with the sonnets. The picture of her as a canny fortune hunter is entirely twentieth-century, and may lead critics so far as to see in her careful disclaimer of any ambition to match with the "royal blood of France" a vulgar foresight, rather than a due sense of rank. Elizabeth's sense of what constituted suitable matches was extremely strict: the Earl of Essex was considered to have committed a shocking impropriety by marrying the widow of Philip Sidney.

from that of Boccaccio's Beltramo, is drawn with a fullness, a kind of uncynical disillusion which makes Hellen as a person still more unsatisfactory. She is a voice of despair breaking into the play; at other times a pliant lay figure on which the characters drape their admiration. No crude and direct personal equation can be thought of; Shakespeare would certainly not wish to unlock his heart on the public stage. But here for once the poet and the dramatist are pulling different ways. He set out to start a discussion on the fashioning of a gentleman and found himself impelled to draw the likeness of one whom Lafeu called an "asse" and Hellen the god of her "idolatrous fancie," but whose portrait stands out clearly as something more complex than either.

JOSEPH WESTLUND

Longing, Idealization, and Sadness in *All's Well That Ends Well*

Psychoanalytic theory takes as its province the often obscure relationship between thought and feeling in human beings, and thus its significance for the interpretation of literature seems inescapable. And in that psychoanalytic theory is largely derived from clinical attempts to *alter* emotional states, it would appear to be ideally suited to clarifying the way in which works of literature affect members of an audience. Nevertheless, many people find psychoanalytic literary criticism reductive. One cause for skepticism is that this school of criticism insists so heavily upon psychosexual stages; another, deeper, reason is that it constantly dwells upon aggression, conflict, and guilt. Other equally basic human feelings such as romantic love, reparation, and elation tend to be swept aside.

Since romantic love and various degrees of elation lie at the heart of most people's view of Shakespeare's comedies, I want to sketch an alternative view, which can help to account for these feelings in psychoanalytic terms. I rely mainly on two innovative, yet essentially Freudian theorists: Melanie Klein and Heinz Kohut. Klein gives full weight to

Adapted and abridged from *Shakespeare's Reparative Comedies: A Psychoanalytic View of the Middle Plays*. Chicago: University of Chicago Press, 1984, pp. 121–46. Reprinted by permission of University of Chicago Press. This is a shortened version of the chapter, with some new introductory material.

people's destructiveness, but argues that they can repair the damage when and if they can admit their guilt; people regularly break the cycle of aggression and destruction by "reparation." Her theory sheds new light on such everyday experiences as marriage, child-rearing, and work; and it helps to account for the cause of art—as reparation on the part of the author—and for its effect upon members of an audience.

In the book from which this abbreviated account of *All's Well That Ends Well* is excerpted, I argue that Shakespeare's comedies are reparative by virtue of their ability to contain and transcend conflict within their own worlds, and by their ability to instill in us some sense of worth or happiness. These plays help to repair our sense of ourselves and life so that living appears, at least for the moment, richer and more benign. In making members of an audience feel better reconciled to our own tough world, these plays must negotiate with the anger and guilt which we bring along with us to the experience of the play as part of human nature.

In *All's Well That Ends Well* this process of reparation can go wildly astray. Most critics call this a "problem" comedy, and for conflicting reasons. I think that this play stirs up so many difficulties because it makes an issue of idealization: the characters tend to elevate one another into models of perfection—or, in a similar and closely related move, to degrade one another for failing to live up to expected perfection. So, too, the play holds out the notion that all will *end well,* and then frustrates this expectation both for the characters and for members of the audience.

Because of this shift in focus in Shakespeare's comedies, I expand Klein's notion to pay particular attention to Heinz Kohut's view of narcissism. Kohut argues that narcissism is, despite its potentially pathological forms, an essential component in each and every one of us. This healthy state of narcissistic self-esteem is induced by a twofold idealization: of self, and of others. Although it is part of a developmental phase, it remains essential and is never completely relinquished. I emphasize the link between Kohut's view of narcissism and Klein's theory of reparation, and suggest that being reparative requires a heightened sense of our own worth and that of others. This vital narcissistic state may well be what gives us the strength to admit our destructiveness and to believe that we can repair it (for further commentary see my "What Comedy Can Do for Us").

In *All's Well That Ends Well*, however, this potentially benign process of idealization gets out of hand. For instance, Helena exalts Bertram as a pattern of perfection: she sees him as someone far above her whom she feels worthy of pursuing as a husband. In a way, her idealization seems to be a defense against her sense of being a lowborn and unworthy orphan, yet she at once disguises this feeling by creating a role for herself as his ideal wife. From this point on her attempts appear to be reparative and benign, but they can readily be interpreted as manipulative and destructive. And this is how Bertram responds to them. He reacts to her protestations of love as an intrusion, and thus he himself grows manipulative. In response to his attempts against her, other characters respond in similarly manipulative fashion: the King forces Bertram to wed her, as does his mother; Helena engages Diana and her mother to trick Bertram; finally, the King and Helena force him to acknowledge her as his wife. In the process of this overcontrol the audience—as the remarks of numerous critics attest—finds itself in a problematic state which is both psychologically realistic and new to Shakespeare's comedies.

I think that critics follow the lead of the characters in their impulse to distort reality in quest of something or someone perfect. Some critics follow Helena by denying Bertram's bad points—deception, cowardice, coldheartedness—in favor of his one good point: honor through battle. They transform his tepid repentance into a sign of his being a better man.

Other critics follow the lead of all the characters but

Bertram in denying Helena's bad points—manipulativeness, willfulness—in favor of her one good point: her heroic persistence. These opposed groups of critics idealize one character at the expense of the other, whom they degrade, and then they pronounce *All's Well* a problem or even a failure.

I think that these responses on the part of the critics indicate that they themselves search for something extremely good in *All's Well*. They give every sign of longing to find perfection in one of the characters or in the outcome of the plot. And this quest fails, as fail it must given the nature of the characterization and plotting—and given the nature of life itself. I think it is more profitable to argue that the uneasiness, strain, and sadness which many seek to explain away are central to the experience of the play and to its psychological value. In life we, like Helena and her society, cannot make all end well, although we want to. *All's Well* makes us experience the longing and sadness which cause us to idealize—and which often result from our attempt to do so. Unless we admit the essential sadness of the human condition, we remain out of touch with reality and unable to feel the concern for others which stimulates reparation.

It is the viewer who can attain such a state through *All's Well*; what Helena and others feel toward the end we do not know. Her persistence and manipulation indicate that she does not feel the sort of sadness caused by being fully in touch with reality. In addition, she lacks a sense of humor that might make us feel that she can observe herself with accuracy. We know that she is not disinterested when she makes bawdy jokes with Parolles; her playfulness, unlike his, seems suspect. Helena's minimal sense of humor helps to account for the play's unpopularity: we are more wary of her than of Viola, or even Vincentio, for she seems to have no humorous detachment from herself—or sad awareness of reality.

One of the attractions of the problem comedies is that by

their inconclusive nature and strained tone they imitate life as we know it. The longing for goodness remains, along with the *awareness* that we long, and that we can be only partly satisfied. To admit the sadness, and that the wish for goodness is just that, a wish, can make us realize that there are no perfect solutions in which all's well. This admission helps us to realize that no omnipotent benign creatures exist: no Helena who can earn a man's love; no one who can make Bertram grow worthy of her or of his station. *All's Well That Ends Well* pulls us up short, and in this lies its reparative effect if we are willing and able to accept it.

Most critics exactly catch the tone of strain and negation; they begin, and sometimes end, by treating a series of negatives: problems, flaws, and failures. The negation, however, is an integral, coherent attitude or even structural device: we find it in the language, character, and plot. The play most often defines character and action, like the language out of which they are created, by "striving through intractable material for effects which hardly justify the struggle." Let us begin with Helena. She denies her father, sets forth her new love for Bertram, and then immediately despairs of gaining him: " 'twere all one / That I should love a bright particular star, / And think to wed it" (1.1.91–93). No one can marry "a bright particular star"; her paradoxes persist into the action itself and haunt us to the very end. So far, all we have seen of Bertram is his vague attention to the elders' talking about loss and death. Helena, as so often during the play, "follows Bertram on stage to interpret his conduct through her love"; perhaps his "conduct is to be reconsidered in the light of her love" (as Price concludes). But this would be *yielding* to her idealization; instead, we should attend to her activity, not simply to his conduct.

Helena severely restricts the terms by which she evaluates Bertram, and talks only about his noble birth and his good looks. On these points she cannot be controverted. She attempts no assessment whatsoever of his honor (apart from birth), his virtue, or his goodness—or any of those qualities so crucial in the discussion which precedes her soliloquy and which concern characters throughout the play. She describes him as ideal without ever employing the terms which she and other characters find so essential. This clearly indicates that she creates him mostly out of her wish. Since she quietly ignores the standards of her world, she more easily deceives herself—and the viewer. She continually evaluates every character except Bertram in terms of honesty, virtue, and goodness. She also condemns herself for her failings in such matters, but only rarely—and late—does she hold Bertram to these standards. Because she idealizes him, viewers are encouraged to do so, and thus to seek what the play will not render up: a clear sense of Bertram being worthy.

That she may know his failings makes her seem not only sadly self-deceived, but willfully wrongheaded. The play never clarifies this, and indeed makes us believe that her whole society shares her propensity for delusion. The elders—the King, Countess, and Lafew—see Bertram's faults, but never try to dissuade Helena. They fail to point out that he is not so desirable or suitable; nor do they suggest that her pursuit may be quixotic or unseemly. No other Shakespearean comedy has so many parental figures who actively support a love match—and no other match is so inappropriate. Helena and her society are at one in their willful idealizing.

In talking to Parolles, Helena suddenly decides that her situation only appears hopeless. With that practicality which makes her at once admirable and, because of the circumstances, willful, she realizes that she can use her virginity to gain Bertram. When Parolles asks "Will you anything with it?" (171), she creates an extraordinarily expansive account of what she will become:

Not my virginity yet!
There shall your master have a thousand loves,
A mother, and a mistress, and a friend.

                                                    (172–74)

(I see no need to emend the Folio punctuation as the Arden
editor does: "Not my virginity; yet . . .") She will not give up
her virginity yet: "there," in her virginity, "shall your master
have a thousand loves." Rather than present a catalogue of
the varieties of love available to Bertram at court (as Hunter
and many others suggest), Helena creates "a definition of
perfect love, which labours for its object's good" (Knight,
p. 140). She defines her role, not his. Knight thinks that
"Helena's love sees Bertram as he potentially is," but she
dwells only on the actual, sexual attraction. She speaks
about moral and social attributes only in relation to herself,
to what she might be: "A mother, and a mistress, and a
friend." She will be "[h]is humble ambition, proud humility"
(178). We learn nothing at all about what she thinks of his
character, or his potential for growth at court. She concen-
trates upon herself and what she might become, which is why
she begins with "a mother," the only unfamiliar term in the
courtly titles and phrases which follow (phoenix, goddess,
traitress). The word "mother" strikes interpreters as out of
place (Arden edition), but not if we realize she talks about
herself, not court ladies. When Bertram takes her virginity
he shall find her a mother: this is the whole point of the task
which he later sets her. Again, this mismatched couple have
one thing in common, sex, but she thinks of it positively as
the means to becoming an ideal wife—and he as the means
to negate her longing.

Helena's feelings progress during this key scene. First she
thinks it impossible to gain Bertram, then the bawdy talk
about her virginity being used leads Helena to list active
roles which she could play as his wife. In her second soliloquy her longing grows less passive, the physical aspect of

love more real, and finally she becomes active and hopeful: "Our remedies oft in ourselves do lie" (223). She abandons her crucial awareness of the difference between longing for something good, and finding it. We all need to believe that "the fated sky / Gives us free scope" (224–25), yet this can be a dangerous wish: it ignores real-life limitations and verges on omnipotent thinking. No one can be certain, although Helena says she is, that "only doth backward pull / Our slow designs when we ourselves are dull" (225–26). She attempts to deny the play's insistent awareness of the inevitable tension between hope and loss.

Helena's invention of an ideal beloved remains constant throughout the play, with minor alterations; now she turns to action. At once, and as always in this play, negation persistently intrudes. For example, the King resists another attempt to cure him. And when Helena succeeds, it is not easy to see her cure as "miraculous" (as Bradbrook does, p. 168). Parolles interrupts and makes fun when Lafew tries to describe the cure for us. Bertram says not a word about the wonder of it all. Also, Helena heals the King not out of affection and altruism but, as she makes clear, to gain Bertram. These details significantly diminish our joy at what ought to be an inspiring moment, and in so doing nicely prepare us for the consequences which lie in store for the King, for Bertram, and for Helena. When Helena exercises her right to choose, she first denies all the courtiers who would accept her. Lafew, in keeping with the play's mood, assumes that they deny *her*. When Bertram refuses Helena he disobeys the King's command; when he capitulates and marries her, he runs away.

When we shift our attention to Bertram and the events in Florence we discern a similar pattern: definition in terms of negation, and yet—this seems crucial—with none of Helena's creativity and resilience in the face of adversity. Bertram seeks an ideal, honor through fighting in Florence. Let us examine the nature of the war. We find France neither officially at war with Siena, nor on the side of Florence. The King states that, for some reason we never learn, "our cousin Austria . . . Prejudicates the business, and would seem / To have us make denial" (1.2.5–9). Austria has "armed our answer, / And Florence is denied before he comes" (11–12). This mysterious business ends in an ambiguous compromise: "Yet, for our gentlemen that mean to see / The Tuscan service, freely have they leave / To stand on either part" (13–15). Shakespeare elaborates the source to intensify the prevailing mood of his play. In Painter's translation of Boccaccio's story, Beltramo leaves his wife and goes to Tuscany "where, understanding that the Florentines and Senoys were at wars, he determined to take the Florentines' part" (this Signet edition, p. 128). Beltramo simply makes a choice. Bertram, on the other hand, fights in a war defined by an ambiguously negative attitude: the King will not openly take sides; his men opt for the very one which Austria wanted the King not to take. A mere setting need not be so elaborately contrived; we certainly do not need to hear about these mysterious political maneuverings for reasons of plot or characterization. All this cannot help but taint the positive value of Bertram's fighting.

No sooner does Bertram gain honor in the field than he begins to sully it. The seduction of Diana has much of the negative coloration so prevalent in *All's Well*. His siege leads to an assignation which, so far as he knows, will be characterized by its negative nature: he deflowers a virgin, neither sees her nor speaks to her in bed, and has no intention to wed her. The trick itself depends upon denial: it assumes that the lovers' bodies exist separately from their personalities. An audience may be troubled by such implications. And rightly so; even Helena, its hopeful perpetrator, expresses dismay that lust plays "[w]ith what it loathes [taking it] for that which is away" (4.4.25). *Her* perversity— or so we are free to assume— is pursuing such a man.

Just after Bertram has been deceived in a trick which

might well trouble us for his sake, and for Helena's, the play forces us to face yet another instance of his unvarying bad character. Before leaving to bed Diana he receives a letter from his mother which the second Lord says "stings his nature, for on the reading it he changed almost into another man" (4.3.4–5). Critics make much of this in an attempt to show a change for the better in Bertram. However, when the same Lord hears that Helena has died, news brought in the letter itself, he remarks: "I am heartily sorry that he'll be glad of this" (66–67). Bertram has not changed "into another man." He immediately enters, breezily listing various "businesses" which he has performed that night: taken leave of the Duke, "done my adieu with his nearest, buried a wife, mourned for her, writ to my lady mother I am returning, entertained my convoy, and between these main parcels of dispatch effected many nicer needs" (that is, bedded Diana) (92–96). Within the space of ninety lines we are told that he has changed, but not with regard to Helena; and then we see him behaving with his usual callousness, eagerly making preparations to return to France now she is dead. We, like the Lords, may *want* to believe that Bertram can grow into a new man, but the play defeats us at every turn.

Dr. Johnson, disturbed by the ending, brings up an aspect which deserves further attention. When Bertram returns from Florence, he should not so readily be forgiven of the "double crime of cruelty and disobedience, joined likewise with some hypocrisy." Johnson sees how the Countess might forgive her son, but asserts that the King "should more pertinaciously vindicate his own authority and Helena's merit." Johnson has good reason to be puzzled here.

Bertram refuses to accept his guilt: he protests that his evil deeds were the unfortunate result of his long-standing love for Maudlin (news to us, and to the characters). We can barely understand what Bertram tries to say (Arden edition, p. lvii). Bertram never before or after attempts such complex metaphorical language; he consistently speaks more simply than any other major character. The King finds it "[w]ell excused. / That didst love her [Helena? Maudlin?], strikes some scores away / From the great compt" (5.3.55–57). An excuse, nevertheless, differs from repentance, as the King indicates in his grand generalization about guilt, loss, and remorse: "remorseful pardon slowly carried . . . turns a sour offense" (58–59). In sum, the King refuses to demand repentance; but Bertram asks pardon, and then excuses his conduct; the King says the excuse is good, but denies its adequacy. That Shakespeare devotes seventy lines of the final scene to such strange stuff is difficult to justify unless he seeks to prepare us for the hauntingly inadequate affirmations at the end.

When the Widow and Diana enter, the King asks Bertram: "do you know these women?" (165) To which he evasively replies: "My lord, I neither can nor will deny / But that I know them" (166–67). He denies Diana is his wife; Lafew denies Maudlin will be his wife. Diana baroquely tells the King to ask Bertram "if he does think / He had not my virginity" (185–86). That she confronts Bertram (rather than Helena, as in the source) allows this series of nullifications: she neither slept with Bertram, nor thinks she has; Bertram never suspects that he did not sleep with Diana. Beyond the situation itself, almost all details incessantly lead to negation. Diana does not want to call Parolles as her witness, for she is loath "to produce / So bad an instrument" (201–2); Bertram tries to undermine Parolles' testimony as coming from a proved liar. When this discredited witness appears, he equivocates; then, after telling the truth, he says, "I will not speak what I know" (265–66).

The King's interrogation produces denial upon denial. To the question of how Diana got the ring, she says: "It was not given me, nor I did not buy it"; "It was not lent me neither"; "I found it not" (272, 273, 274). Exasperated, the King asks: "If it were yours by none of all these ways, / How could you give it him?" Diana caps this dizzying series: "I never gave it him" (275–76). She persists in refusing, then produces a flourish of negatives which create a larger paradox (289–93) and lead to the statement which introduces Helena: "So there's my riddle: one that's dead is quick. / And now behold the meaning" (303–4). We expect Helena's appearance to clear the air, but instead of resolving the tension she manages to prolong it. The King wonders if she is real; she replies: "No, my good lord, / 'Tis but the shadow of a wife you see, / The name and not the thing" (306–8). Whatever strength Bertram's affirmation and request for pardon have must derive from our relief at its being simple, straightforward, and positive: "Both, both. O, pardon!" (308) Yet we have good reason, by his previous lies, not to believe him.

A minor detail of great significance helps to sustain the uncertainty at the end: Helena alters the terms which Bertram set in his letter. When she appears she reads the crucial parts: "When from my finger you can get this ring, / And is by me with child, &c" (312–13). The startling shift in grammar, knowledge of the old tale, or a good memory would remind us that Bertram actually wrote: "and show me a child begotten of thy body that I am father to" (3.2.59–60). Perhaps this alteration is a slip, or change of mind, on Shakespeare's part; yet it alters the mood exactly the way all his other changes do. In the source Giletta produces two sons rather than the one son demanded of her; they are not mere babes, but "carefully . . . nursed and brought up" to be "fair young boys" (this Signet edition, pp. 133–34). In contrast to Giletta's characteristic overachievement of the tasks set her, Helena is simply pregnant: she cannot as yet show the requisite child to Bertram.

In a scene so much more elaborate than in the story, this alteration shows the coherence of Shakespeare's design. The denouement involves a highly punctilious working out of questions about identifiable rings replete with histories and symbolic meanings (especially the ring Shakespeare adds). At the same time, he alters the actual, realized child of

Bertram's instructions (and the source) into a potential child, one not yet born let alone "carefully nursed and brought up." Critics ignore this detail—perhaps because of their search for an unambiguously happy, or unhappy, ending. Until recently it was not possible to assume that being pregnant almost means having a child in one's arms. Giletta's two sons add joy because they better ensure succession than one easily lost son. That Helena is simply pregnant suits the insistently tentative quality of the play. She stands as a perfect symbol of potential, one which contributes to the play's haunting sense of longing for something good which may, or may not, be realized.

The obliquely positive, conditional tone extends throughout the conclusion. Helena asks Bertram: "Will you be mine, now you are doubly won?" (5.3.314) Her tone seems poignant, "doubly won"; or, this phrase may convey her intolerable persistence, especially to Bertram, who again (as when she chose to wed him) turns to the King, not her: "If she, my liege, can make me know this clearly, / I'll love her dearly, ever, ever dearly" (315–16). Helena herself counters with a conditional statement rather than an affirmation: "If it appear not plain and prove untrue, / Deadly divorce step between me and you!" She then asks: "O my dear mother, do I see you living?" (317–19) Helena and Bertram seem determined to be uncertain about everything, no matter how obvious it may be. In this they are wise, given what they have experienced.

This might have been a conclusion in which Bertram fully admitted guilt for his scorn of Helena and "requited" it—as Benedick does in *Much Ado*. But Helena herself has been so manipulative that she—like Beatrice—should meet him halfway; in doing so she would have to free him, for we have no sign that Bertram loves her. Straightforward reparation vanishes in the problem comedies, and may be the reason why they rarely get a positive reception.

As I suggested at the start, *All's Well* can restore us in a deeper, more basic sense of clarifying the relationship between ideals which sustain (such as many of those in *Twelfth Night*) and idealizations which prove limiting and dangerous (such as most of those in *All's Well*). *Twelfth Night* blurs this crucial distinction. *All's Well* clarifies it by mirroring and confirming our need to find something extremely good, and then frustrating it so that we recognize the wish is a wish—a longing. The play tempers the sort of near-grandiose elation which such plays as *Twelfth Night* can create. Now the sadness implicit, say, in Viola's quest is openly revealed (too openly, many feel). We can see *All's Well* as precipitating *Measure for Measure* and its more radical questioning of ideals. What makes these two comedies so problematic is not their arbitrary plots or unattractive characters, but their focus on what is problematic in life itself: not the grandeur of tragedy or the elation of the earlier and final comedies, but the mixed sadness and pleasure of our condition.

Works Cited

Bradbrook, M. C. *Shakespeare and Elizabethan Poetry*. London: Chatto and Windus, 1951.

Hunter, G. K. "Introduction," in *All's Well That Ends Well*, Arden ed. London: Methuen, 1959. Throughout this excerpt all references to G. K. Hunter are to his introduction and editorial comments.

Johnson, Samuel. *Yale Edition of the Works of Samuel Johnson*. Ed. Arthur Sherbo. New Haven: Yale University Press, 1968. Vol. 7.

Klein, Melanie. "Love, Guilt and Reparation." Rept. in *Love, Guilt and Reparation and Other Works, 1921–1945*. Ed. R. E. Money-Kyrle. London: Hogarth Press, 1975.

Knight, G. Wilson. *The Sovereign Flower*. London: Methuen, 1958.

Kohut, Heinz. *The Restoration of the Self*. New York: International Universities Press, 1977.

Price, Joseph G. *The Unfortunate Comedy: A Study of "All's Well That Ends Well" and Its Critics*. Toronto: University of Toronto Press, 1968.

Westlund, Joseph. "What Comedy Can Do for Us: Reparation and Idealization in Shakespeare's Comedies." In *Psychoanalytic Approaches to Literature and Film*. Ed. Maurice Charney and Joseph Reppen. Rutherford, N.J.: Fairleigh Dickinson University Press, 1987.

BRUCE R. SMITH

What Doing It in the Dark, Without Words, Tells Us About Early Modern Sexuality

"Married women—Drama," "Runaway husbands—Drama," "Florence (Italy)—Drama": the three Library of Congress subject headings for *All's Well That Ends Well* make Shakespeare's play sound something like E. M. Forster's novel *Where Angels Fear to Tread,* a romantic tale of a troubled marriage that finds its denouement amid the sunshine and the passions of Italy.* Where modern readers, given these subject headings and remembering Merchant-Ivory films, might expect a cinematic encounter in a sun-drenched piazza, followed by a no less cinematic session in the candlelit bedroom of a small *pensione,* Shakespeare gives us, instead, the darkness and the silence of the bed trick. The bed trick—there's the rub. Since the nineteenth century, readers, actors, and audiences have had a hard time with the husband-deceiving device Helena contrives in Act 3, Scene 7. Rather than consummate his forced wedding to Helena, Bertram has fled the arms of the marriage bed for the arms of the battlefield. Following him to Florence in the guise of a religious pilgrim, Helena takes lodging with a widow, whose daughter, Diana, has, like a military target, been the object of Bertram's "wanton siege" (3.7.18) in the form of letters, love tokens, fancy speeches, and consorts of

Library of Congress Subject Headings, 5 vols. (Washington: Library of Congress, 2002), 3:3848, 4:5494, 2:2276.

music.* Helena convinces Diana to pretend to accept Bertram's advances, to demand that Bertram give Diana his ancestral ring, to insist on darkness and silence during their assignation—and to let Helena take Diana's place in bed.

What the original audiences thought about this stratagem can perhaps be gauged by the fact that no fewer than forty-four surviving scripts datable from 1594 to 1630 deploy some form of bed trick.† For spectators through the 1630s, having sex with a person you don't suspect seems to have been one of the ways they liked it. As for later audiences, Samuel Johnson finds the events of *All's Well* unlikely but not, it would seem, unlikable. "This play has many delightful scenes," Johnson observes in his 1765 edition of Shakespeare, "though not sufficiently probable, and some happy characters, though not new, nor produced by any deep knowledge of human nature." The bed trick comes in for particular notice: "The story of *Bertram* and *Diana* had been told before of *Mariana* and *Angelo* [in *Measure for Measure*], and, to confess the truth, scarcely merited to be heard a second time."‡ Coleridge, lecturing on Shakespeare in 1811–12, likewise registers incredulity, but nonetheless expresses no regrets: "The poet in this play . . . was always uppermost and little was drawn from real life. His judgement

---

*Quotations from *All's Well That Ends Well* are taken from this revised Signet Classics edition. Quotations from Shakespeare's other plays are also from the Signet Classics editions, and are cited in the text by act, scene, and line numbers.

†Marliss C. Desens, *The Bed-Trick in English Renaissance Drama: Explorations in Gender, Sexuality, and Power* (Newark: University of Delaware Press, 1994), 143–51, supplies an appendix that catalogues and describes these forty-four plays. Desens distinguishes four ways in which critics have attempted to negotiate the challenges posed by the bed trick: by treating it (1) as a plot expedient that ignores psychological reality, (2) as evidence of historical differences in attitudes toward matrimony, (3) as a dramatic device, sometimes used with metatheatrical effect, and (4) (Desens's own approach) as an index of gender politics (12–16). In her account of *All's Well* (63–67), Desens casts Helena as "a person fighting for a place in a society that severely limits the options available to a woman" (67).

‡Samuel Johnson, endnote to *All's Well That Ends Well*, in Brian Vickers, ed., *Shakespeare: The Critical Heritage*, 5 (London: Routledge and Kegan Paul, 1979), 114.

only was shown in placing the scenes at such a period when we could imagine the transactions of the play natural."* Distant from 1811–12, perhaps. Nothing in Shakespeare's script suggests that the events in *All's Well* take place earlier than 1602, when the play was likely first produced. By 1832, however, a writer in *The Theatrical Observer* could declare that "the plot is in itself so objectionable to modern refinement, that it has long been acknowledged not to be fit for representation."† The objections heard in classrooms and theater lobbies today have less to do with moral refinement than with commonsense skepticism and with sentiments about romantic love. How could anyone, however dark it might be, possibly be deceived about the person with whom he was having sex? Even if the trick worked, how could a sustainable relationship result from such a deception?

The uneasiness of most modern readers, actors, and spectators has been expressed by one of the play's recent editors, Susan Snyder, who notices how strangely the folktale qualities of the bed trick sort with the circumstantial physicality of Helena's encounter with Bertram.‡ On the one hand, Helena enacts a plot device that has its own number in Stith Thompson's structuralist encyclopedia of folktales from cultures all over the world—number K1843.2, to be precise: "Wife takes mistress's place in husband's bed. Brings about reconciliation." Thompson cites five texts from medieval and early modern Europe, as well as examples from India and Africa.§ On the other hand, Helena exults afterward to the Widow over the "sweet use" Bertram has made of her body (4.4.22), a physical consummation of desires that have

*Samuel Taylor Coleridge, *Lectures 1808–1818 in Literature,* ed. R. A. Foakes in *Collected Works,* gen. ed. Kathleen Coburn, 5 (Princeton: Princeton University Press, 1987), 276, spelling modernized.
†Quoted in William Shakespeare, *All's Well That Ends Well,* ed. Russell Fraser (Cambridge: Cambridge University Press, 1985), 30.
‡William Shakespeare, *All's Well That Ends Well,* ed. Susan Snyder (Oxford: Clarendon Press, 1993), 10–11.
§Stith Thompson, *Motif-Index of Folk-Literature,* rev. ed., 6 vols. (Bloomington: Indiana University Press, 1955–58), 4:443.

taken a somatic solidity from the very beginning. "What power is it which mounts my love so high,/That makes me see, and cannot feed mine eye?" she asks the audience in the second of the two soliloquies she speaks in the play's first scene. "The mightiest space in fortune nature brings/To join like likes, and kiss like native things" (1.1.227–30). On the male side, a conversation between two Lords substitutes onstage for the dark and silent business that is taking place offstage, at that very moment, in Diana's chamber—a space situated somewhere else, somewhere "within" the house, perhaps just behind the upstage curtain or arras that other scripts call for. (*Hamlet,* acted just the season before *All's Well,* is an example.) In many of these scripts—*Romeo and Juliet* and *Othello* are examples—a bed stands behind the curtain, waiting to be "thrust forth."* What gets "thrust forth" on this occasion is not a bed, however, but something that could never have been shown onstage. "[T]his night he fleshes his will in the spoil of her honor," the First Lord tells the Second Lord (4.3.16–17). The pun on "will" as sexual desire and "will" as sexual equipment is a page out of Shakespeare's sonnets 135 and 136. When Bertram joins the two Lords moments later, he boasts of having just "dispatched sixteen businesses" (4.3.90). What? *Sixteen* times? If these businesses turn out, a few words later, to be attendance on the Duke, Bertram nonetheless claims to have "effected many nicer needs" in between. "[T]he last was the greatest, but I have not ended yet" (4.3.96–97). On Helena's part, as well as on Bertram's, there is no escaping the physicality of the bed trick. The deception may be a folktale motif, but it involves bodies, eyes, lips, and genitals. If readers and audiences today are uncomfortable with Helena's ploy, it is because we entertain ideas about sexuality that are fundamentally different from the ideas of Shakespeare and his

*Alan C. Dessen and Leslie Thomson, *A Dictionary of Stage Directions in English Drama, 1580–1642* (Cambridge: Cambridge University Press, 1999), sv. "thrust," 229–30.

contemporaries.* Those differences present two aspects, one public and one private. Let us examine the two aspects in turn.

For us, the public face of a marriage ceremony stands in sharp contrast to the privacy of a honeymoon. The public way in which characters in Act 5 of Shakespeare's comedies refer to the sexual consummation coming up in Act 6 should alert us to the anachronism of our assumptions. "Come, Kate, we'll to bed," bellows Petruccio six lines from the end of *The Taming of the Shrew* (5.2.184). Would Nerissa rather wait one more night "or go to bed now," Graziano wonders facetiously at the end of *The Merchant of Venice* (5.1.303). Duke Senior, at the end of *As You Like It,* commands, "Proceed, proceed. We'll so begin these rites/As we do trust they'll end, in true delights" (5.4.197–98). The "delights" he has in mind are connubial, as Rosalind confirms in the Epilogue when (s)he hopes aloud to the men in the audience "that between you and the women the play may please" (Ep. 16), all puns intended. The putting to bed of bride and groom was a very public part of early modern weddings. Women in the wedding party undressed the bride, men prepared the groom, the entire group put the two to bed; in some cases, they waited up all night to see how things went.† *A Midsummer Night's Dream* catches this public character in the blessing that the fairies dance out in the play's last scene. Oberon and Titania will take charge of "the best-bride bed" (5.1.405), Theseus and Hippolyta's. The audience is invited to imagine the sexual intercourse taking place there as Oberon wishes away any mole, harelip, scar, or prodigious mark that might disfigure the children the Duke of Athens and his new bride engender. A flourishing genre in Shakespeare's time was the wedding-celebration poem known as

---

*In this essay I develop, with specific reference to *All's Well*, ideas that I first presented in "L[o]cating the●Sexual Subject" in *Alternative Shakespeares 2,* ed. Terence Hawkes and John Drakakis (London: Routledge, 1996), 95–121.

†David Cressy, *Birth, Marriage, and Death: Ritual, Religion, and the Life-Cycle in Tudor and Stuart England* (Oxford: Oxford University Press, 1997), 350–76.

epithalamium, literally, "at the nuptial chamber."* John Donne's epithalamium for the marriage of King James's daughter Elizabeth to the Count Palatine in 1613 is altogether typical in situating the poem's readers and listeners within the bridal suite, right outside the bed curtains. Donne imagines what is going on within, just as the two Lords do in *All's Well.* Donne depicts the couple's sexual play as the fiery union of sun and moon—but with the usual genders reversed: "Here lies a she sun, and a he moon here,/She gives the best light to his sphere/Or each is both, and all."† In one sense, there is nothing unusual in the voyeurism that attends the consummation of Helena's marriage to Bertram.

In another sense, there is. The relationship of sex to marriage was no less controversial in Shakespeare's time than it is today. As feminist critics have made us see, the institution of marriage in early modern England served as a way of controlling women's sexual activity so as to ensure efficient transfer of male power and male property across generations.‡ For these transactions to work, it was essential that the sexual behavior of women be subject to male control. For a male to sow his wild oats wherever he liked made no difference to the property/power transfer system; for the female to be planted with the wrong oats undermined the system entirely. The control that Helena wields from the moment she cures the king's fistula is fundamentally disturbing. She chooses Bertram, and

---

*On representations of sexual consummation in epithalamia see Heather Dubrow, *A Happier Eden: The Politics of Marriage in the Stuart Epithalamium* (Ithaca, NY: Cornell University Press, 1990), 44–45, 86–90; and Virginia Tufte, *The Poetry of Marriage: The Epithalamium in Europe and Its Development in England* (Los Angeles: Tinnon-Brown, 1970), 127–38.

†John Donne, "An Epithalamium, or Marriage Song, on the Lady *Elizabeth* and Count *Palatine* being married on St. *Valentine's* Day," in *Poems* (London: John Marriot, 1633), sig. R1, spelling modernized.

‡A series of feminist studies of Shakespeare that continues to the present day was inaugurated by Carolyn Ruth Swift Lenz, Gayle Greene, and Carol Thomas Neely, eds., *The Woman's Part: Feminist Criticism of Shakespeare* (Urbana: University of Illinois Press, 1980). Particularly relevant to *All's Well* are Carol Thomas Neely, *Broken Nuptials in Shakespeare's Plays* (New Haven, CT: Yale University Press, 1985) and Marilyn L. Williamson, *The Patriarchy of Shakespeare's Comedies* (Detroit: Wayne State University Press, 1986).

it is she, not he, who engineers consummation of the marriage. *Consummare,* to sum up, complete, finish: the *con-* in that word usually entails a mutual "with," not a one-sided con game or trick. Betrothal/ceremony/sexual consummation: Helena stage-manages all three episodes in the traditional rite of passage. In the bed trick she says, not that she will take Diana's place, but that she will "fill the time" (3.7.33). As several social historians have demonstrated, not every marriage in early modern England proceeded according to the expected sequence. Common law recognized the legality of so-called *per verba de presenti* contracts in which two people would make a pronouncement before one or more witnesses that they *intended* to marry. In the eyes of many local communities, such a pronouncement served as legitimation for sexual relations before a formal ceremony took place later. First there was a contract, then sex, then marriage.* In the case of aristocrats, however, where a great deal of property and power was at stake, the sequence was usually the traditional one: first a contract, then marriage, then sex. The last stage was absolutely essential for the match to be legal. Otherwise, it could be annulled. Bertram, as Count Rousillon, constitutes a case in point. His decampment to Florence has less to do with personal repugnance toward Helena than with avoiding legal consummation of a marriage to a social inferior. "A poor physician's daughter my wife!" Bertram exclaims to the King. "Disdain/Rather corrupt me ever!" (2.3.116–117). To achieve her upwardly mobile desires, Helena pulls off a legal trick just as clever as Portia's in *The Merchant of Venice.* The word "law" is much on Helena's lips. What she intends, she tells the Widow, "Is wicked meaning in a lawful deed, / And lawful meaning in a lawful act" (3.7.45–46). The bed trick in *All's Well That Ends Well* shapes up as a publicly visible consummation of a legal contract, not as the private moment of genuine affection that modern readers and spectators want it to be. Helena has a contract, and she is determined to make it good.

At the same time, there is an intensely private side to the bed trick that we likewise tend to miss because we entertain such different ideas about reason and imagination. When it comes to sex, we have wanted since Freud to have it both ways: to indulge libido but to confirm the ego's rational control and to satisfy the superego's social scruples, all at the same time. In early modern conceptualizations of sexual intercourse, imagination, for better not worse, for richer not poorer, is given much larger scope. We can see that in the early modern spaces where sex took place. Mendoza in John Marston's tragedy *The Malcontent,* likely acted in the same season as *All's Well,* sets the scene for wanton sex: "sweet sheets, wax lights, antique bedposts, cambric smocks, villainous curtains, arras pictures, oil'd hinges, and all the tongue-tied lascivious witnesses of great creatures' wantonness" (1.7.38–41).* The bedposts are "antique" (i.e. "antic," fantastic, grotesque) because they are carved with what Edward Phillips in *The New World of English Words* (1658) describes as "a disorderly mixture of divers shapes of men, birds, flowers, etc."† The bed head made for Henry VIII and Anne of Cleves, preserved today in the Burrell Collection, Glasgow, features a male figure grabbing his penis on Henry's side of the bed and a female figure exposing her genitals on Anne's.‡ The curtains that Mendoza describes are "villainous" because they are woven with sexual escapades out of Ovid's *Metamorphoses,* as several surviving panels attest.§

---

*John Marston, *The Malcontent,* ed. M. L. Wine (Lincoln: University of Nebraska Press, 1964), 37. Further quotations are cited in the text by act, scene, and line numbers.

†Edward Phillips, *The New World of English Words* (London: E. Tyler, 1658), sv. "*Antike* work," sig. C2, spelling modernized.

‡Glasgow Museums, Burrell Collection, inventory 14/236, illustrated in Simon Thurley, *The Royal Palaces of Tudor England: Architecture and Court Life 1460–1647* (New Haven, CT: Yale University Press, 1993), 237.

§See, for example, three valences usually on display in the British Galleries, Victoria and Albert Museum, London: one showing the story of Venus and Adonis (inventory T.879-1904), one the story of Myrrha (T.879-A-1904), and one the story of Lucrece (T.125–1913). The last of these can be viewed online at http://www.scran.ac.uk. A fourth panel depicting the story of Philomel, present location unknown, is illustrated in Preston Remington,

In two extensive inventories of beds and curtains, one devoted to actual furniture in upper-class houses and one to stage properties in plays like *Romeo and Juliet* and *Othello,* Sasha Roberts traces the intricate connections among curtained beds, sexual imaginings, and moveable goods that signify social status.* Later in *The Malcontent,* the play's satirist Malevole provides yet another catalogue of bedchamber amenities—in this case, specifically *Italian* amenities—and imagines their seductive effects on "a lady guardianless," that is to say, on just such a lady as Helena. All such effects Malevole attributes to "Strong fantasy tricking up strange delights" (3.2.40). In *All's Well,* however, it is not so much the lady who is swept up in sensual imaginings but her husband. Justifying to the King in Act 5 why he would give up his ancestral ring, Bertram blames Diana's cunning. She got the ring, he explains, because she kept holding back, and he succumbed, "As all impediments in fancy's course/Are motives of more fancy" (5.3.214–215). In early modern epistemology, fancy or fantasy is the faculty that gathers sense experience—sights, sounds, smells, tastes, feelings—and puts them together in creative, constantly changing new ways.† The carvings on early modern bedposts and the woven subjects in early modern bed curtains were products of fancy, just as were the sexual acts that took place within them.

In his medical encyclopedia, *Microcosmographia: A Description of the Body of Man* (1616 and 1631), Helkiah Crooke devotes several pages to human reproductive organs—and to the movements of mind that activate them. Crooke realizes that

---

English Domestic Needlework of the XVI, XVII, and XVIII Centuries (New York: Metropolitan Museum of Art, 1945), fig. 34.

*Sasha Roberts, "Lying among the Classics: Ritual and Motif in Elite Elizabethan and Jacobean Beds," in *Albion's Classicism: The Visual Arts in Britain, 1550–1660,* ed. Lucy Gent (New Haven, CT: Yale University Press, 1995), 325–57, with numerous illustrations, and " 'Let Me the Curtains Draw': The Dramatic and Symbolic Properties of the Bed in Shakespearean Tragedy," in *Staged Properties in Early Modern English Drama,* ed. Jonathan Gil Harris and Natasha Korda (Cambridge: Cambridge University Press, 2002), 153–74.

†Katharine Park, "The Organic Soul," in *The Cambridge History of Renaissance Philosophy,* ed. Charles B. Schmitt, Quentin Skinner, Eckhard Kessler, and Jill Kraye (Cambridge: Cambridge University Press, 1988), 464–84.

human sexual acts are not just "natural" or instinctual; they are also "animal" or spiritual, a term he derives from the Latin word *anima* or soul. "The action of erection," Crooke explains, "is neither merely animal nor mere natural, but a mixed action. In respect of the imagination and the sense it is animal, because it is not distended unless some luxurious [i.e., lustful, lascivious] imagination go before, and the distention when it is made is always accompanied with a sense of pleasure and delight; but in respect of the motion [itself] we rather think it to be natural which yet is somewhat holpen [i.e., helped] by the animal."* Elsewhere Crooke is absolutely insistent that "luxurious imagination" on the part of both parties is necessary for conception of a child to take place.† *All's Well That Ends Well*, like Shakespeare's source story in William Painter's *The Palace of Pleasure*, relates that Helena and Bertram did not just copulate during the bed trick but conceived a child together. In Painter, the Helena figure waits until the offspring—twins, in fact—are born and recognizable as Bertram's issue before she confronts her reluctant husband. If we accept fancy and imagination as creative states of flux, as comings-to-be, then perhaps the married future of Helena and Bertram is not so bleak as modern readers, actors, and audiences are apt to assume. In their fancies, in their bodily coition, Helena and Bertram have *imagined* a child together. The darkness and the silence of the curtained bed have encouraged that happy result.

In both its aspects, in its privateness as in its publicness, *All's Well That Ends Well* embodies a sexual imaginary that challenges modern complacencies.

---

*Helkiah Crooke, *Microcosmographia: A Description of the Body of Man* (London: Thomas and Richard Cotes, 1631), 248, spelling modernized. I am grateful to Mary-Ann Davis for bringing this passage to my attention.

†Early modern physiology regarded the female sexual organs as operating just like the male, so that ejaculation was just as necessary for the female as for the male. See Thomas Laqueur, *Making Sex: Body and Gender from the Greeks to Freud* (Cambridge, MA: Harvard University Press, 1990), 98–103; and Valerie Traub, *The Renaissance of Lesbianism in Early Modern England* (Cambridge: Cambridge University Press, 2002), 89–90.

All's Well That Ends Well on Stage and Screen

One of the minor and indeed relatively harmless myths of our age is the belief that not until our own time have Shakespeare's plays been adequately presented on the stage. We think with horror of Nahum Tate's stage version of *King Lear* (1681), with its happy ending, or of Beerbohm Tree's *A Midsummer Night's Dream* (1900), with its real rabbits in the forest, and we congratulate ourselves that we have got rid of all that—forgetting that (for instance) in our own age Peter Brook's much-acclaimed *King Lear* omitted all the lines that did not suit Brook's interpretation of the play, and that it is almost impossible today to see a production of *A Midsummer Night's Dream* that is not rooted in Jan Kott's view of the play as a nightmare of lechery.

Still, we probably can rightly claim that (putting aside productions in Shakespeare's day) not until the second half of the twentieth century did *All's Well That Ends Well* achieve reasonably competent productions. In fact, we can't assert categorically that it was produced (competently or not) even in Shakespeare's own day, since there is no record of any production in the early seventeenth century, or, for that matter, at any date in the seventeenth century.

The first recorded performance of *All's Well That Ends Well* took place in London in 1741—about a hundred and forty years after it was written—when Henry Giffard produced it for eight performances in his theater at Goodman's Fields. Giffard, who had already done some of the highly popular plays such as *Hamlet* and *Macbeth,* perhaps turned to *All's Well* in search of a novelty. In the next season it was added to the repertory at Drury Lane, but after the first performance Peg Woffington, who played Helena, fell ill, and scheduled performances were canceled. When Woffington recovered, the actor who played the King fell ill, causing additional postponements. Ultimately, however, ten performances were given in 1742; apparently the chief attraction was Theophilus Cibber's Parolles.

In *The Unfortunate Comedy,* an invaluable stage history of *All's Well* up to 1964, Joseph G. Price points out that in the first five years of its revival, *All's Well* was fairly successful; it was performed twenty-two times in four theaters (true, *As You Like It* was performed sixty-five times in the same seasons, but *Twelfth Night* was performed only ten times); then followed ten years when it was absent from the London stage, though it was occasionally done in the provinces. In 1756, however, David Garrick restored the play to the stage, this time in an adaptation (probably of his own devising) with the part of Helena much reduced, so that she became not much more than a passive wife. For instance, Garrick deleted most of her important soliloquy at the end of 1.1, beginning: "Our remedies oft in ourselves do lie. . . ."

Garrick's adaptation, which not only trimmed the role of Helena but also fattened the role of Parolles, held the stage for eighteen years, chiefly as the farcical comedy of Parolles. Another version, made by Frederick Pilon in 1785 for the farcical actor John Bannister, cut almost all of the first three acts, and apparently was chiefly a comedy about the exposure of Parolles and of Bertram. Speaking only a little broadly one can say that most versions of the play continue this emphasis on comedy at the expense of the more serious or darker scenes, such as those with the King in the second act. The last version of the eighteenth century, however, published by John Philip Kemble in 1793 though not staged until the following year, cut much of the comedy of Parolles and increased interest in the love plot. One obvious sign of this shift of interest is that Kemble played Bertram, a part that no leading actor after Giffard had played. It also diminished Helena's energy and cleverness, choosing instead to emphasize her patience. The play was now a sentimental drama of a long-suffering, docile wife; although Kemble omitted the explicit talk about the bed trick, he kept the passage in which Bertram sets as a condition that she bear him a child, and so (since Helena fulfills this condition, though Kemble's version doesn't clearly say how) the play is not quite so bawdlerized as one might expect. The last production in the eighteenth century (it was the first in America) took place in Boston in 1799; Kemble's text was used, and Kemble's sister, Mrs. Elizabeth Kemble-Whitlock, played Helena. No reviews are known.

In the nineteenth century the first production of *All's Well* was Charles Kemble's adaptation (1811) of his brother's adaptation; although the play was elaborately costumed, it was (like John Philip Kemble's own production) not a popular success. An operatic version of 1832, made by Frederick Reynolds, added not only songs from several other plays but also spoken dialogue from other plays—for instance from *Romeo and Juliet*—now set to music for this version, which emphasized the sentimental and the comic. In 1852 Samuel Phelps staged *All's Well,* probably in John Philip Kemble's adaptation but with further expurgations. Although Phelps' production emphasized sentiment and romance, it also emphasized Phelps' role, Parolles. Reviewers found the play itself objectionable but Phelps' production nevertheless had an acceptable run. The last revival in the nineteenth century, given by the Irving Dramatic Club in 1895, is remembered only because it evoked a review by Bernard Shaw, who in later writings saw the play as an anticipation of Ibsen's *A Doll's House*.

The twentieth century did not do much better until relatively recently. Frank Benson's production at Stratford-upon-Avon in 1916 was chiefly notable for restoring Shakespeare's text; William Poel's production in London in 1920, deemphasizing the comedy and emphasizing Helena as a woman free from society's conventions, was something of a tribute to the success (in the previous year) of the suffragette movement and to the activity of Sylvia Pankhurst, the feminist who with much publicity opposed the institution of marriage. In 1921 Robert Atkins, who had been the stage manager of Poel's production, directed the play for the Old Vic (he directed it again in 1932 and in 1940); Atkins retained some of the sweetness of the nineteenth-century Helena, but he also included much of the bawdry that the nineteenth century had deleted. That is, he apparently tried to combine both romance and somewhat crude satire. The production received polite attention, as did W. Bridges-Adams' 1922 production at Stratford-upon-Avon. In 1924 *All's Well* was produced in Norwich, and in 1927 Barry Jackson's Birmingham Repertory Theatre produced it in modern dress, with Laurence Olivier as Parolles.

What probably is the first important revival of the play took place in 1953, when Tyrone Guthrie staged *All's Well* in a new theater—more or less Elizabethan—at the Shakespeare Festival at Stratford, Ontario. The audience was seated, sixteen rows deep (and with no spectator further from the stage than sixty-five feet), in an amphitheater that extended 220 degrees around the platform stage. Guthrie used vaguely Edwardian costumes for the court scenes, and vaguely contemporary costumes for the scenes in the military camp, and though he omitted the Clown he included most of the rest of the play in a production that aimed at high comedy. Irene Worth (Helena) and Alec Guinness (the King of France, in a wheelchair) were immensely popular, and their success in their roles helped to make the play a popular success. In 1959 Guthrie staged the play again, this time at Stratford-upon-Avon, with Zoe Caldwell as Helena and Edith Evans as the Countess. Again he used Edwardian settings and costumes, but this version was in passages more farcical than its predecessor. Apparently Guthrie had come to feel that the play, unable to stand by itself, needed broad comedy. Both Caldwell and Evans were widely acclaimed, though Kenneth Tynan, in a review in *The New Yorker,* reprinted in Tynan's *Curtains,* spoke of Dame Edith's "characteristic later manner—tranquillized benevolence cascading from a great height, like royalty opening a bazaar." Tynan spoke, too, of Guthrie's

> infuriating blend of insight and madness. On the one hand we have the great conductor, the master of visual orchestration . . . ; on the other hand we have this zany *Doppelgänger,* darting about with his pockets full of fireworks and giving the members of the orchestra hotfeet whenever genuine feeling threatens to impend . . . We get—among other things—a long scene, performed mainly in mime, wherein a deaf general reviews the French troops and exhorts them to battle through a faulty public-address system. Two hours of this can be fun; three and a quarter is too much. Lavache, the Countess of Roussillon's clown, who has some of the most haunting prose in Shakespeare, is entirely omitted; to cut a play, yet make what remains last longer than the whole, must argue, I suppose, a kind of dotty genius.

The farcical business to which Tynan refers (an amplification of 3.3, which in the original runs to eleven lines) is described in greater detail by Alan Brien, in a review in *The Spectator,* quoted in Price's *The Unfortunate Comedy*:

> The Duke of Florence, a goateed parody of General Smuts, dodders along the line with his officers falling over him every

time he halts to peer at a mysterious medal. When he turns suddenly his sword becomes entangled between the legs of his
staff officer. When he tries to make a speech from the top of an
observation tower, the microphone gets a fit of metallic
coughing. When he attempts to salute the flag, it slides slowly
down the post again. Meanwhile every man on the stage is
improvising some ludicrous pranks such as few amateur enter-
tainers at a Stag Night Sergeants' Mess could hope to equal.

Diana was played as a tart, her mother as a coarse and comic
creature; but Guthrie still sought to present Helena as a character in a world of high romance. Rousillon, at first a
neglected garden with withered leaves and broken branches,
was later, after Helena's return from Florence, transformed
into a handsome room of state.

In between Guthrie's 1953 and 1959 productions were
two other major productions of the play, Michael Benthall's
Old Vic production of 1953 in Edinburgh, and Noel
Willman's production at Stratford-upon-Avon in 1955. Benthall cut the play heavily, and treated it as a comic fairy tale:
Helena (Claire Bloom) was the sweet princess, and Bertram
(John Neville) was the dashing prince. The Countess, instead
of being aristocratic and sympathetic, was a crotchety semi-
comic and almost witchlike figure. Lafew, another older figure
who strikes most readers as highly sympathetic, was presented as a pompous dotard, and the sick King, attended by
a pair of comic physicians and by a friar who chanted every
time the King had a seizure, was burlesqued. As in many
productions that seek to make the young male lover acceptable, much of Bertram's nastiness was in effect attributed to
Parolles. Thus, when Helena requests a kiss from Bertram at
the end of 2.5, he was about to respond when Parolles hus-
tled him off. (This bit of stage business has very nearly become
standard operating procedure.) Despite the grossness of the
interpretation, the production was relatively successful, running for thirty-five performances.

In 1955, the same year that Ashland, Oregon, staged the play as a lighthearted comedy (repeated at Ashland in 1960), Noel Willman directed *All's Well* at Stratford-upon-Avon, presenting the play as a dark comedy with an earnest and even solemn Helena who seemed transported out of one of Shaw's plays. The last production of the 1950s, given a few months after Guthrie's second version, was John Houseman's version, produced at the American Shakespeare Festival at Stratford, Connecticut, in August 1959. Like Willman, Houseman directed the play as a dark comedy; Helena (Nancy Wickwire), somewhat older than the usual romantic heroine, had a tragic intensity. Houseman in *Full Dress* (one of his three autobiographies) says Wickwire "had simplicity, clarity, beauty, and a sense of passionate independence that made of Helena, instead of a lovesick ninny, a 'new woman' determined to get her man, almost in the Shavian manner." There was little farce; even in his affair with Diana, Bertram was presented seriously rather than sportively. In a review in *Saturday Review* Henry Hewes wrote:

> The most moving scene in the play . . . is the one in which a pretty Italian virgin must deceive the married Bertram into an assignation in which he will believe he is making love to her, but will really be bedding his wife. Barbara Berrie brings to this scene a touching full measure of emotion. Without it detracting from the speed or humor of the action, we are conscious that she is suffering the bittersweet pain of vicarious anticipation of a lovers' tryst and at the same time learning how perfidious the most noble of men can be when they are quail-hunting.

The 1960s were less interesting. In 1967, a year after Joseph Papp directed the play in New York, John Barton directed the Royal Shakespeare Company's production. Barton cut about 500 lines (including much of the Clown's satire), and minimized Bertram's nastiness. He managed to suggest that Bertram was genuinely in love with Helena (even if he didn't know it) but was unwilling to admit it to Parolles.

The first production of the 1970s, Michael Kahn's at the American Shakespeare Festival at Stratford, Connecticut, turned away from the dark view that John Houseman had offered eleven years earlier in the same theater, and sought instead to emphasize both fun and elegance. Parolles again was somewhat farcical (as usual he stuck himself with his own sword), and Helena, without sharp edges, was certainly no Shavian superwoman. Most of the reviewers were especially enthusiastic in their praise of Eva Le Gallienne, who played a warm, aristocratic Countess. Seven years later, in 1977, David Jones directed the play at Stratford, Ontario. His Helena (Martha Henry) was a woman overcome by passion; in the scene where she asks Bertram for a kiss, when Bertram lightly kissed her hand she seized him and held him in a prolonged kiss. Reviewers found the production Chekhovian—the usual autumnal setting—and at the end of the play it seemed that Bertram was not quite the cad we had thought, for the couple appeared to be heading toward a lifetime of happiness, since Bertram displayed no reservation in accepting Helena. Roger Warren, in *Shakespeare Survey* 31 (1978), gives a capsule description:

> The colors underlined the changing moods: scattered autumnal leaves and creepers for the opening Roussillon scenes, the sombre furs of a bitter winter campaign for Parolles' baiting and Bertram's growing up, touches of spring green, sunny light, and soft cream colors for the clothes of the Countess and Helena in the hopeful final scene.

In 1975 Jonathan Miller directed a surprisingly straight production in Elizabethan costume in Greenwich, near London; in 1978, in New York, Wilford Leach directed a genial but simplistic production using a set that resembled a miniature golf course. Fairy-tale-like structures (Rousillon Castle, Notre Dame, the Duomo), about five feet tall, were placed on a greensward with little hills, in an effort to evoke something of the sense of a medieval picture. There were no traces of a dark comedy; instead, all was farce and good feeling, with Helena a tomboy and Bertram—a bit petulant but finally likable—a mischievous stripling. A good deal of music was added, including serenades and, for soldiers, marching songs. Much fun was had by all (some at the expense of a doddering King), but it was hard to find Shakespeare's abrasive play in this production.

In the 1980s, three stage productions and one television production deserve comment here. The first, directed by Trevor Nunn in London in the 1981–82 season with the Royal Shakespeare Company, presented an almost uncut text. But the aim was not museum theater; Nunn used Edwardian costumes and a set that consisted of elegant metal arches with glass panels, suggesting a greenhouse. In the court scene this set, designed by John Gunter, served as a gymnasium in which young men practiced fencing; in Rousillon it served as the Countess's country house; in Florence, it served as a railway station and temporary housing for soldiers being posted to war, and also as a café in which the blindfolded Parolles was interrogated. This imaginative and adaptable set received uniformly favorable praise, and so did most other aspects of the production, including the ending, in which Bertram tentatively took Helena's offered hand, but did not kiss her. The production was brought to New York in 1983, perhaps because New York audiences had welcomed Nunn's spectacular productions of *Cats* and *Nicholas Nickleby,* but audiences at *All's Well* were (predictably?) relatively sparse.

A second production of the 1980s, a curious thing offered in 1986 in New York by the American Shakespeare Repertory, was subtitled *A Passion Play,* partly alluding to Helena's passionate love but partly alluding also to Christ's suffering on the cross. Incantatory repetitions, sometimes sung as madrigals, presumably were supposed to evoke a ritualistic world; actors were present on stage even when not acting, and when Helena confessed her love one of these actors—not Bertram—caressed her, thus (gratuitously) indicating her longings. Taken as an independent work, perhaps it had merit, but it was not Shakespeare's play.

In 1989, only eight years after Nunn's Royal Shakespeare Company production, Barry Kyle directed another RSC production of *All's Well,* this one using Jacobean (i.e., early-seventeenth-century) costumes. Several actors spoke with Scots accents, and in the final scene the King of France, wearing a tartan, appeared before a portrait of King James I (who had been James VI of Scotland). Moreover, the Countess, wearing an Elizabethan costume, stood before a portrait of Queen Elizabeth I. Kyle's explanation was that the play—whose date is uncertain, but may be any time between 1602 and 1605—reflects nostalgia for Elizabeth I, who died in 1603, and disillusionment with her successor, James VI of Scotland, who became James I of England. The production was handsome—including some handsome young men around the King, emphasizing the connection with the homosexual James I—but spectators found it hard to accept the director's unambiguous happy ending, marked by the embrace of Bertram, Helena, and the Countess. Readers will recall that Helena reads from Bertram's letter, in which he says he will marry her only when she can get his ring and is with child by him. She asserts that she has fulfilled the conditions, shows him the ring, and then says, "Will you be mine, now you are doubly won?" Bertram replies:

> If she, my liege, can make me know this clearly,
> I'll love her dearly, ever, ever dearly   (5.3.314–16)

This is hardly an unambiguously loving remark, and the second of these lines certainly is not Shakespeare at his most memorable.

The problem, in short—and this is largely why the play has been regarded as one of the "problem plays" rather than as one of the "romantic comedies"—is that at the end of *All's Well* the spectators do not feel that they are seeing the union of lovers who are made for each other and who have been kept apart by troublemakers or by misunderstandings. Rather, Bertram still seems churlish, or at least grudging, not at all what audiences want at the end of a romantic comedy. To many spectators at Kyle's production, the embrace was not consistent with what they had been seeing on the stage. (We will return to this issue of an audience's response to the ending, and will compare the response to that of a reader of the story.)

A few words should be added about the BBC television program of 1981, directed by Elijah Moshinsky, with Angela Dow as Helena (dignified yet deeply in love), Ian Charleson as Bertram (petulant but handsome and not without dignity), Donald Sinden as the King (unfortunately turned into a lecher), and Michael Hordern as Parolles (Hordern had already played a superb Parolles, sometimes farcical, sometimes bitingly realistic, in Michael Benthall's production of 1953–54). The settings remind one of Dutch paintings, say the interiors of Vermeer, and considerable use is made of mirrors, giving the play an appropriate sense of a puzzling reality. G. K. Hunter, in a talk reprinted in J. C. Bulman and H. R. Coursen, *Shakespeare on Television* (1988), comments on the extremely effective use of the television camera.

> On the stage, as the tension builds up through the intrigue, the reservation of Helena for a miraculous, knot-cutting entry places an intolerable burden on that entry: can one simple step

through the door cause all this? *We* see her as she is and not as
she is received. The television production solved the problem,
brilliantly I thought, by concealing the entry. The family and
its supporters have lined up imperceptibly, facing the door
through which Diana is being taken to prison. At the door she
stops and pleads her final stay of execution. . . . As the cast
looks through the door music begins to play. "Behold the
meaning," says Diana. But the camera does not allow us to
behold: Instead it does what the camera does best—it shows us
a set of mouths and eyes. As it tracks along the line we are
made witness to a series of inner sunrises, as face after face
responds to the miracle and lights up with understanding and
relief. I confess to finding it a very moving experience.

The last decade of the twentieth century saw several
important productions. In 1992 Peter Hall directed the Royal
Shakespeare Company in an almost uncut text at the Swan
Theatre, with Sophie Thompson as Helena, Barbara Jefford
as the Countess, Paul Venables as Bertram, and Richard
Johnson as the King. Robert Smallwood in *Shakespeare
Quarterly* 44 (1993), describes the set Hall used:

His production, designed by John Gunter, presented a full text
in mid-seventeenth-century costume, the Swan stage bare
except for the sloping back wall, a misted mirror with little
hinged openings that displayed models of a pretty little
château for the Rossillion scenes and of the Duomo for those
set in Florence; for the French court scenes a Sun King
emblem was suspended over the stage. (356)

Alan C. Dessen, in an extremely informative review in *Shakespeare Bulletin* 11:2 (Spring 1993): 34–37, calls attention to
Hall's use of music at three especially significant points when
Helena is connected with supernatural powers. In the first of
these, Helena tells the Countess of the medicine:

> There's something in't
> More than my father's skill, which was the great'st
> Of his profession, that his good receipt
> Shall for my legacy be sanctified
> By th' luckiest stars in heaven; and would your honor
> But give me leave to try success, I'd venture
> The well-lost life of mine on his Grace's cure
> By such a day, an hour.   (1.3.244–51)

The second passage that evoked music to heighten Helena's powers was at the end of 2.1, when Helena responded to the King's "Within what space / Hops't thou my cure?" (161–62) In answering, she spoke in a prophetic manner, a manner well suited to the lines with their allusions to classical mythology ("the horses of the sun," "moist Hesperus"). The third use of music, again with supernatural overtones, was at her entrance in the final scene, when Diana says,

> So there's my riddle: one that's dead is quick.
> And now behold the meaning.

> *Enter Helena and Widow.*

> *King.*   Is there no exorcist
> Beguiles the truer office of mine eyes?
> Is't real that I see?   (5.3.303–6)

"The key to any production of *All's Well*," Dessen rightly says, "is the problematic ending where many options are available." He goes on to describe Hall's choice:

At the climax, Helena entered dressed in a white wedding gown, pregnant, and accompanied by the distinctive music, and, with her back to the audience, knelt, with Bertram by her side. They faced each other but did not kiss. After reading and then tearing the letter, she paused and made her final move to the countess; mother, son, and daughter-in-law then joined

> hands and formed a circle, the final image for the playgoer,
> with the king in a spotlight slightly downstage to deliver the
> Epilogue (and with Lafew-Parolles further downstage in a
> decidedly unemphatic position for their final exchange). The
> circle of three provided . . . physical contact . . . but the absence
> of a kiss forestalled any upbeat ending. [Peter Hall] therefore
> provided little sense of romantic climax or love fulfilled or
> Helena as victor. (37)

In short, despite the the title of the play, although *something*
was well, *all* was not yet well. In keeping with the cautious
or even unromantic (which is not by any means to say antiro-
mantic) view, the clown, Lavatch, was in the tradition of the
bitter fool, not the sweet fool. And speaking of comic material, spectators found the humiliation of Parolles in 4.3 dis-
tressing rather than amusing.

If Peter Hall never let the audience regard the play as a
romantic comedy, Richard Jones, director of the 1993 New
York Shakespeare Festival production in the Delacorte Theater in Central Park, similarly kept romance in check. A
child dressed in a Halloween skeleton costume and holding
a scythe occasionally appeared. For instance at the start,
where the sick King of France was on a table, this small representative of death stood nearby, and he was present, too,
when Helena, waiting to complete the bed trick, was lying
on the same table, and yet again when the French army
returned in victory. But this is not to say that the production
was macabre: summer productions in a theater in the park
inevitably have a romantic air.

In 1997 Irina Brook directed the Oxford Stage Company
(at the Oxford Playhouse) in a modern-dress version, set in
Africa, with black and white actors. When not onstage, the
actors sat at the edges of the stage, sometimes playing drums
or ringing bells. When Helena cured the King, she did not do
so offstage, unseen by her fellows; rather, this Helena cured
the King by means of a witch doctor's dance that was pro-

jected onto a screen watched by the other actors. The Epilogue was spoken by a witch doctor, not by the King, though it was not clear what was gained thereby.

All's Well got off to a good start in the twenty-first century with Richard Monette's production in 2002 at Stratford, Ontario (Lucy Peacock was an attractive Helena). The play was amusing, not disquieting, and it followed the pattern of romantic comedy in moving from a somber beginning to a happy ending (early scenes were black, gray, silver; later scenes were washed in orange, with soldiers wearing red). The darker aspects of the play were not ignored, but finally the play was treated as a romance.

At the time of this writing (March 2005), the strongest production of this young century has been the one (2003–4) by the Royal Shakespeare Company, directed by Gregory Doran, which opened at the Swan Theatre in Stratford and moved to the Gielgud Theatre in London. It began with a wintry setting (bare trees on a backdrop and on translucent screens), though later scenes gave an occasional hint of spring in the choice of flowers. The costumes were exuberant—at least two reviewers were reminded of *The Three Musketeers*—and Helena (Claudia Bailey) and Bertram (James Glover) were highly effective but the Countess (the incomparable Judi Dench) inevitably stole the show. In discussing Peter Hall's 1992 production I quoted at some length a reviewer's comments about the end; here is another reviewer, Russell Jackson, commenting in *Shakespeare Quarterly* 55 (2004): 195, on the end of Doran's production:

> Suddenly, as Diana, resisting arrest, pronounced her riddle, silence fell. To a mysterious sustained chord from the offstage band, Helena entered, veiled, from the left-hand gangway. (This was the direction from which she had emerged out of the shadows to bring her cure to the king.) She did not remove her veil until she reached the center of the stage. The moment of magic and stillness carried into the next speeches of the dia-

logue, and when she claimed "this is done," she placed
Bertram's hand on her abdomen. "If she, my liege, can make
me know this clearly" was spoken by Bertram on his knees,
head bowed. . . . The play's modulation out of wonderment
came with Lafeu's request for Parolles's handkerchief and his
refusal of the filthy rag when it was offered. There was [a]
moment of comic consternation among his courtiers when the
king invited Diana to choose a husband, and a general exit followed "All yet *seems* well. . . ." But the king and Countess
moved upstage and lingered to look back at Bertram and
Helena, who remained facing each other from opposite sides
of the stage as the lights faded. The epilogue was not spoken.

The ending of this production was implicitly optimistic—
one felt that Bertram was on his way to becoming a suitable
husband—but it lacked the evident joy that marks such
romantic comedies as *A Midsummer Night's Dream, As You
Like It,* and *Much Ado about Nothing.* We return, then, to the
question of the nature of the play: Is *All's Well* a "problem
play," and if so, what is the problem?

To the present writer, it seems that the greatest problem is
this: Shakespeare took what essentially are motifs from folk
tales—the prodigal son, the clever woman, the bed trick—
and from these narratives made a play. When instead of
reading short plots we hear the words and see them performed at length by actors, do we respond to them in the
same way? This is not a mere academic question, as any
director will assure us. After all, directors cannot merely
instruct actors to read the lines and then exit; they must
decide on costumes, sets, gestures, intonations, and all of
these decisions will shape the production and the audience's
response.

Consider the ending of the Boccaccio story (mid four-
teenth century) as Shakespeare read it, in the third edition
(1575) of William Painter's *The Palace of Pleasure.* (The
full text is given earlier in this edition of the play.)

The Countess . . . rehearsed unto them in order all that which
had been done, and the whole discourse thereof. For which
cause the Count, knowing the things she had spoken to be true
(and perceiving her constant mind and good wit . . . and to
please his subjects and the ladies that made suit unto him to
accept her from that time forth as his lawful wife and to honor
her . . .) embraced and kissed her, acknowledging her again for
his lawful wife. And after he had appareled her according to
her estate, to the great pleasure and contentation of those that
were there and of all his other friends, not only that day but
many others, he kept great cheer, and from that time forth he
loved and honored her as his dear spouse and wife.

Notice that in Boccaccio, the Count, a cad by our standards,
apparently is a thoroughly acceptable figure. He had be-
haved badly (again by our standards), and now, perceiving
that the woman is telling the truth, and perceiving her "constant mind and good wit," *and* "to please his subjects," he
accepts his wife, and we are told that "from that time forth
he loved and honored her." Good enough; in this fairy-tale
world we accept the narrator's statement. This sort of per-
functory assurance apparently is (or was) acceptable to
readers of a short narrative, but, as the stage history of *All's
Well That Ends Well* indicates, audiences in the theater are
not so willing to find the happy ending fully satisfactory.

When Jon Jory directed *All's Well* at the Oregon Shakespeare Festival in 1975, he shrewdly suggested that it ought
to be "played in repertory with itself." An audience thus
might see, on one night, "a dark production, emphasizing its
melancholy pronouncements on age, its many portraits of
betrayal both of others and of self, and the callow villanies
of its young hero juxtaposed with the shrewd machina-
tions of its heroine." On another night the audience might
see "the tomfoolery . . . of a youth who learns slowly but
well, and a man who when he finds himself a fool, makes it
his profession and is even self-forgiving." (Quoted by Alan

C. Dessen, in *Shakespeare Quarterly* 27 [1976].) All of this (and more) is in the play; whether a single production can catch it remains to be seen.

Bibliographic note: Two books are devoted to the stage history of *All's Well*: 1) Joseph G. Price, *The Unfortunate Comedy: A Study of "All's Well That Ends Well" and Its Critics* (Toronto: University of Toronto Press, 1968); 2) J. L. Styan, *"All's Well That Ends Well": Shakespeare in Performance* (Manchester: Manchester University Press, 1984). Price's book is a thorough study, chronologically organized, of the play on the stage up to 1964; Styan's much shorter book discusses in some detail the ways in which various scenes were handled in recent productions.

Reviews of modern productions can be found in *Shakespeare Bulletin, Shakespearean Criticism,* and *Shakespeare Survey*.

Suggested References

The number of possible references is vast and grows alarmingly. (The *Shakespeare Quarterly* devotes one issue each year to a list of the previous year's work, and *Shakespeare Survey*—an annual publication—includes a substantial review of biographical, critical, and textual studies, as well as a survey of performances.) The vast bibliography is best approached through James Harner, *The World Shakespeare Bibliography on CD-Rom: 1900–Present.* The first release, in 1996, included more than 12,000 annotated items from 1990–93, plus references to several thousand book reviews, productions, films, and audio recordings. The plan is to update the publication annually, moving forward one year and backward three years. Thus, the second issue (1997), with 24,700 entries, and another 35,000 or so references to reviews, newspaper pieces, and so on, covered 1987–94.

For guidance to the immense amount that has been written, consult Larry S. Champion, *The Essential Shakespeare: An Annotated Bibliography of Major Modern Studies,* 2nd ed. (1993), which comments briefly on 1,800 publications.

Though no works are indispensable, those listed below have been found especially helpful. The arrangement is as follows:

1. Shakespeare's Times
2. Shakespeare's Life
3. Shakespeare's Theater
4. Shakespeare on Stage and Screen
5. Miscellaneous Reference Works
6. Shakespeare's Plays: General Studies
7. The Comedies
8. The Romances

The titles in the first five sections are accompanied by brief explanatory annotations.

1. Shakespeare's Times

Andrews, John F., ed. *William Shakespeare: His World, His Work, His Influence,* 3 vols. (1985). Sixty articles, dealing not only with such subjects as "The State," "The Church," "Law," "Science, Magic, and Folklore," but also with the plays and poems themselves and Shakespeare's influence (e.g., translations, films, reputation).

Byrne, Muriel St. Clare. *Elizabethan Life in Town and Country* (8th ed., 1970). Chapters on manners, beliefs, education, etc., with illustrations.

Dollimore, John, and Alan Sinfield, eds. *Political Shakespeare: New Essays in Cultural Materialism* (1985). Essays on such topics as the subordination of women and colonialism, presented in connection with some of Shakespeare's plays.

Greenblatt, Stephen. *Representing the English Renaissance* (1988). New Historicist essays, especially on connections between political and aesthetic matters, statecraft and stagecraft.

Joseph, B. L. *Shakespeare's Eden: the Commonwealth of England 1558–1629* (1971). An account of the social, political, economic, and cultural life of England.

Kernan, Alvin. *Shakespeare, the King's Playwright: Theater in the Stuart Court 1603–1613* (1995). The social setting and the politics of the court of James I, in relation to *Hamlet, Measure for Measure, Macbeth, King Lear, Antony and Cleopatra, Coriolanus,* and *The Tempest.*

Montrose, Louis. *The Purpose of Playing: Shakespeare and the Cultural Politics of the Elizabethan Theatre* (1996). A poststructuralist view, discussing the professional theater "within the ideological and material frameworks of Elizabethan culture and society," with an extended analysis of *A Midsummer Night's Dream.*

Mullaney, Steven. *The Place of the Stage: License, Play, and Power in Renaissance England* (1988). New Historicist analysis, arguing that popular drama became a cultural institution "only by . . . taking up a place on the margins of society."

Schoenbaum, S. *Shakespeare: The Globe and the World* (1979). A readable, abundantly illustrated introductory book on the world of the Elizabethans.

Shakespeare's England, 2 vols. (1916). A large collection of scholarly essays on a wide variety of topics, e.g., astrology, costume, gardening, horsemanship, with special attention to Shakespeare's references to these topics.

2. Shakespeare's Life

Andrews, John F., ed. *William Shakespeare: His World, His Work, His Influence,* 3 vols. (1985). See the description above.

Bentley, Gerald E. *Shakespeare: A Biographical Handbook* (1961). The facts about Shakespeare, with virtually no conjecture intermingled.

Chambers, E. K. *William Shakespeare: A Study of Facts and Problems,* 2 vols. (1930). The fullest collection of data.

Fraser, Russell. *Young Shakespeare* (1988). A highly readable account that simultaneously considers Shakespeare's life and Shakespeare's art.

———. *Shakespeare: The Later Years* (1992).

Schoenbaum, S. *Shakespeare's Lives* (1970). A review of the evidence and an examination of many biographies, including those of Baconians and other heretics.

———. *William Shakespeare: A Compact Documentary Life* (1977). An abbreviated version, in a smaller format, of the next title. The compact version reproduces some fifty documents in reduced form. A readable presentation of all that the documents tell us about Shakespeare.

———. *William Shakespeare: A Documentary Life* (1975). A large-format book setting forth the biography with facsimiles of more than two hundred documents, and with transcriptions and commentaries.

3. Shakespeare's Theater

Astington, John H., ed. *The Development of Shakespeare's Theater* (1992). Eight specialized essays on theatrical companies, playing spaces, and performance.

Beckerman, Bernard. *Shakespeare at the Globe, 1599–1609* (1962). On the playhouse and on Elizabethan dramaturgy, acting, and staging.

Bentley, Gerald E. *The Profession of Dramatist in Shakespeare's Time* (1971). An account of the dramatist's status in the Elizabethan period.

———. *The Profession of Player in Shakespeare's Time, 1590–1642* (1984). An account of the status of members of London companies (sharers, hired men, apprentices, managers) and a discussion of conditions when they toured.

Berry, Herbert. *Shakespeare's Playhouses* (1987). Usefully emphasizes how little we know about the construction of Elizabethan theaters.

Brown, John Russell. *Shakespeare's Plays in Performance* (1966). A speculative and practical analysis relevant to all of the plays, but with emphasis on *The Merchant of Venice*, *Richard II*, *Hamlet*, *Romeo and Juliet*, and *Twelfth Night*.

———. *William Shakespeare: Writing for Performance* (1996). A discussion aimed at helping readers to develop theatrically conscious habits of reading.

Chambers, E. K. *The Elizabethan Stage*, 4 vols. (1945). A major reference work on theaters, theatrical companies, and staging at court.

Cook, Ann Jennalie. *The Privileged Playgoers of Shakespeare's London, 1576–1642* (1981). Sees Shakespeare's audience as wealthier, more middle-class, and more intellectual than Harbage (below) does.

Dessen, Alan C. *Elizabethan Drama and the Viewer's Eye* (1977). On how certain scenes may have looked to spectators in an Elizabethan theater.

Gurr, Andrew. *Playgoing in Shakespeare's London* (1987). Something of a middle ground between Cook (above) and Harbage (below).

———. *The Shakespearean Stage, 1579–1642* (3rd ed., 1992). On the acting companies, the actors, the playhouses, the stages, and the audiences.

———, and Mariko Ichikawa. *Staging in Shakespeare's Theatres* (2000). Like Alan C. Dessen's book, cited above, a careful analysis of what the Elizabethans saw on the stage.

Harbage, Alfred. *Shakespeare's Audience* (1941). A study of the size and nature of the theatrical public, emphasizing the representativeness of its working class and middle-class audience.

Hodges, C. Walter. *The Globe Restored* (1968). A conjectural restoration, with lucid drawings.

Hosley, Richard. "The Playhouses," in *The Revels History of Drama in English*, vol. 3, general editors Clifford Leech and T. W. Craik (1975). An essay of a hundred pages on the physical aspects of the playhouses.

Howard, Jane E. "Crossdressing, the Theatre, and Gender Struggle in Early Modern England," *Shakespeare Quarterly* 39 (1988): 418–40. Judicious comments on the effects of boys playing female roles.

Orrell, John. *The Human Stage: English Theatre Design, 1567–1640* (1988). Argues that the public, private, and court playhouses are less indebted to popular structures (e.g., innyards and bear-baiting pits) than to banqueting halls and to Renaissance conceptions of Roman amphitheaters.

Slater, Ann Pasternak. *Shakespeare the Director* (1982). An analysis of theatrical effects (e.g., kissing, kneeling) in stage directions and dialogue.

Styan, J. L. *Shakespeare's Stagecraft* (1967). An introduction to Shakespeare's visual and aural stagecraft, with chapters on such topics as acting conventions, stage groupings, and speech.

Thompson, Peter. *Shakespeare's Professional Career* (1992). An examination of patronage and related theatrical conditions.

———. *Shakespeare's Theatre* (1983). A discussion of how plays were staged in Shakespeare's time.

4. Shakespeare on Stage and Screen

Bate, Jonathan, and Russell Jackson, eds. *Shakespeare: An Illustrated Stage History* (1996). Highly readable essays on stage productions from the Renaissance to the present.

Berry, Ralph. *Changing Styles in Shakespeare* (1981). Discusses productions of six plays (*Coriolanus*, *Hamlet*, *Henry V*, *Measure for Measure*, *The Tempest*, and *Twelfth Night*) on the English stage, chiefly 1950–1980.

———. *On Directing Shakespeare: Interviews with Contemporary Directors* (1989). An enlarged edition of a book first published in 1977, this version includes the seven interviews from the early 1970s and adds five interviews conducted in 1988.

Brockbank, Philip, ed. *Players of Shakespeare: Essays in Shakespearean Performance* (1985). Comments by twelve actors, reporting their experiences with roles. See also the entry for Russell Jackson (below).

Bulman, J. C., and H. R. Coursen, eds. *Shakespeare on Television* (1988). An anthology of general and theoretical essays, essays on individual productions, and shorter reviews, with a bibliography and a videography listing cassettes that may be rented.

Coursen, H. P. *Watching Shakespeare on Television* (1993).

Analyses not only of TV versions but also of films and videotapes of stage presentations that are shown on television.

Davies, Anthony, and Stanley Wells, eds. *Shakespeare and the Moving Image: The Plays on Film and Television* (1994). General essays (e.g., on the comedies) as well as essays devoted entirely to *Hamlet, King Lear*, and *Macbeth.*

Dawson, Anthony B. *Watching Shakespeare: A Playgoer's Guide* (1988). About half of the plays are discussed, chiefly in terms of decisions that actors and directors make in putting the works onto the stage.

Dessen, Alan C. *Elizabethan Stage Conventions and Modern Interpretations* (1984). On interpreting conventions such as the representation of light and darkness and stage violence (duels, battles).

Donaldson, Peter. *Shakespearean Films/Shakespearean Directors* (1990). Postmodernist analyses, drawing on Freudianism, Feminism, Deconstruction, and Queer Theory.

Jackson, Russell, and Robert Smallwood, eds. *Players of Shakespeare 2: Further Essays in Shakespearean Performance by Players with the Royal Shakespeare Company* (1988). Fourteen actors discuss their roles in productions between 1982 and 1987.

———. *Players of Shakespeare 3: Further Essays in Shakespearean Performance by Players with the Royal Shakespeare Company* (1993). Comments by thirteen performers.

Jorgens, Jack. *Shakespeare on Film* (1977). Fairly detailed studies of eighteen films, preceded by an introductory chapter addressing such issues as music, and whether to "open" the play by including scenes of landscape.

Kennedy, Dennis. *Looking at Shakespeare: A Visual History of Twentieth-Century Performance* (1993). Lucid descriptions (with 170 photographs) of European, British, and American performances.

Leiter, Samuel L. *Shakespeare Around the Globe: A Guide to Notable Postwar Revivals* (1986). For each play there are about two pages of introductory comments, then discussions (about five hundred words per production) of ten or so productions, and finally bibliographic references.

McMurty, Jo. *Shakespeare Films in the Classroom* (1994). Useful evaluations of the chief films most likely to be shown in undergraduate courses.

Rothwell, Kenneth, and Annabelle Henkin Melzer. *Shakespeare on Screen: An International Filmography and Videography* (1990). A reference guide to several hundred films and videos produced between 1899 and 1989, including spinoffs such as musicals and dance versions.

Smallwood, Robert. *Players of Shakespeare 4* (1998). Like the volumes by Brockbank and Jackson, listed above, contains remarks by contemporary performers.

Sprague, Arthur Colby. *Shakespeare and the Actors* (1944). Detailed discussions of stage business (gestures, etc.) over the years.

Willis, Susan. *The BBC Shakespeare Plays: Making the Televised Canon* (1991). A history of the series, with interviews and production diaries for some plays.

5. Miscellaneous Reference Works

Abbott, E. A. *A Shakespearean Grammar* (new edition, 1877). An examination of differences between Elizabethan and modern grammar.

Allen, Michael J. B., and Kenneth Muir, eds. *Shakespeare's Plays in Quarto* (1981). One volume containing facsimiles of the plays issued in small format before they were collected in the First Folio of 1623.

Blake, Norman. *Shakespeare's Language: An Introduction* (1983). On vocabulary, parts of speech, and word order.

Bullough, Geoffrey. *Narrative and Dramatic Sources of Shakespeare*, 8 vols. (1957–75). A collection of many of the books Shakespeare drew on, with judicious comments.

Campbell, Oscar James, and Edward G. Quinn, eds. *The Reader's Encyclopedia of Shakespeare* (1966). Old, and in some ways superseded by Michael Dobson's *Oxford Companion* (see below), but still highly valuable.

Cercignani, Fausto. *Shakespeare's Works and Elizabethan Pronunciation* (1981). Considered the best work on the topic, but remains controversial.

Champion, Larry S. *The Essential Shakespeare: An Annotated Bibliography of Major Modern Studies* (2nd ed., 1993). An invaluable guide to 1,800 writings about Shakespeare.

Dent, R. W. *Shakespeare's Proverbial Language: An Index* (1981). An index of proverbs, with an introduction concerning a form Shakespeare frequently drew on.

Dobson, Michael, ed. *The Oxford Companion to Shakespeare* (2001). Probably the single most useful reference work for information (arranged alphabetically) about Shakespeare and his works.

Greg, W. W. *The Shakespeare First Folio* (1955). A detailed yet readable history of the first collection (1623) of Shakespeare's plays.

Harner, James. *The World Shakespeare Bibliography*. See headnote to Suggested References.

Hosley, Richard. *Shakespeare's Holinshed* (1968). Valuable presentation of one of Shakespeare's major sources.

Kökeritz, Helge. *Shakespeare's Names* (1959). A guide to pronouncing some 1,800 names appearing in Shakespeare.

———. *Shakespeare's Pronunciation* (1953). Contains much information about puns and rhymes, but see Cercignani (above).

Muir, Kenneth. *The Sources of Shakespeare's Plays* (1978). An account of Shakespeare's use of his reading. It covers all the plays, in chronological order.

Miriam Joseph, Sister. *Shakespeare's Use of the Arts of Language* (1947). A study of Shakespeare's use of rhetorical devices, reprinted in part as *Rhetoric in Shakespeare's Time* (1962).

The Norton Facsimile: The First Folio of Shakespeare's Plays (1968). A handsome and accurate facsimile of the first collection (1623) of Shakespeare's plays, with a valuable introduction by Charlton Hinman.

Onions, C. T. *A Shakespeare Glossary*, rev. and enlarged by R. D. Eagleson (1986). Definitions of words (or senses of words) now obsolete.

Partridge, Eric. *Shakespeare's Bawdy*, rev. ed. (1955). Relatively brief dictionary of bawdy words; useful, but see Williams, below.

Shakespeare Quarterly. See headnote to Suggested References.

Shakespeare Survey. See headnote to Suggested References.

Spevack, Marvin. *The Harvard Concordance to Shakespeare* (1973). An index to Shakespeare's words.

Vickers, Brian. *Appropriating Shakespeare: Contemporary Critical Quarrels* (1993). A survey—chiefly hostile—of recent schools of criticism.

Wells, Stanley, ed. *Shakespeare: A Bibliographical Guide* (new edition, 1990). Nineteen chapters (some devoted to single plays, others devoted to groups of related plays) on recent scholarship on the life and all of the works.

Williams, Gordon. *A Dictionary of Sexual Language and Imagery in Shakespearean and Stuart Literature*, 3 vols. (1994). Extended discussions of words and passages; much fuller than Partridge, cited above.

6. Shakespeare's Plays: General Studies

Bamber, Linda. *Comic Women, Tragic Men: A Study of Gender and Genre in Shakespeare* (1982).

Barnet, Sylvan. *A Short Guide to Shakespeare* (1974).

Callaghan, Dympna, Lorraine Helms, and Jyotsna Singh. *The Weyward Sisters: Shakespeare and Feminist Politics* (1994).

Clemen, Wolfgang H. *The Development of Shakespeare's Imagery* (1951).

Cook, Ann Jennalie. *Making a Match: Courtship in Shakespeare and His Society* (1991).

Dollimore, Jonathan, and Alan Sinfield, eds. *Political Shakespeare: New Essays in Cultural Materialism* (1985).

Dusinberre, Juliet. *Shakespeare and the Nature of Women* (1975).

Granville-Barker, Harley. *Prefaces to Shakespeare*, 2 vols. (1946–47; volume 1 contains essays on *Hamlet, King Lear, Merchant of Venice, Antony and Cleopatra,* and *Cymbeline*; volume 2 contains essays on *Othello, Coriolanus, Julius Caesar, Romeo and Juliet, Love's Labor's Lost*).

———. *More Prefaces to Shakespeare* (1974; essays on *Twelfth Night, A Midsummer Night's Dream, The Winter's Tale, Macbeth*).

Harbage, Alfred. *William Shakespeare: A Reader's Guide* (1963).

Howard, Jean E. *Shakespeare's Art of Orchestration: Stage Technique and Audience Response* (1984).

Jones, Emrys. *Scenic Form in Shakespeare* (1971).

Lenz, Carolyn Ruth Swift, Gayle Greene, and Carol Thomas Neely, eds. *The Woman's Part: Feminist Criticism of Shakespeare* (1980).

Novy, Marianne. *Love's Argument: Gender Relations in Shakespeare* (1984).

Rose, Mark. *Shakespearean Design* (1972).

Scragg, Leah. *Discovering Shakespeare's Meaning* (1994).

———. *Shakespeare's "Mouldy Tales": Recurrent Plot Motifs in Shakespearean Drama* (1992).

Traub, Valerie. *Desire and Anxiety: Circulations of Sexuality in Shakespearean Drama* (1992).

Traversi, D. A. *An Approach to Shakespeare,* 2 vols. (3rd rev. ed, 1968–69).

Vickers, Brian. *The Artistry of Shakespeare's Prose* (1968).

Wells, Stanley. *Shakespeare: A Dramatic Life* (1994).

Wright, George T. *Shakespeare's Metrical Art* (1988).

7. The Comedies

Barber, C. L. *Shakespeare's Festive Comedy* (1959; discusses *Love's Labor's Lost, A Midsummer Night's Dream, The Merchant of Venice, As You Like It, Twelfth Night*).

Barton, Anne. *The Names of Comedy* (1990).

Berry, Ralph. *Shakespeare's Comedy: Explorations in Form* (1972).

Bradbury, Malcolm, and David Palmer, eds. *Shakespearean Comedy* (1972).

Bryant, J. A., Jr. *Shakespeare and the Uses of Comedy* (1986).

Carroll, William. *The Metamorphoses of Shakespearean Comedy* (1985).

Champion, Larry S. *The Evolution of Shakespeare's Comedy* (1970).

Evans, Bertrand. *Shakespeare's Comedies* (1960).

Frye, Northrop. *Shakespearean Comedy and Romance* (1965).

Leggatt, Alexander. *Shakespeare's Comedy of Love* (1974).

Miola, Robert S. *Shakespeare and Classical Comedy: The Influence of Plautus and Terence* (1994).

Nevo, Ruth. *Comic Transformations in Shakespeare* (1980).

Ornstein, Robert. *Shakespeare's Comedies: From Roman Farce to Romantic Mystery* (1986).

Richman, David. *Laughter, Pain, and Wonder: Shakespeare's Comedies and the Audience in the Theater* (1990).

Salingar, Leo. *Shakespeare and the Traditions of Comedy* (1974).

Slights, Camille Wells. *Shakespeare's Comic Commonwealths* (1993).

Waller, Gary, ed. *Shakespeare's Comedies* (1991).

Westlund, Joseph. *Shakespeare's Reparative Comedies: A Psychoanalytic View of the Middle Plays* (1984).

Williamson, Marilyn. *The Patriarchy of Shakespeare's Comedies* (1986).

8. The Romances (*Pericles, Cymbeline, The Winter's Tale, The Tempest, The Two Noble Kinsmen*)

Adams, Robert M. *Shakespeare: The Four Romances* (1989).
Felperin, Howard. *Shakespearean Romance* (1972).
Frye, Northrop. *A Natural Perspective: The Development of Shakespearean Comedy and Romance* (1965).
Mowat, Barbara. *The Dramaturgy of Shakespeare's Romances* (1976).
Warren, Roger. *Staging Shakespeare's Late Plays* (1990).
Young, David. *The Heart's Forest: A Study of Shakespeare's Pastoral Plays* (1972).

9. The Tragedies

Bradley, A. C. *Shakespearean Tragedy* (1904).
Brooke, Nicholas. *Shakespeare's Early Tragedies* (1968).
Champion, Larry S. *Shakespeare's Tragic Perspective* (1976).
Drakakis, John, ed. *Shakespearean Tragedy* (1992).
Evans, Bertrand. *Shakespeare's Tragic Practice* (1979).
Everett, Barbara. *Young Hamlet: Essays on Shakespeare's Tragedies* (1989).
Foakes, R. A. *Hamlet versus Lear: Cultural Politics and Shakespeare's Art* (1993).
Frye, Northrop. *Fools of Time: Studies in Shakespearean Tragedy* (1967).
Harbage, Alfred, ed. *Shakespeare: The Tragedies* (1964).
Mack, Maynard. *Everybody's Shakespeare: Reflections Chiefly on the Tragedies* (1993).
McAlindon, T. *Shakespeare's Tragic Cosmos* (1991).
Miola, Robert S. *Shakespeare and Classical Tragedy: The Influence of Seneca* (1992).
———. *Shakespeare's Rome* (1983).
Nevo, Ruth. *Tragic Form in Shakespeare* (1972).
Rackin, Phyllis. *Shakespeare's Tragedies* (1978).

Rose, Mark, ed. *Shakespeare's Early Tragedies: A Collection of Critical Essays* (1995).

Rosen, William. *Shakespeare and the Craft of Tragedy* (1960).

Snyder, Susan. *The Comic Matrix of Shakespeare's Tragedies* (1979).

Wofford, Susanne. *Shakespeare's Late Tragedies: A Collection of Critical Essays* (1996).

Young, David. *The Action to the Word: Structure and Style in Shakespearean Tragedy* (1990).

———. *Shakespeare's Middle Tragedies: A Collection of Critical Essays* (1993).

10. The Histories

Blanpied, John W. *Time and the Artist in Shakespeare's English Histories* (1983).

Campbell, Lily B. *Shakespeare's "Histories": Mirrors of Elizabethan Policy* (1947).

Champion, Larry S. *Perspective in Shakespeare's English Histories* (1980).

Grene, Nicholas. *Shakespeare's Serial History Plays* (2002).

Hodgdon, Barbara. *The End Crowns All: Closure and Contradiction in Shakespeare's History* (1991).

Holderness, Graham. *Shakespeare Recycled: The Making of Historical Drama* (1992).

———, ed. *Shakespeare's History Plays: "Richard II" to "Henry V"* (1992).

Jones, Robert C. *Those Valiant Dead: Reviving the Past in Shakespeare's Histories* (1991).

Knowles, Ronald. *Shakespeare's Arguments with History* (2002).

Leggatt, Alexander. *Shakespeare's Political Drama: The History Plays and the Roman Plays* (1988).

Levine, Nina S. *Women's Matters: Politics, Gender, and Nation in Shakespeare's Early History Plays* (1998).

Ornstein, Robert. *A Kingdom for a Stage: The Achievement of Shakespeare's History Plays* (1972).

Pugliatti, Paola. *Shakespeare the Historian* (1996).

Rackin, Phyllis. *Stages of History: Shakespeare's English Chronicles* (1990).

Reese, Max Meredith. *The Cease of Majesty: A Study of Shakespeare's History Plays* (1961).

Ribner, Irving. *The English History Play in the Age of Shakespeare* (rev. ed., 1965).

Saccio, Peter. *Shakespeare's English Kings* (2nd ed., 1999).

Spiekerman, Tim. *Shakespeare's Political Realism* (2001).

Tillyard, E.M.W. *Shakespeare's History Plays* (1944).

Velz, John W., ed. *Shakespeare's English Histories: A Quest for Form and Genre* (1996).

11. *All's Well That Ends Well*

Especially useful modern editions of *All's Well That Ends Well* have been prepared by G. K. Hunter (1959), Susan Snyder (1993), and Russell Fraser (updated edition, 2003).

Shakespearean Criticism, a massive series, reprints essays from many sources—including scholarly journals, books, and (for reviews of productions) newspapers. Volumes 7, 26, 38, 55, 63, 75, and 86 include numerous essays on all aspects of the play.

For readings concerned with stage and television productions, see the Bibliographic Note above, following *All's Well That Ends Well* on Stage and Screen, and see the material, also above, in Section 4 of this list of Suggested References.

For the play in the context of Shakespeare's other comedies, see above, Section 7.

Brooke, Nicholas. *"All's Well That Ends Well."* *Shakespeare Survey* 30 (1977): 73–84.

Cole, Howard C. *The "All's Well" Story from Boccaccio to Shakespeare* (1981).

Dash, Irene. *Women's Worlds in Shakespeare's Plays* (1997).

Dessen, Alan C. *Shakespeare and the Late Moral Plays* (1986).

Donaldson, Ian. *"All's Well That Ends Well:* Shakespeare's Play of Errors." *Essays in Criticism* 27 (1977): 34–55.

Erickson, Peter. *Rewriting Shakespeare, Rewriting Ourselves* (1991).

Findlay, Alison. *A Feminist Perspective on Renaissance Drama* (1999).

Frye, Northrop. *The Myth of Deliverance* (1982).

Haley, David. *Shakespeare's Courtly Mirror: Reflexivity and Prudence in "All's Well That Ends Well"* (1993).

Hodgdon, Barbara. "The Making of Virgins and Mothers: Sexual Signs, Substitute Scenes, and Doubled Presences in *All's Well That Ends Well." Philological Quarterly* 66 (1987): 47–71.

Honigman, Ernst. *Myriad-Minded Shakespeare: Essays, Chiefly on the Tragedies and Problem Plays* (1989).

Hunter, Robert Grams. *Shakespeare and the Comedy of Forgiveness* (1965).

Kirsch, Arthur. *Shakespeare and the Experience of Love* (1981).

Knight, G. Wilson. *The Sovereign Flower* (1958).

McCandless, David Foley. *Gender and Performance in Shakespeare's Problem Comedies* (1997).

Parker, R. B. "War and Sex in *All's Well That Ends Well." Shakespeare Survey* 37 (1984): 99–113.

Price, Joseph G. *The Unfortunate Comedy: A Study of "All's Well That Ends Well"* (1968).

Sullivan, Garrett A. " 'Be this sweet Helen's knell, and now forget her': Forgetting, Memory, and Identity in *All's Well That Ends Well." Shakespeare Quarterly* 50 (1999): 51–69.

Westlund, Joseph. *Shakespeare's Reparative Comedies: A Psychoanalytic View of the Middle Plays* (1981).

Zitner, Sheldon. *All's Well That Ends Well* (1989).